MONETARISM AND LIBERALIZATION

MONETARISM AND LIBERALIZATION
The Chilean Experiment

Sebastian Edwards

and

Alejandra Cox Edwards

BALLINGER PUBLISHING COMPANY
Cambridge, Massachusetts
A Subsidiary of Harper & Row, Publishers, Inc.

International Standard Book Number: 0-88730-105-3

Library of Congress Catalog Card Number: 86-25959

Printed in the United States of America

Library of Congress Cataloging in Publication Data

Edwards, Sebastian.
  Monetarism and liberalization.

  Bibliography: p.
  Includes index.
  1. Chile—Economic policy.   2. Monetary policy—Chile.
  3. Economic stabilization—Chile.   4. Chile—Economic
  conditions—1970-   . I. Edwards, Alejandra Cox,
  1954-   . II. Title.
  HC192.E249   1987   338.983   86-25959

  ISBN 0-88730-105-3

To Magdalena, who loves Chile.

"No one could understand such fatal coincidences."

"For years we couldn't talk about anything else. Our daily conduct, dominated then by so many linear habits, had suddenly begun to spin around a single common anxiety. The cocks of dawn would catch us trying to give order to the chain of many chance events that had made absurdity possible. . . ."

— *Gabriel García Márquez*
"Chronicle of a Death Foretold"

CONTENTS

LIST OF FIGURES

LIST OF TABLES

PREFACE

During the 1970s the countries of the Southern Cone of South America — Argentina, Chile, and Uruguay — embarked on major attempts to liberalize their economies through reforms directed at increasing the role of the market mechanism and reducing existing barriers to international trade and capital movements. The more ambitious of these episodes took place in Chile where under the aegis of an authoritarian military regime major free market–oriented reforms were pursued at the same time that a monetarist-type stabilization program aimed at reducing a 600 percent rate of inflation was implemented. For a moment, the initial economic success of the Chilean experience captured the imagination of the international financial press, economists, and conservative politicians. In fact, in the (very) early 1980s the Chilean and Thatcher experiments became important symbols for the supporters of monetarism and free market liberalization policies. However, a decade after the Chilean reforms were first implemented the verdict was far from enthusiastic. In 1982 the Chilean economy entered into a deep recession: Real income declined by almost 20 percent; open unemployment climbed to almost 30 percent; and the financial system experienced a major collapse.

This book deals with the Chilean experiment with monetarist and free market policies. In it we analyze the different policies pursued by the military during the first decade (1973–83) of the regime. The book analyzes both the stabilization program and the free market liberalization reforms and discusses the factors behind the initial success and subsequent collapse of the Chilean economy. We emphasize some of the most novel aspects of the experiment — for example, the use of exchange rate management as the major stabilization tool. We also discuss the more "puzzling" aspects of the Chilean economy, including the persistence of unemployment and the exorbitantly high interest rates that prevailed throughout the period.

This book revolves around the important question of what went wrong in Chile. A particularly important issue that we address — and one that has far-reaching implications for other developing countries — is whether the disappointing outcomes of the Chilean experiment was the consequence of the liberalization itself or whether it was the consequence of other events, including adverse foreign shocks and inappropriate macroeconomic policies.

The book consists of eight chapters. In Chapter 1 we present some background information and an overview of the experiment. Here we briefly discuss the evolution of the Chilean economy before 1973, placing special emphasis on the *Unidad Popular*'s socialist experience during 1970–73. In Chapter 2 we analyze the military's stabilization program. Here the discussion emphasizes how the monetarist thinking in Chile — and for that matter in most of Latin America — evolved during this period. In Chapter 3 we analyze the behavior of two key prices — the interest rate and the real exchange rate — and we discuss the way in which they reacted to the liberalization reforms and to the macroeconomic policies. Both in Chapters 2 and 3 we discuss the process that lead to a significant real overvaluation of the exchange rate. Chapter 4 is devoted to the discussion of the privatization and deregulation process. Here the role of the *grupos* or major conglomerates is analyzed. This chapter also deals with some of the more profound structural reforms, such as the new labor law that regulated unions' behavior and the reform of the social security system. In Chapter 5 we discuss the more important aspects of the liberalization of international trade. Chapter 6 deals with unemployment, wages, and income distribution. Here we develop a simple model of the labor market in a developing economy to explain the persistence of unemployment. In Chapter 7 we discuss some issues related to the sequencing of the economic reforms, emphasizing the appropriate order of liberalization of the current and capital accounts of the balance of payments. In Chapter 8 we present our conclusions and discuss the more important lessons that emerge from the Chilean experiment.

During the long gestation of this book we have incurred numerous intellectual debts. Throughout the years we have benefited from discussions with Vittorio Corbo, Jim de Melo, Jim Hanson, Marcelo Selowsky, and Sweder van Wijnbergen. Our long conversations with Al Harberger have always been very fruitful. We are grateful to Bob Topel, Horng Ji Liu, Hernan Cortes, Evan Tanner, Phil Brock, Ken Sokoloff, Arye Hillman, and Patricio Mujica for their comments on one or more chapters. Our special thanks go to Edgardo Barandiarán who, in spite of his numerous obligations as an international civil servant, always found time to comment on a chapter, check on some obscure fact, or discuss some of our interpretations. Lorraine Grams typed diligently the innumerable drafts of the manuscript. Sebastian Edwards gratefully acknowledges financial support from the National Science Foundation (Grant SES 84 19932), UCLA's International Studies and Overseas Programs and from a UCLA Academic Senate Research Grant.

1 THE CHILEAN EXPERIMENT
An Overview

The study of Chile's modern economic history usually generates a sense of excitement and sadness: excitement, because during the last fifty years Chile has been a social laboratory of sorts, where almost every possible type of economic policy has been experimented; sadness, because to a large extent all these experiments have ended in failure and frustration.

The most recent of these "experiments" began in 1973, after the military overthrew President Salvador Allende. In the ten years following the coup, the military implemented deep reforms directed at transforming Chile from an economy semi-isolated from the rest of the world, with strong government intervention, into a liberalized world-integrated economy where market forces were freely left to guide most economic decisions. These liberalization reforms were carried out at the same time that a major stabilization program aimed at reducing a rate of inflation of approximately 600 percent was being implemented. Many of the liberalization policies undertaken roughly correspond to what a vast number of economists have been advocating for developing countries: International trade was liberalized; the capital account was opened; prices, including interest rates, were freed; an active domestic capital market was developed; the fiscal system was reformed, and a value added tax implemented; the social security system was reformed; and the private sector began to play an active role in the growth process.[1]

1

The period 1973–83 was characterized by acute contrasts. For example, while in 1973 Chile had the highest rate of inflation in the world (600 percent), in 1981 it had one of the lowest (9 percent). On the other hand, the rate of growth of real GDP fluctuated drastically: It was −13 percent in 1975; it then averaged almost 7 percent per annum during 1977–81 and dropped to −15 percent in 1982.

The rapid growth of real GDP in Chile during 1977–81 and the apparent success of other policies prompted some observers to (prematurely) talk about the Chilean miracle. By the end of 1981, however, the euphoria came to a sudden end, as it became evident that the growth pace of the previous years was not sustainable. The inflow of foreign capital was halted, the foreign debt could not be paid, real interest rates skyrocketed, and a severe financial crisis erupted. These events, and a drastic deterioration of the terms of trade—which amounted to 26 percent between 1979 and 1983—provoked one of the worst recessions faced by the country, from which, by early 1986, it still has not fully recovered. In addition, some of the reforms were partially reversed: Tariff rates were hiked; capital movements were tightly controlled; the financial sector was plagued with bankruptcies and was virtually nationalized.

The ultimate failure of Chile's experiment with liberalization policies has added considerable interest to this case.[2] Perhaps the most relevant question—and one that has far-reaching policy implications for other developing countries—is whether this failure was the consequence of the liberalization itself or whether it was the result of other events, including foreign shocks and inappropriate macroeconomic policies. Also, the political environment in which these reforms and liberalization programs evolved—an authoritarian dictatorship—has generated interest not only among economists but also among other social scientists. An important question here is whether it is possible to have a truly liberal and free market–oriented economic system within the context of a dictatorial political regime.

The purpose of this book is to provide a detailed analysis of Chile's most recent economic experiment. The book focuses on the ten first years of the experiment (1973–83) and analyzes both the stabilization program and the free market liberalization reforms implemented by the military government. Emphasis is placed on the more novel aspects of this experience—for example, the use of the preannouncement of the rate of devaluation as a major stabilization tool. Also, the analysis tries to shed some light on the more puzzling aspects of the Chilean economy, including the persistence of unemployment and the very high interest rates that prevailed throughout the experience.[3] The book revolves around the important question of what went wrong in Chile. In particular the analysis tries to extract lessons from this experience that will be helpful both to policymakers in other countries and to development economists that are, at the present time, rethinking the framework traditionally used in their analyses. This chapter provides an overview of the military experiment with free market policies, including a brief description of the behavior of the Chilean economy before 1973, with special emphasis given to the *Unidad Popular* government of 1970–73, as well as a discussion of the record of growth during 1973–83.

THE CHILEAN ECONOMY BEFORE 1973

The 1950–72 Period[4]

Between 1950 and 1972 the Chilean economy grew at modest rates. Real GDP grew at an average rate of 3.9 percent per annum, whereas real GDP per capita increased at an average yearly rate of 1.7 percent.[5] This performance is particularly meager if compared with that of other countries in the region. Over this period, for example, Chile's economic performance was the poorest of Latin America's large and medium-size countries.[6]

In the 1940s Chile, as well as most other Latin American countries, embarked on an ambitious industrialization program based on import substitution. This inward-looking development strategy was based on the idea that small developing economies would grow sufficiently rapidly only if they were able to develop a large and diversified industrial sector. This, in turn, could be achieved only if sufficiently high protection, in the form of import tariffs or quotas, was granted to the incipient domestic industries. Most proponents of the import substitution strategy also pointed out that the high degree of protection would be necessary only as a temporary measure; after an initial learning period, these "infant industries" would move into their "adolescence" and would not require tariffs. Reality, however, showed this view to be wrong. Protectionism became a permanent feature of the Chilean economy.[7]

During the first years of the industrialization process, important heavy industries were created — mostly under the guidance of the government's *Corporacion de Fomento de le Producción* (CORFO) —

and the bases for the manufacturing sector were set. Between 1937 and 1950 the manufacturing sector grew at an average yearly real rate of almost 7 percent (Munoz 1966: 158). However, with the industrialization process evolved an impressive array of restrictions, controls, and often contradictory regulations. It was, in fact, because of these import restrictions that many of the domestic industries were able to survive. For example, a number of comparative studies have indicated that Chile had one of the highest, and more variable, structures of protection in the developing world (Balassa 1971). As a consequence, many (if not most) of the industries created under the import substitution strategy were quite inefficient. In a carefully done empirical study Corbo and Meller (1981) found that this inward-looking strategy resulted in the use of very capital-intensive techniques, which hampered the creation of employment, among other inefficiencies.[8]

As in most historical cases, the Chilean import substitution strategy was accompanied by an acute overvalued domestic currency that precluded the development of a vigorous nontraditional (that is, noncopper) export sector. The agricultural sector was particularly harmed by the real exchange rate overvaluation. The lagging of agriculture became, in fact, one of the most noticeable symptoms of Chile's economic problems of the 1950s and 1960s. Over this period mining — which is mainly composed of copper — and manufacturing significantly increased their share in total output (see Table 1-1).

During the 1950s and early 1960s the import substitution strategy

Table 1-1.   The Structure of Production in Chile: 1950, 1960, 1970 (percentages of GDP).[a]

Sector	1950	1960	1970
Agriculture, forestry, and fishing	14.0	12.2	7.5
Mining	5.9	10.3	11.8
Construction	2.0	4.8	4.1
Manufacturing	22.9	24.9	27.9
Energy, transportation, and commerce	N.A.	24.5	20.0
Other services	N.A.	23.3	28.7
GDP	100.0	100.0	100.0

Sources: For 1950 CORFO (various issues); for 1960 and 1970 ODEPLAN (1972).
[a] These data correspond to shares of sectoral production measured at current prices.

began to run out of steam. At that time most of the easy and obvious substitutions of imported goods had already taken place, and the process was rapidly becoming less dynamic. For example, between 1950 and 1960 total real industrial production grew at an annual rate of only 3.5 percent – almost half of the rate of the previous decade.[9]

During the 1950s inflation, which had been a chronic problem in Chile since at least the 1880s, became particularly serious; the rate of increase of consumer prices averaged 36 percent per annum during the decade, reaching a peak of 84 percent in 1955. The roots of Chile's inflationary pressures rested mainly on excessive money creation and a remarkably lax fiscal policy. Chile's economic history is plagued with failed attempts to curb inflation. During the 1950s and 1960s three major stabilization programs – one in each administration – were launched. In spite of the initial success of the Ibañez and Alessandri efforts, inflation maintained on average its rampant pace during these two decades, averaging a rate of 31 percent per annum. In 1970, the last year of the Frei administration, the inflation rate stood at 35 percent.[10]

During the late 1950s and early 1960s politicians and economists came to a virtual agreement that Chile was facing a long-run economic crisis. Remarkably, perhaps, many analysts agreed on some of the principal aspects of the crisis. They recognized that the easy phase of the import substitution process had ended and that inflation and the recurrent crises of the external and agricultural sectors had become serious obstacles for reassuming growth. Further, the uneven distribution of income and the solution of the unemployment problem represented serious challenges to any new economic program. Although most experts pointed out that the traditionally low rates of domestic savings and investment represented an important obstacle for growth, they differed on some other aspects of their analyses and on the proposed policy packages recommended to take the country out of its relative stagnation.[11]

During the 1960s, and especially during the Frei administration, some efforts to reform the Chilean economy were launched: an agrarian reform, a mild liberalization of the external sector, and an exchange rate policy based on mini-devaluations that aimed at avoiding the erosion of the real exchange rate. In spite of these and other reforms, toward the end of the 1970s it appeared that the performance of the Chilean economy had not improved in relation to the previous twenty years. Moreover, the economy was still plagued with regulations and controls—including very high levels of taxes to international trade—that greatly hampered any efforts to develop an efficient and rapidly growing economy. In 1970 all three presidential candidates pointed out that the Chilean economy was in crisis.[12]

The Unidad Popular Government: 1970-73

In the September 1970 presidential elections Dr. Salvador Allende obtained a plurality with almost 39 percent of the votes. In October of that year he was elected president by both chambers of the Chilean Congress.[13] As the candidate of the *Unidad Popular* (UP)—a political coalition comprised of left and center-left parties, including Communists and Socialists—Allende became the first Marxist to be freely elected president of a Western democracy. The political aim of the UP was to transform Chile into a socialist society. This was to be achieved through the implementation of deep institutional and economic reforms—including the abolition of Congress and its replacement by a People's Assembly, the nationalization of the mining, banking, agricultural sectors, and the nationalization of most of the manufacturing sector. All of this was to be accomplished within the existing legal framework; the program called for a democratic "Chilean road to socialism."[14]

The analysis of the behavior of the Chilean economy during this period is well beyond the scope of the present book; that task warrants a volume of its own. However, a brief description of this period is provided, since in order to fully understand the evolution of Chilean economic policy during the military regime, it is essential to have a general idea of what went on during the UP period.

The UP program, and most of the technical literature generated by the UP economists, characterized the pre-1970 economy as "monopolistic" and "dependent." It was argued that the most serious problems faced by the country were the unequal income distribution, chronic inflation, and unemployment. It was further argued that the structure of internal demand, the semipermanent crisis in the external sector, and the low level of capital accumulation conspired to preclude a sufficiently high rate of growth. It was then postulated that the implementation of deep institutional—or revolutionary—reforms plus the improvement of the distribution of income would not only constitute an important step toward the construction of socialism but would also generate a fast pace of economic growth.[15]

An essential assumption of the UP economic program was that in 1970 there was substantial unutilized capital capacity in the manufacturing sector (see Zorrilla 1971: 17; Alaluf 1972: 6; Guardia 1979: 61–62). The existence of a high stock of international reserves plus the unutilized capacity would allow the government to generate major increases of aggregate demand without provoking major inflationary pressures in the short run. It was expected that this higher demand would be mostly absorbed by an increase in domestic production.

After Dr. Allende took office in early November of 1970, the UP program was rapidly implemented. In 1971 a policy of expansionary aggregate demand — through generalized wage increases, higher rates of money creation, and significantly higher government expenditure — was combined with major institutional reforms. By the end of the year the fiscal deficit had jumped from 3 percent of GDP (in 1970) to 11 percent of GDP. In the fourth quarter of 1971 the rate of money creation had surpassed 100 percent per annum, and the rate of growth of domestic credit to the public sector was approaching 300 percent per year. In order to avoid a major outburst of inflation, prices were tightly controlled. On the reforms side, the banking sector was nationalized, the large copper mines were nationalized, and the agrarian reform was greatly intensified. Also, a number of manufacturing firms were de facto expropriated through a procedure called "government intervention."[16]

According to the traditional economic indicators the year 1971 was a good one. Inflation was only 22 percent, real GDP grew at 7.7 percent, real wages increased by 29 percent, and the rate of unemployment was reduced from around 6 percent to below 4 percent.

However, these accomplishments were of a short-run nature and had been obtained through the implementation of a macroeconomic policy that was not sustainable in the medium to long run. In particular, the ever-increasing fiscal deficit constituted a very weak spot in the overall economic picture. In 1972 the deficit reached almost 13 percent of GDP, and in 1973 that ratio surpassed 24 percent. The process of massive increases of money coupled with tight price controls resulted in a classical case of *represented inflation*.[17] Black markets rapidly developed, and in 1972 the level of production began to drop. A particularly serious problem evolved around the de facto process of expropriation of manufacturing firms. The government intervention was almost always preceded by long labor strikes and by the seizure of the firms' installations by their workers. This process disrupted production not only in the seized firms but also in the rest of the sector where uncertainty was rapidly mounting. Also the level of efficiency in the nationalized firms dropped dramatically. Contrary to what the UP economists had thought no surpluses were generated; nationalized firms reduced output and ran large losses.[18]

The expansionary fiscal and monetary policies also generated an acute crisis in the external sector. International reserves dropped sharply and in the first quarter of 1973 reached less than two months' worth of imports, which was a dramatic decline from their 1970 level of almost six months' worth of imports. A system of tight exchange controls and multiple exchange rates was implemented. For example, in 1973 there were fifteen different official exchange rates, with the ratio of the highest to lowest rate exceeding 8,000 percent! Partially as a result of these policies the incentives to the agricultural sector were greatly reduced. This, plus the mode of organization of the land expropriated during the agrarian reform — large state-owned farms — resulted in a significant decline in agricultural output. The arbitrariness that characterized the process of de facto expropriation of industrial firms also generated a heightened level of uncertainty, which was translated into very low gross investment and private sector savings (Guardia 1979). For example, in 1972 gross investment was only 15 percent of GDP, significantly lower than the 21.3 percent average ratio attained between 1965 and 1970.

By late 1972 the economic and political situations were extremely chaotic. In August of that year inflation reached a monthly rate of 23 percent, and the existence of pervasive black markets was a fact almost incorporated into everyday life. As a way to combat the generalized scarcity of goods and in particular food, the government tried to organize a rationing scheme that made available a certain amount of food (the so-called popular basket) to each household through neighborhood organizations specially created for this purpose. This rationing scheme, however, generated a massive reaction by the opposition, which argued that Chile was being transformed into another Cuba. In August of 1972 the government also launched a major stabilization attempt mainly based on the expansion of aggregate supply. The Communist party main slogan during this period was "Let's win the battle for increased production." Also a drastic devaluation was implemented, and an attempt to control money creation was made. The fiscal deficit, however, was left untouched, and, not surprisingly, the stabilization effort failed.

In October of 1972 the opposition parties organized a national strike as a protest to what were considered to be erroneous and antidemocratic government policies. The protest was particularly directed against the government economic and educational policies. This strike generated significant economic costs and greatly aggravated the situation. It could be solved only after President Allende incorporated representatives of the armed forces into his cabinet.

The first part of the year 1973 was characterized by a deepening of the crisis. The economic situation became increasingly precarious, with the inflationary process tending toward hyperinflation. Production decreased in all sectors, and the external sector began to face an extremely serious crisis. At the political level things were not better. The opposition, after an important victory in the parliamentary elections of March 1973, became increasingly impatient. Toward mid-1973 the opposition parties were demanding the resignation of President Allende. However, even more serious, was that at this time the UP parties – and in particular Communists and Socialists – had entered into an increasingly serious feud, strongly disagreeing on how to face the crisis.

On September 11, 1973, the Allende presidency came to a sudden end. That day the armed forces staged a coup. When the military took over, the country was politically divided, and the economy was in shambles. Inflation was galloping, relative price distortions – stemming mainly from massive price controls – were widespread; black market activities were rampant; real wages had dropped drastically; the economic circumstances of the middle class had been greatly damaged; the foreign trade sector was facing a serious crisis; production and investment were steeply falling; and government finances were completely out of hand.[19] Table 1–2 contains some indicators for the period 1970–73.

THE MILITARY EXPERIMENT

The military coup of 1973 marked an important turning point in Chile's economic and political history. The ten years that followed witnessed one of the most ambitious attempts to reform an isolated and tightly government-controlled economy into a world integrated market-oriented society. These policies – which were undertaken at the same time as a major stabilization program was underway – can be viewed as a reaction to the long tradition of government intervention and controls that had characterized the Chilean economy since the 1930s. It is important to point out, however, that initially the military did not

Table 1-2.   Selected Economic Indicators during the Unidad Popular Government: 1970–73.

Year	(A) Rate of Inflation (December to December)	(B) Real GDP (1970 = 100)	(C) Industrial Production (1970 = 100)	(D) Government Deficit/ GDP	(E) International Reserves (Millions U.S. $)	(F) Current Account Deficit/ GNP	(G) Unemployment Rate — Santiago Area	(G) Unemployment Rate — Total	(H) Real Wages (1970 = 100)
1970	34.9%	100.0	100.0	2.9%	394	1.3%	7.1%	3.5%	100.0
1971	34.5%	109.0	110.8	11.2%	163	2.1%	5.5%	3.3%	129.0
1972	216.7%	107.6	113.6	13.5%	76	3.9%	3.7%	3.3%	114.5
1973	605.9%	101.6	106.2	24.6%	168	2.9%	4.7%	N.A.	64.4

Sources: Column A from Yañez (1978). Columns B, F, and H from Banco Central de Chile (1981, 1983, 1984). Column G from IMF and Instituto de Economia y Planificación (1973). Column E from the IFS. Column H from Banco Central de Chile (1981, 1983, 1984). The total unemployment rate refers to September–December for 1970 and to October–December for rest of years. The Santiago unemployment rate is an average for the year. Real wages were computed using the GDP deflator.

have a very clear long-run economic program; only slowly during the first two years were the more conservative aspects of the free market policies were adopted.[20]

The Record of Growth: 1973-83

In terms of economic growth the period 1973-83 was characterized by a highly variable record. Table 1-3 presents data on real GDP and real per capita GDP between 1970 and 1983. As may be seen, the first full year of the military regime (1974) was characterized by a small increase in real GDP and by a *decline* in real per capita GDP. In 1975, on the other hand, economic activity dropped dramatically, partially as a consequence of the stabilization program and partially due to worsening world economic conditions (see below and Chapter 2).

In the years 1977 through 1980 extraordinarily high rates of growth of GDP, which averaged 8.5 percent per year, were achieved. These were the years of the "miracle." However, as may be seen from Table 1-3, real per capita GDP did not regain its 1971 level until 1980. A crucial question, then, is to what extent these high growth rates were due only to a recovery process, starting from a very low initial level of GDP in 1975. As will be argued below the increase in the degree of utilization of the capital stock between 1976 and 1979 accounts for some of Chile's growth during the period. This table also shows the steep decline in real GDP in 1982, and the further drop in 1983. As can be seen, in 1983 real GDP per capita was below its 1970 level!

Table 1-3 shows that the average rate of growth of real GDP for 1974-83 was only 1.4 percent. An issue that has usually come up in discussions on the recent behavior of the Chilean economy relates to the year that should be used as a base to compute the relevant growth indicators and to establish comparisons. There are, of course, good reasons to use 1973 as the base year; it was the year the military took over the government. Yet some have argued that the poor performance of 1974-76 was a legacy of the Unidad Popular government and that 1976 is a more relevant benchmark to be used to evaluate the growth performance of the economy. When 1976 is used as the base, the average rate of growth for 1976-83 turns out to be 3.2 percent, significantly higher than 1.4 percent but still below the historical average for 1950-72.[21]

Table 1–3. Real Gross Domestic Product and Real Gross
Domestic Product per Capita in Chile: 1970–83.

Year	(1) Real Gross Domestic Product (Millions of 1977 Pesos)	(2) Rate of Growth of Real GDP	(3) Per Capita Real GDP (Thousands of 1977 Pesos)	(4) Rate of Growth of per Capita Real GDP
1970	283,097	2.1%	30.2	0.2%
1971	308,449	9.0%	32.4	7.1%
1972	304,707	−1.2%	31.4	−2.9%
1973	287,750	−5.6%	29.2	−7.1%
1974	290,554	1.0%	30.0	−0.7%
1975	253,043	−12.9%	24.8	−14.4%
1976	261,945	3.5%	25.3	1.8%
1977	287,770	9.9%	27.3	8.0%
1978	311,417	8.2%	29.0	6.4%
1979	337,207	8.3%	30.9	6.5%
1980	363,446	7.8%	32.7	6.0%
1981	383,551	5.5%	34.0	3.8%
1982	329,523	−14.1%	28.7	−15.5%
1983	327,180	−0.7%	28.0	−2.4%
Average Growth 1974–83	—	1.4%	—	−0.8%

Source: Banco Central de Chile (1984).

Table 1–4 contains data on sectoral growth. During the initial years
of the military government most sectors performed very poorly. By
the late 1970s, however, there was a marked recuperation, with the
commerce and financial services sectors leading the economy. This was
largely a result of the liberalization reforms that, among other things,
resulted in a significant increase in the number of financial intermediaries and commerce activities. The data reported in Table 1–4 also
show that the construction sector experienced very wide swings during the period. It declined by 26 percent in 1975. In 1976 it experienced
a further decline, even though the other sectors and the economy as
a whole were experiencing an important recovery. However, between

Table 1-4. Rate Growth of Real GDP by Sectors (percentage).

Sector	1970	1975	1976	1977	1978	1979	1980	1981	1982
Agriculture and forestry	3.6	4.8	-2.9	10.4	-4.9	5.6	1.8	2.2	-2.1
Fishery	-5.4	-6.7	33.9	15.4	17.9	14.3	7.5	18.1	9.4
Mining	-3.0	-11.3	12.2	2.7	1.6	5.4	5.2	7.7	5.7
Manufacturing	2.0	-25.5	6.0	8.5	9.3	7.9	6.2	2.6	-21.0
Electricity, gas, and water	5.3	-3.8	5.8	5.8	6.7	6.8	5.0	2.1	0.1
Construction	5.5	-26.0	-16.0	-0.9	8.1	23.9	23.9	21.1	-23.8
Commerce	-1.5	-17.1	2.5	24.8	20.0	11.0	12.4	4.3	-17.3
Transport and communication	4.7	-7.7	4.7	10.8	8.4	9.0	11.1	1.8	-11.8
Financial services	15.4	-4.2	9.3	14.5	20.2	28.0	22.6	11.9	-5.4
Services of dwellings	3.7	1.8	0.7	0.6	0.9	0.5	1.0	1.5	1.0
Public administration	1.5	1.9	5.9	1.8	-3.1	-1.2	-3.2	-1.8	-2.9
Education	2.6	1.8	-2.3	2.4	2.2	1.9	-1.1	-2.3	-0.3
Health	3.1	-1.7	4.2	2.7	3.2	5.7	3.3	3.2	-8.0
Other services	1.4	-4.5	3.5	5.7	5.7	6.4	5.7	3.3	-16.2
Aggregate GDP	2.1	-12.9	3.5	9.9	8.2	8.3	7.8	5.5	-14.1

Source: Banco Central de Chile (1981, 1983, 1984).

1979 and 1981 the construction sector went through a steep recovery, leading most sectors.

Domestic savings were very low throughout the 1973–83 period. This is perhaps surprising, since due to the liberalization of the domestic financial market, real interest rates were positive for the first time in a long period of time. In fact, as discussed in detail in Chapter 3, during this period domestic savings were at one of the lowest historical levels. Moreover, contrary to what was expected by the authorities, foreign direct investment was very limited throughout the period. Partially as a result of this, gross investment was increasingly financed by foreign savings. In 1980 foreign savings reached 8.5 percent of GDP, while in 1981 they rose to 14.5 percent of GDP, representing 66 percent of total gross domestic investment. The current account deficits associated with these high levels of foreign savings began to generate a serious foreign indebtedness problem in 1980–81. In 1981 total foreign debt increased almost 50 percent – from $10,987 million U.S. to $15,546 million U.S. – reaching 50 percent of GDP. As is explained in more detail in Chapter 3, it was thought at the time by the economic authorities and other observers that since most of the new debt had been contracted by the private sector (without any government guarantee), this increase in foreign indebtedness did not represent a threat for the country as a whole. As the facts showed later, this distinction between private and public debt was highly artificial, and the Chilean government ended up taking over all of the private sector foreign debt, independently of the fact that the original borrowers went bankrupt and there were no previous government guarantees on those loans.

In general, it appears that Chile's inability to increase domestic savings and gross domestic investment indicated, from the early years of the military dictatorship, that the rate of growth of the economy could not be consistently high for a long period of time. In fact, an early study on the subject pointed out that unless Chile's *total* savings reached 28 percent of GNP by 1979 it would be impossible to achieve the high sustained rates of growth of real GDP forecasted by some optimistic observers.[22]

Although capital accumulation is hardly the only source of growth, the extremely modest level of investment in 1977–80 makes one wonder how Chile managed to grow so fast during this period. Some studies have suggested that this rapid period of growth can be partially explained by an increase in the degree of capacity utilization during

1977-80.[23] The other important source of growth between 1977 and 1980 is related to the efficiency gains associated to the process of resource reallocation generated by the liberalization reforms. In fact some studies have attempted to estimate the (static) welfare gains resulting from a reduction, or total elimination, of distortions in Chile. More than twenty-five years ago, Harberger (1959) estimated that the elimination of *all* distortions would result in a static increase in Chile's national welfare of about 15 percent of national income. He also indicated that this static effect would result in a higher rate of growth of one to two percentage points per year, for a limited period of time. Coeymans (1978), more recently estimated that the military tariff liberalization process would result in a static improvement of Chile's welfare of around 3 percent of national income. Schmidt-Hebbel (1981), on the other hand, estimated that the recent liberalizations policies (both trade and others) resulted in a static increase in welfare of approximately 10 percent of national income. He also suggests that this welfare improvement would be spread through ten years, contributing approximately one percentage point per annum to the growth rate during this period. Data from a study by Meller, Livacich, and Arrau (1984) strongly suggest that during the military regime there were extremely important gains in efficiency and productivity. In Chapter 5 below, these productivity improvements are discussed in more detail.

In order to obtain a better sense of the relative importance of some of the different sources of growth during 1975-80, we applied a conventional growth-accounting framework to compute the contributions to growth of changes in the stock of physical capital and changes in employment. If it is the case that changes in the degree of capital utilization and efficiency improvements made important contributions to growth, we would expect that the residuals obtained from this exercise would be very large — that is, larger than the residuals obtained in this type of computation for Chile before 1970. Table 1-5 shows the contribution to growth of changes in the quantities of capital and labor between 1970 and 1979 and of imputed contributions to growth of changes in capacity utilization and gains in efficiency generated by the liberalization program. These latter figures were taken from Schmidt-Hebbel (1981) and are 1.5 percent per year. In these computations labor was assigned a share of 52 percent of GDP, while capital was assigned a 48 percent share. The data on changes in the stock of capital were taken from Edwards (1985b), and the data on the evolution of employment were obtained from S. Edwards (1980a).

Table 1-5. The Sources of Growth in Chile: 1975–80.

	(1) Actual Rate of Growth of GDP	(2) Contributions of Changes in Physical Capital	(3) Contributions of Changes in the Quantity of Labor	(4) "Grand" Residual [(1)-(2)-(3)]	(5) Contribution of Efficiency Gains	(6) Contribution of Change in Capacity Utilization	(7) Residual [(1)-(2)-(3)-(5)-(6)]
1975	-12.9	-3.7	0.3	-9.5	—	-5.4	-4.1
1976	3.5	1.3	0.3	1.9	—	1.0	0.9
1977	9.9	3.8	0.6	5.5	1.5	1.6	2.4
1978	8.2	1.4	1.2	5.6	1.5	0.4	3.7
1979	8.3	1.1	1.9	5.3	1.5	0.7	3.1
1980	7.5	3.2	2.8	1.5	1.5	—	0.0

Sources: Column 1, Banco Central de Chile (1981, 1983, 1984); Column 2 taken from table 9; Column 3 computed from S. Edwards (1980a); Column 5 estimated from Schmidt-Hebbel (1980); Column 6 computed from data presented in Schmidt-Hebbel (1980).

Column (4) in Table 1-5 shows the "grand residual" obtained after having taken into account the contributions of the quantities of capital and labor to growth. As expected, these residuals are very high — indeed much higher than those obtained in earlier accounting studies on the sources of growth in Chile — indicating that during the recent period factors other than changes in the quantities of capital and labor played an important role in growth.[24] As discussed above, the most plausible variables that would explain this "grand" residual are efficiency gains and change in the degree of capital utilization. Indeed, if following Schmidt-Hebbel (1981) we assume that between 1977 and 1980 the resource reallocation process contributed with 1.5 percentage points to annual growth, and we use his estimates of the degree of capital utilization, these residuals are significantly reduced.[25] This is shown in columns (5), (6) and (7) of Table 1-5. However, these residuals are still fairly large — in fact, larger than what can be attributed to higher "quality" of labor and capital and to "technical progress" — suggesting that there are still some measurement problems that should be accounted for.

Stabilization and Liberalization Policies

In terms of economic policy — as well as overall performance — the first decade of the military regime was by no means homogeneous. In fact, it is possible to distinguish four different phases. The first covers September 1973 through April 1975 and was characterized by an attempt to correct the most serious economic distortions introduced during the Allende regime. During this phase a gradual anti-inflationary policy was implemented, and inflation declined only slightly. Output experienced a very mild recovery, and the first steps of some of the liberalization reforms were delineated. Perhaps the most important characteristic of this period is that the process of privatization of banks and public enterprises — some of them previously nationalized during the Allende regime — began. Partially as a result of this privatization process some very big conglomerates (the so-called *grupos*) emerged. As is discussed throughout the rest of the book — and in particular in Chapters 3 and 4 — the *grupos* played an important role in the main events that took place during the first ten years of the military regime.

1975-78

The second phase runs from April 1975 until early 1978 and corresponds to the first serious effort to curb inflation. This was attempted by following an orthodox closed economy stabilization program based on tight monetary policy and on the elimination of the fiscal deficit. During this time the free market character of the military program was accentuated, and important steps toward reforming and liberalizing the domestic financial sector and international trade were implemented. It was during this phase that the group of economists popularly known as the "Chicago boys" began to gain great influence and, in fact, to fully run the economic policy. Many of these economists had been trained at the University of Chicago and other U.S. universities and had a strong ideological stance against any kind of government intervention in the development process.

The early part of this phase saw a dramatic reduction of output — 12.9 percent decline in GDP in 1975 — and a steep increase in unemployment. This phase was also characterized by a marked deterioration in the international environment, as real copper prices fell to their lowest level in two decades, inducing a resource loss to the economy equivalent to about 10 percent of GDP. Additional resources, equivalent to 2.5 percent of GDP, were used to service the debt. Over and above this, oil prices increased, introducing further constraints on the already weak economic structure.

During this phase the anti-inflationary policy made some important progress with annual inflation declining from 343 percent in 1975 to 84 percent in 1977. Also, and as can be seen in Table 1–4 the year 1977 is the first year of a marked recovery in the level of economic activity.

1978-81

The third phase goes from early 1978 through the first half of 1981 and is characterized by a marked change in emphasis in the stabilization program. As noted, during the initial phases of the experiment the anti-inflation program was based on quite traditional monetary principles, where the emphasis was placed almost exclusively on controlling the rate of growth of money and the fiscal deficit. In early 1978, with the fiscal deficit virtually under control and with the rate of inflation still standing at 80 percent per annum, a drastic change in the monetarist approach took place. At this time the policymakers began to emphasize the fact that Chile had become an open economy, and the manipulation of the exchange rate replaced the control of the quantity of money as the main stabilization tool. In January 1978 Chile introduced the preannouncement of the rate of devaluation (the so-called *tablita*) as the main anti-inflation measure.[26] This novel approach to stabilization was later adopted by Argentina and Uruguay. In 1979 the policy of preannouncing the rate of devaluation was replaced by a fixed exchange rate. It was expected that this move would help to finally eliminate inflation.

This third phase corresponds to the days of the "miracle" — or the "boom" as the Chileans referred to these few years. Output grew at fast rates, the availability of imported goods increased drastically and inflation — Chile's almost eternal malaise — finally subsided, reaching 9 percent in 1981. Unemployment, however, stubbornly remained at high levels — with open unemployment still surpassing 10 percent — constituting one of the unresolved puzzles of the military regime.

A number of important reforms were implemented during this phase, including the enactment of the labor law, which among other things legally established a mechanism of 100 percent wage indexation with respect to past inflation for those workers subject to collective bargaining. The financial reform was pushed further, by relaxing a series of controls on capital inflows. Also, as is discussed in more detail in Chapter 4, during this phase the deregulation reforms pursued by the government became more drastic and far-reaching. The social security system was reformed, the educational system was decentralized, and the health services system underwent important changes.

Another important and puzzling aspect of this phase relates to the behavior of two key prices — the real interest rate and the real exchange rate. Whereas the first remained at very high levels during most of the period, the real exchange rate experienced a steady real appreciation since mid-1979, greatly harming the degree of competitiveness of the domestic sector, including nontraditional exports. In fact, according to some popular accounts, this real appreciation was the single most important cause of the failure of the Chilean experiment. In Chapter 3 we attempt to explain the behavior of these two key variables and argue that they basically responded to erroneous policy measures.

1981-83

Finally, the fourth phase begins in late 1981 and is characterized by the collapse of the "miracle." By late 1981 it became apparent that the high rates of growth experienced during the previous years were coming to an end. The fourth quarter of 1981 was characterized by extraordinarily high real interest rates; by a huge current account deficit; rising unemployment; and a reduction of real GDP of 3.3 percent with respect to the fourth quarter of 1980. On the positive side, inflation was only 9 percent that year. In 1982 the economic situation worsened and became almost chaotic. GDP declined by 14.3 percent; in September of that year open unemployment (excluding the emergency employment programs) reached 23.7 percent; the exchange rate was devalued by almost 100 percent; a major financial crisis developed; and there were serious problems to service the foreign debt.

The causes that led to this crisis are extensively discussed throughout the book, and especially in Chapters 3 and 8. In Chapter 8 we analyze whether the ultimate failure of the Chilean experiment can be attributed to the liberalization policies themselves or to other features including the macroeconomic policies implemented with the liberalization reforms or to a combination of different factors. In that chapter the possible role of external factors—including the steep worsening in Chile's terms of trade—is also discussed in detail.

The 1981-82 crisis was first manifested by a very sharp increase in the real interest rate. In the third quarter of 1981 the real borrowing rate reached 30 percent per annum, significantly higher than its level in the third quarter of 1980—5 percent. These hikes in real interest rates plus the real appreciation of the peso placed important financial strains on most firms, with those in the import competing and export sectors being hit in a particularly hard way. (Chapter 3 includes a detailed discussion on interest rate behavior.)

Many firms reacted to the crisis by increasing their borrowing from the banking sector. Banks, on their turn, were willing to make additional loans as a way to avert a series of bankruptcies that would have greatly affected their parent holding companies.[27] In late 1981 and early 1982 the level of activity dropped, and firms' operational profits were greatly squeezed. The situation was aggravated by a generalized belief that a devaluation of the peso would be implemented in an attempt to correct the perceived real overvaluation. In trying to anticipate the

THE CHILEAN EXPERIMENT: AN OVERVIEW   21

devaluation the public exercised additional pressure on domestic interest rates, making things worse.

In a way, businesspeople decided to survive a day at a time. They tried to avert or delay bankruptcy in every possible way. Many firms, especially small and medium size, could not do it and had to close down. The rest waited, hoping for some miraculous government intervention. Nothing of that sort happened; on the contrary, throughout this period the government had a remarkably passive attitude. As is explained in Chapter 2 the macroeconomic policy adopted at that time called for an "automatic adjustment." This situation was greatly aggravated by the somewhat abrupt cut in capital inflows that took place in early 1982. At that time, as a result of the evident troubles the economy was going through and the extraordinary increase in foreign borrowing in the previous two years, the foreign banks halted most of their operations with Chile. In mid-1982 the government finally reacted and tried to avert the crashlanding by devaluing. It was, however, too little and too late. The Pinochet economic miracle had seen its final days.

In late 1982 the Pinochet government approached the IMF in order to obtain financial assistance to service the foreign debt. Private banks were also approached, and a rescheduling of the foreign debt was proposed. A standby agreement with the IMF, which called for a typical IMF-type stabilization program, was signed. In late 1983, ten years after Pinochet had taken over the government and had embarked on sweeping market-oriented reforms, Chile was once again struggling to put her economy together.

What Went Wrong?

There has been a tendency among some observers, and especially in the popular press, to oversimplify the causes of the collapse of the Chilean economy in 1982. Most of these accounts have tried to single out only *one* factor as responsible for the disappointing outcome of the free market attempt. The principal suspects in these searches for "the" failure's cause have usually been the exchange rate policy (that is, the *tablita* and subsequent fixing of the peso) and the marked deterioration of the terms of trade in 1981–82.

As we show in the rest of the book, the Chilean experiment is extraordinarily complex, and its failure was the consequence of not one but many interwoven factors. Ignoring the role played by all these factors is indeed a gross oversimplification, which does not allow us to extract all of the many and important lessons of the Chilean experiment.

There is no doubt that there were some serious policy mistakes, related both to the way in which the liberalization reforms were implemented and to the conduct of macroeconomic policy. Chief among these mistakes were the lack of supervision of the financial sector, which allowed the banks to amass a large proportion of "bad loans"; the combination of a 100 percent backward wage indexation mechanism and a fixed exchange rate, which resulted in a steady process of real overvaluation; and the timing of the opening of the current account of the balance of payments. But perhaps the most serious of the policy mistakes was the passive stance toward macroeconomic policy adopted by the government in the early 1980s. As the crisis unraveled in 1981 and early 1982 the authorities passively waited for the economy to "automatically adjust." As the adjustment failed to materialize quickly enough and in the way predicted by the authorities, the crisis deepened and the social costs increased. There is little doubt, as we argue in Chapter 8, that if a more active macro policy had been adopted in late 1980 or even during the first half of 1981 that the magnitude of the crisis would not have reached the proportion it did.

The drastic deterioration of the external environment in late 1981 and in 1982, and in particular the decline in the price of copper and the increase in world interest rates, conspired with the policy mistakes to make things even worse. The sudden drain of capital inflows in 1982 also had an important negative effect. However, contrary to the drop in copper prices and the increase in interest rates the halt of capital inflows was not a completely exogenous phenomenon; it was largely a consequence of the policy mistakes. In Chapter 8 we show how the decline in real income generated by these external shocks greatly affected production of the nontraded sectors and of the import competing manufacturing industries.

The political system in which the free market experiment took place also played a role in determining the magnitude of the crisis. There is no doubt, as we argue in Chapter 8, that the lack of democratic channels and institutions to check on policymakers — congressional hearings, for example — allowed the Chilean authorities to pursue what from an economic perspective were at least questionable policies such as the macroeconomic "automatic adjustment," for a prolonged period of time.

In spite of the dramatic collapse of the economy in 1982 there were some significant, and possibly lasting, achievements. Particularly important among them was the elimination of a great number of atavistic regulations and distortions that had penalized the Chilean economy and Chilean society for many decades. The freeing of domestic prices, the tax reform of 1975, the elimination of discriminatory laws, the rationalization of the foreign trade regime, and the imports tariff reforms were, by and large, very important achievements that greatly helped to increase the efficiency and level of productivity in Chile. In fact, as we point out in Chapter 8, there is a fairly generalized agreement among Chilean experts of very diverse political inclination that these were important and major achievements that should be maintained, perhaps with some variations, by the future democratically elected governments.

NOTES

1. The liberalization of the domestic economies, and especially of the external sector, has for a long time been one of the main policy recommendations of a large group of economists that include both "conservatives" and "liberals." See, for example, Little, Scitovsky, and Scott (1971), Balassa (1982), Krueger (1978), Bhagwati (1978), Bhagwati and Srinivasan (1979), and Díaz-Alejandro (1971).

2. Whether the Chilean experience with free markets was or was not a failure may be subject to debate. If failure is defined as a reversal of the reforms, the Chilean experiment didn't fail; until at least early 1986 most of the reforms were in place. Moreover, the economy is recovering. However, if failure is defined as a significant deviation between expected and actual results of the policies, then the Chilean experience was a failure.

3. Different aspects of the recent Chilean experiment have been analyzed by Hachette (1978), Harberger (1982, 1983a, 1983b), Foxley (1982, 1983), Ffrench-Davis (1983), Corbo (1985a), Parkin (1983), Hanson (1985), Balassa (1985), Walton (1985), and S. Edwards (1985a, 1986a).

4. In this section the main characteristics of the Chilean economy during the twenty years prior to the 1973 military coup are discussed. By necessity this discussion is brief and only highlights some of the more important aspects of the economy. Interested readers are referred to some of the existing more detailed accounts of the evolution of Chile's economic conditions during this period. On the Chilean economy before 1973 see, for example, Mamalakis and Reynolds (1965), Mamalakis (1978), Behrman (1976, 1977), Corbo (1974), and Ffrench-Davis (1973).

5. Before 1950 Chile's economic performance was also somewhat modest. For example, Ballesteros and Davis (1963) estimated that between 1908 and 1957 output per capita grew at approximately 1 percent per year. It is interesting to note that in spite of the economy's poor performance, in 1960 Chile's income per capita was still one of the highest in Latin America.

6. Between 1950 and 1972 Argentina's real GDP grew at a yearly average rate of 4.1 percent, Brazil's at 7 percent, Colombia at 5.2 percent, Mexico at 6.5 percent, Peru at 5.7 percent, and Venezuela at 6.2 percent.

7. For a theoretical analysis on the import substitution strategy see, for example, Chenery (1960). See also Chenery (1975). For a criticism of this approach see Krueger (1978). For a historical analysis of the process within the Latin American context see Furtado (1970). Muñoz (1966) carefully analyzes the case of Chile. See Díaz-Alejandro (1971) for the case of Argentina.

8. Almost all analysts agree that the import substitution protectionist strategy resulted in significant inefficiencies and low rates of employment creation. See, for example, Behrman (1976), de la Cuadra (1969), Martner (1971), and Guardia (1979). Cortes, Butelmann, and Videla (1981) provide a historical analysis of the evolution of protectionism in Chile.

9. See Muñoz (1966). On the exhaustion of the easy phase of import substitution in Latin America see Furtado (1970). On Chile see Pinto (1964).

10. On the early inflationary experience see Fetter (1932) and Subercaceaux (1922). For the 1940s and 1950s see Hirschman (1961) and Harberger (1963). For the 1960s see Corbo (1974), Behrman (1977), and Ffrench-Davis (1973). It should be pointed out that the analysis of the causes of Chile's inflation had been characterized by an acute debate between "monetarists" and "structuralists." For the former, money creation was the main *cause* of inflation (see, for example, Luders (1968) and Luders and Arbildua (1969)). For the latter, however, money creation was only the *propagation* mechanism, with the *causes* of inflation being closely related to the *structure* of the economy, including the system of land tenure. See, for example, Hirschman (1961), Sunkel (1958), and Felix (1960).

11. Undoubtedly, the most influential economic work of this period was the book by Ahumada (1958). In this volume the author argued that the Chilean economic crisis stemmed from four basic causes: (a) the stagnation of agriculture, (b) the chronic inflation, (c) the uneven distribution of income, and (d) the economic and institutional centralism. For other analyses of the crisis see, for example, Pinto (1959, 1964).

12. The presidential candidates were Socialist Salvador Allende, Conservative Jorge Alessandri, and Christian Democrat Radomiro Tomic.

13. According to the Chilean Constitution, if there was no majority in the popular vote, Congress elected the president among the two candidates with higher votes.

14. See Unidad Popular (1970) and Allende et al. (1971).

15. For the UP economic diagnosis see, for example, Vuskovic (1970), Martner (1971), Aranda and Martínez (1970), Zorrilla (1971), Alaluf (1972), and Guardia, Martínez, and Ramos (1979).

16. From a legal standpoint the ownership of most of these firms still remained with the original private owners. However, after "intervening" them the government could exercise *complete* control. For a detailed description of the process used to expropriate these firms see Instituto de Economía y Planificación (1973: 85–161). See also Martinez (1979).

17. See, for example, the discussion in Cauas and Corbo (1972).

18. Between 1971 and 1972 318 firms were seized by the government through "intervention" or similar procedures. See Instituto de Economía y Planificación (1973). An important assumption of the UP model was that after the nationalization of the "monopolistic firms" the state would capture the "surplus," with those funds used to increase investment (see Guardia 1979). However, as mentioned, the great majority of these firms didn't generate surpluses; quite on the contrary, losses were generalized, and both output and investment dropped.

19. Of course, the UP supporters have long recognized that during the period serious economic mistakes were made and that the UP had plunged the country into "economic chaos" (Sideri 1979). The papers in Sideri's volume (1979) contain interesting self-criticisms by former senior UP officials, including Clodomiro Almeyda, a former Minister of Foreign Affairs and Defense during the Allende administration. The main point of these criticisms is that there were mistakes in the short-run economic conduction. According to this view the short-run behavior of the economy—galloping inflation, pervasive shortages, black markets, and so on—was inconsistent with the long-run institutional reforms. It should be pointed out that in this volume, as in most of the UP self-criticism literature, the behavior of the economy is evaluated not so much by the use of traditional indicators but in terms of how far the revolutionary program was pushed. See also Vuskovic (1975) for an insider's critical view of the UP economic policy.

20. For a more detailed discussion, see Chapter 4. See also S. Edwards (1985a, 1985b) and Foxley (1983).

21. When compared to other countries in the region Chile's performance during the military regime was also quite meager. For 1973–83, for example, Chile's real GDP growth was well below middle-income countries' average. For these ten years, however, Chile did better than a number of the Latin American countries.

22. Some optimists actually predicted that Chile would grow at an average real rate of 8.0 percent between 1980 and 1990.
23. See, for example, S. Edwards (1985a) and Schmidt-Hebbel (1981).
24. For previous studies on the sources of growth see, for example, Harberger and Selowsky (1966), Elias (1978), and Schmidt-Hebbel (1981).
25. One has to be careful, however, in interpreting these results. A serious problem is that Schmidt-Hebbel's measure of capacity utilization does not take into account the changes in the structure of production generated by the liberalization of trade and other reforms. On this subject see Chapter 5.
26. The main rationale for this policy was the belief that in an open economy the domestic rate of inflation very rapidly converges to the level of world inflation plus rate of devaluation of the domestic currency. See the detailed discussion in Chapter 2.
27. As discussed in detail in Chapters 3 and 4 during the military experiment banks and big conglomerates established intricate ownership relationships.

2 THE STABILIZATION PROGRAM
From Monetarist Orthodoxy to Exchange Rate Management

In October 1973 the military government announced that the reduction of inflation — which had exceeded 600 percent in the previous twelve months — was one of its main economic goals. During the next eight years the government combated inflation using a variety of tools. Eventually inflation subsided, and, as can be seen from Table 2-1, in 1981 it was at the one-digit level for the first time since 1964.[1]

Other important short-run objectives stated by the government in late 1973 were the eradication of black markets and food shortages, the reduction of government controls, the reorganization of the productive sector, and the avoidance of a major balance of payments crisis. As part of the initial policy package aimed at achieving these goals, the government rationalized the exchange rate system, reducing the fifteen multiple exchange rates to three, and a massive devaluation was implemented in late 1973.[2] Prices of almost 3,000 goods were decontrolled, and measures to reduce tax evasion were undertaken. As an immediate result of the devaluation and of the relaxation of price controls, the official price level increased in October 1973 by 87.5 percent.

During the first eighteen months of the regime some of these objectives were partially achieved — relative prices were realigned, the balance of payments crisis was avoided, and government finances were somewhat straightened. Also during this period the initial steps toward

27

Table 2-1. Rate of Inflation in Chile: 1970–84 (rate of change of the Consumer Price Index: December to December).

	Percent
1970	34.9
1971	34.5
1972	216.7
1973	605.9
1974	369.2
1975	343.2
1976	197.9
1977	84.2
1978	37.2
1979	38.0
1980	31.2
1981	9.9
1982	20.7
1983	23.1
1984	23.0

Sources: From Instituto Nacional de Estadisticas as published in Banco Central de Chile, *Boletín Mensual* for 1979–84; from Cortazar and Marshall (1980) for 1973–78; from Yañez (1978) for 1970–73.

liberalizing some of the key economic sectors — domestic capital markets and international trade — were undertaken, and some firms nationalized during the UP government began to be privatized.[3]

Although the reduction of inflation had been termed the main objective of the government's short-run economic policy, until April 1975 a relatively timid gradualist anti-inflationary approach was deliberately followed. The decision to adopt this gradualist policy was based on the supposed costs of an abrupt alternative and was rationalized in the Minister of Finance's 1974 Economic Report (Mendez 1979: 103–04):

> The first decision in the anti-inflationary policy consisted in adopting a gradualist point of view instead of one of violent containment. . . . To detain inflation suddenly would imply the immediate elimination of the fiscal deficit, and the reduction of credit to the private sector. . . . A simple analysis of these measures gives us an idea of the catastrophic consequences of this type of [abrupt] policy. . . . [T]he social cost, in terms

of loss of production, employment and income from an [abrupt anti-inflationary] economic policy...would be very high and we are sure the majority of Chilean[s] would not be willing to accept it.

The gradualist character of the policy was reflected mainly in the behavior of monetary growth. In June of 1974 the rate of growth of money (M1) stood at an annual rate of 333 percent, only slightly lower than the most expansionary month of the Allende regime—342 percent in August of 1973. On the fiscal side, however, fairly substantial progress was made. The fiscal deficit, which in 1973 reached the unprecedented level of 24.6 percent of GDP was reduced in 1974 to 10.5 percent of GDP. Most of this reduction was attained via a lower government expenditure—the ratio of expenditure to GDP was reduced from 45 percent of GDP in 1973 to 32.4 percent in 1974—which was achieved through a combination of measures, including the elimination of most subsidies, and the firing of a substantial number of civil servants (according to Decree Law 534 of 1974 more than 50,000 government employees had to be fired in a period of eighteen months.) Another important source of decreased expenditure was the sale to the private sector of a number of ailing firms owned by the government. Some of these industries had been nationalized during the Allende government, and most of them were in a precarious financial condition and required permanent injections of fresh funds from the government. This privatization process is discussed in detail in Chapter 4.

Another important characteristic of the initial stabilization effort—which was to be maintained throughout the experiment—was the reluctance to use any type of price controls or guidelines. The government view on this subject is clearly reflected in the already quoted 1974 Minister of Finance report (Mendez 1979: 105): "A particular inappropriate tool for restraining inflation...is price controls. As long as the inflationary pressures generated by fiscal deficit and excessive monetary expansion are not eliminated, it is impossible to prevent price levels from increasing." Of course, this reluctance to use price controls—or other forms of incomes policies—stemmed from Chile's long history of unsuccessful attempts to curb inflation using these types of policies. The most recent of these attempts, the failed UP stabilization effort of 1972, was still fresh in the minds of the military authorities. In particular, the effects of a repressed inflation situation—including generalized shortages, black markets, and the possibility of rationing—had been very traumatic.

In spite of the gradualist stabilization policy and the stated desire of avoiding an excessive "social cost" in reducing inflation, the rigor of the fiscal measures began to be felt in the economy by late 1974. October industrial production fell to 12 percent compared to October of 1973; in November and December further reductions in manufacturing output at annual rates of 11 percent and 12 percent took place. On average, industrial production declined by almost 4 percent during 1974. Unemployment also experienced a marked increase late in that year. In September the rate of unemployment in the greater Santiago area had reached 8.4 percent, drastically up from the 4.1 percent rate of September of 1973.

Perhaps not surprisingly given the relatively lax monetary policy followed during this early period, in 1974 the stabilization program made only very limited progress in attaining its goal of reducing inflation. At the end of the year the rate of inflation stood at 370 percent. Moreover, during the first quarter of 1975, while the level of output continued to decline, inflation began to experience an alarming upward trend, with the official rate of change in the consumer price index reaching 14 percent per month in January, 17 percent in February, and 21 percent in March. At this time the deterioration of the terms of trade made things even more complicated, as the projected deficit in the balance of payments for 1975 as a whole was alarmingly high. In a way Chile was in the worst of worlds. On one hand, the gradualism of the stabilization effort was clearly failing to reduce inflation, and on the other hand the measures undertaken on the fiscal side were negatively affecting production and employment. The Chilean economy was paying the costs of a stabilization program without getting any of its benefits.

THE CLOSED ECONOMY APPROACH TO STABILIZATION: 1975–77

In April 1975, and due to the very slow progress achieved until that point, the gradual approach to anti-inflationary policy was abandoned, and the so-called shock treatment began.[4] On the twenty-fourth of that month Finance Minister Jorge Cauas – a Columbia University trained economist and former World Bank senior staff member – announced on national television that the government had declared a frontal war on inflation. In this speech Cauas noted that General Pinochet had asked him to "design and carry out an economic program with the fundamental purpose of eradicating the inflation that has affected our country for more than seventy five years..." (Mendez 1979: 157). This program was based on traditional views regarding abrupt economic stabilization and called for a drastic reduction in inflation in one year. The main characteristics of the program were (a) an across-the-board reduction in government expenditure (between 15 percent and 25 percent); (b) a 10 percent temporary hike in income taxes; (c) an acceleration of the program of reducing the size of the public sector, which had begun in 1974; and (d) a tight monetary policy. Table 2–2 presents data on inflation and stabilization during the 1970s and early 1980s.

In designing and applying the "shock" anti-inflationary policy, social cost consideration that had greatly preoccupied Minister Cauas in 1974 were set aside. This change in attitude was partly due to the fact that, as noted, the economy was already incurring in some of the costs of stabilization without reaping any substantial benefits and partially due to the recognition that given the dictatorial character of the government the economic costs of disinflation had little, if any, political consequences.

On the fiscal side the "shock" anti-inflationary program was aided by a sweeping tax reform enacted in March 1975. The main purposes of this reform were to generate a substantial increase in tax revenues and to reduce the efficiency distortions generated by the old system. The principal features of this reform include the replacement of a cascade sales tax with a flat rate value added tax at a 20 percent rate; a full indexation of the tax system; an elimination of the remaining tax exemptions and subsidies; a unification of the corporation and non-corporation income taxes into a flat business tax; and the integration of the personal and business income taxes.[5] As may be seen in Table 2–2 the combination of increased tax revenues and reduced government expenditure rapidly affected the fiscal deficit, which declined from over 10 percent of GDP in 1974 to 2.6 percent in 1975 and to less than 1 percent in 1978. In the years that followed and for the first time in more than twenty years Chile experienced a fiscal surplus. This situation changed only in 1983 when in the midst of the recessive crisis the reduction of tax collection generated a small deficit.

The stabilization effort of 1975 also relied on a tighter monetary policy. Although Harberger (1982) has pointed out that it can hardly be said that there was a monetary crunch, during the initial phase of

Table 2-2. Inflation and Stabilization: 1973–83.

	(A)	(B) Government Expenditure		(C) Government Revenue		(D) Fiscal Deficit		(E)	(F)	(G)	(H)
Year	Inflation Rate % (December–December)	1977 Millions of U.S. $	% GDP	1977 Millions of U.S. $	% GDP	1977 Millions of U.S. $	% GDP	Rate of Growth of M1 % (December–December)	Proportion of Total Credit Received by Government	Rate of Devaluation of Peso % (December–December)	Balance of Payments (Millions U.S. $)[a]
1970	34.9	3681	28.1	3301	25.2	380	2.9	—	.56	20.0	—
1971	34.5	4633	32.4	2989	21.2	1644	11.2	110	.69	33.3	—
1972	216.7	4540	32.2	2637	18.7	1903	13.5	157	.77	56.3	—
1973	605.9	5990	44.7	2693	20.1	3297	24.6	317	.88	1340.0	-21
1974	369.2	4374	32.4	2957	21.9	1417	10.5	272	.85	419.4	-55
1975	343.2	3206	27.4	2902	24.8	304	2.6	258	.85	354.5	-344
1976	197.9	3148	25.8	2867	23.5	281	2.3	194	.75	104.9	414
1977	84.2	3337	24.9	3095	23.1	242	1.9	108	.59	60.5	113
1978	37.2	3451	23.8	3335	23.0	116	.9	67	.40	21.4	712
1979	38.0	3627	23.1	3878	24.7	-251	-1.7	65	.29	14.9	1,047
1980	31.2	4200	25.0	4284	25.5	-84	-.6	57	.10	0.0	1,244
1981	9.9	4195	23.7	4726	26.7	-531	-3.0	-6	.02	0.0	70
1982	20.7	4379	29.0	4032	26.7	347	-2.3	9	.07	88.3	-1,165
1983	23.1	N.A.	28.4	N.A.	24.6	N.A.	3.8	27	.09	19.2	-541

Sources: Column A is taken from Yañez (1978) for years 1970–72 and 1979–82 as published in Banco Central de Chile, *Boletín Mensual* (various issues); from Cortazar and Marshall (1980) for 1973–78. Columns B through D are taken from de Castro (1981); columns E and F are taken from *International Financial Statistics* (IFS). Columns G and H are taken from Banco Central de Chile (1983) and from IFS. Column G refers to the peso U.S. $ exchange rate.
[a] A minus sign means deficit. Data for 1970–72 are not available because in 1980 the Central Bank changed the way balance of payment statistics are recorded.

the "shock" stabilization program the control of monetary aggregates was a central aspect of the overall policy, and the Central Bank made serious efforts to control the rate of growth of domestic credit. In particular, in 1975 the monetary tightness was significant, with the real quantity of money (M1) declining almost 20 percent in relation to the previous year.[6]

The April 1975 stabilization program was largely based on traditional monetarist views regarding inflation in closed economies and considered that money creation to finance the fiscal deficit was the basic and most fundamental cause of inflation. This position was consistent with the diagnosis made by some of the government technicians before the coup. A document elaborated during the UP government by a group of economists, then in the opposition, stated that since Chile was largely a closed economy, the control of inflation required (only) the reduction of the fiscal deficit and a tight monetary policy.[7] The government's view on the inflation and on its eradication are clearly summarized by the following quote from Cauas (Mendez 1979: 109).

> The monetary policy that we have been applying recognizes that there is a close relation between the rhythm of growth in the level of prices and the rate of expansion of month supply. . . . The high degree of sensitivity of the money supply to variations in the fiscal deficit necessarily implies that the success of this policy is intimately bound to the maintenance of solid discipline in fiscal matters.

Consistent with the belief that fiscally induced money creation was the most fundamental cause of inflation, the April 1975 stabilization program did not consider using the exchange rate as an anti-inflationary tool. In fact it was decided to maintain a crawling peg exchange rate system that consisted on periodically adjusting the nominal exchange rate at approximately the same rate as lagged inflation.[8] As Minister Cauas himself put it in his April 24 speech, "the exchange rate shall continue to be adjusted in relation to domestic prices" (Mendez 1979: 161). The motivations behind this policy were twofold. First, it was intended to help avoid a balance of payments crisis that was beginning to emerge as a result, among other things, of the drastic drop in the price of copper by more than 50 percent since April of 1974. Second, it responded to the desire to maintain a stable and "realistic" real exchange rate that would encourage nontraditional exports and help the adjustment process following the import tariff reduction that was already underway.[9] In fact, as may be seen in Table

2–2 during 1975 the rate of nominal devaluation of the peso with respect to the U.S. dollar exceeded the rate of inflation (354 percent versus 343 percent). In Chapter 5 we provide a more detailed account of the way in which the tariff reduction and exchange rate policies interacted during this phase.

In terms of wage rates policy, the April 1975 stabilization program called for prudence. Although Cauas asked wage earners to share in the "sacrifice," he also pointed out that the policy of automatic periodic wage adjustments approximately based on past inflation, which had been started in 1974, would continue. In fact, as a result of this policy, during 1975 real wages experienced an increase of 6.5 percent from the depressed level they had attained in 1974. (See Chapter 6 for a detailed discussion of wage behavior.)

The 1975 "shock" stabilization program promptly impacted on inflation, with the rate of growth of prices declining from 69 percent in the second quarter of 1975 to 26 percent in the fourth quarter of 1975. On the production side, the immediate short-run effect of the stabilization program was to aggravate the already serious crisis, generating a large reduction in the level of economic activity in 1975. The fiscal shock plus the sharp decline in Chile's terms of trade resulted in a reduction of GDP in 1975 of 12.9 percent and in a steep increase in the rate of unemployment to almost 20 percent in September of that year. Even though the economy rapidly began to recover after 1975, with real GDP reaching its 1974 level in 1977, unemployment remained at extraordinarily high levels through the period. Real GDP per capita, however, attained its 1974 level only in 1979. In spite of the initial success of the "shock" stabilization program, by early 1976 it seemed that even though the major source of money creation — the fiscal deficit — had been greatly reduced, the rate of growth of prices was regaining its old pace, with the rate of inflation climbing, in the first quarter of 1976, to 47 percent.

With the fiscal deficit under control, and a lower rate of growth of money, inflationary expectations began to play an increasingly important role in the perpetuation of inflation. In fact, it seemed that inflationary expectations had been stabilized at a level of around 200 percent per annum. It also became clear at the time that the behavior of the exchange rate had become an important element in the process of formation of inflationary expectations.[10] Not too surprisingly, given the long inflationary tradition of the country, the public had quickly realized that inflation and nominal exchange rate devaluation were closely linked; bankers, businesspeople, and housewives increasingly began to look at the exchange rate to form their expectations of inflation. In June of 1976, as a means to break inflationary expectations, the government revalued the peso by 10 percent.[11] Following this revaluation the process of minidevaluations, where the nominal exchange rate (with respect to the U.S. dollar) was adjusted at approximately the same rate as past inflation, was reassumed. In March 1977, in order to further break expectations, the nominal exchange rate was again revalued by 10 percent. Once again this appreciation was followed by periodic devaluations that, as discussed in Chapter 5, tried to compensate firms for the loss in competitiveness generated by the tariff reduction process.

During 1976 and 1977 substantial progress was made in the battle against inflation. The rate of increase of prices had been reduced almost by half in each of those years (see Table 2-2). However, by late 1977 inflation was still very high in absolute levels — 87 percent.

The revaluation of the peso of 1976 and 1977 marked the first steps toward a major change in the Chilean stabilization strategy and in the authorities' conception of the role of macroeconomic policy. In late 1977, with the rate of inflation standing at a yearly level of 84 percent, the government authorities argued that given the increasingly open character of the Chilean economy, traditional anti-inflationary programs based on closed economy premises were becoming clearly ineffective. It was then pointed out that a drastic change in the orientation of the stabilization policy was required to make further progress against inflation.

OPEN ECONOMY MONETARISM: 1978–82

Exchange Rate Management

In February 1978 the manipulation of the exchange rate completely took over as the most important anti-inflationary tool. At that time a novel policy of preannouncing a declining rate of devaluation for a fairly long period of time (up to a year) was introduced as a way of further reducing the rate of inflation. This system, popularly known as the *tablita*, deliberately set the starting declining rate of devaluation at a lower rate than ongoing inflation. With the trade reform having substantially reduced most import barriers, it was expected that this system of preannounced devaluations would have two important effects on inflation. First, it would channel inflationary expectations downward for a fairly long period of time. Second, and more important, it was expected that the system would work in a way similar to a textbook-type fixed exchange rate regime, where the law of one price holds. Consequently, it was thought that domestic inflation would rapidly converge to the level of world inflation plus the rate of devaluation of the peso.[12]

This new open economy approach to stabilization policies was largely influenced by the simplest version of the monetary approach to the balance of payments (MABP). This view, which enjoyed some popularity in the United States and other academic circles during the early 1970s, focuses on the relation between the economy's balance of payments and its monetary sector. In its simplest incarnation the monetary approach postulates, among other things, that the law of one price holds permanently and that the domestic rate of inflation will be equal to the world rate of inflation plus the rate of devaluation. At a more general level the MABP has important implications regarding the effectiveness of macroeconomic policy in an open economy. For example, under the most basic set of assumptions if there are fixed (or preannounced) exchange rates, the nominal quantity of money becomes an endogenous variable and monetary policy has no effect on inflation or on the rest of the economy even in the short run. All the monetary authorities can hope to do is affect the composition of high-powered money; changes in domestic credit result in instantaneous and opposite changes in the stock of international reserves, with total nominal money being unaffected.

The monetary approach has a long tradition emanating, at least, from Hume. The MABP provides only a very general framework to analyze balance of payments behavior. Its central proposition is that the balance of payments will reflect conditions of excess demand or supply for money in the domestic economy. This proposition, of course, is little more than a tautology derived from the balance sheet of the monetary system. In order for the MABP to be of analytical interest, some structure has to be added through a macroeconomic model of the behavior of the economy. The textbook version of the MABP, which seems to have influenced (some) of the Chilean authorities, uses a caricature-type macromodel that assumes that there are only tradable goods, that PPP (or the law of one price) holds permanently, that interest arbitrage holds continuously, and that both output and domestic credit are exogenous variables.[13]

The economic authorities, in line with the predictions of the MABP, expected that given the *tablita* any attempts by local firms to raise prices at a pace faster than the preannounced rate of devaluation plus rate of world inflation, would be frustrated by the price arbitrage mechanism, where cheaper imports would crowd out the domestically produced good from the market. The way in which this price arbitrate-type mechanism was expected to work was explained by Minister de Castro in 1978 (Banco Central de Chile, *Boletín Mensual*, (October 1978): 1677):

> [W]e have modified our exchange rate policy. . . . [T]he rate of devalua-tion. . .has been determined at 21.4% for 1978. As the year progresses both the monthly rates of devaluation and import tariffs will be reduced. . . . [T]hus, if there is a higher inflation. . .the cost of imports would de-cline. . . . [I]n this way foreign competition. . .would increase.

Moreover, in his February 3, 1978, speech, where he announced the adoption of the *tablita*, Minister de Castro provided a more complete view of the way in which the system was expected to work (Banco Central, *Boletín Mensual* (February 1978): 241):

> [T]he openness of the economy to international trade and the prean-nouncement of the rate of devaluation until the end of 1978 will rapidly generate competitive imports for those domestic products whose internal prices are increased above reasonable limits. . . . This mechanism will also allow us to generate important increases in internal liquidity, without risking higher inflationary pressures.

The guidance of expectations was the other objective of the prean-nounced devaluation *tablita* system. In Minister de Castro's words (Mendez 1979: 287): "[E]xchange rate policy has provided a reason-able orientation of inflationary expectations on the part of the public, because it was solidly supported by the absence of the need for money creation for the public sector."

The use of a preannounced exchange rate as the fundamental form of combatting inflation was later also adopted in Argentina and Uru-guay.[14] A crucial difference between Chile and these countries, how-ever, was that in Chile, before the *tablita* was adopted, the fiscal deficit had been controlled. In this way the maintenance of the pre-announced exchange rate policy was (somewhat) credible. The Chilean authorities, in fact, repeatedly pointed out that the *tablita* strategy was only possible because fiscal pressures had already been eliminated. In the Argentinian case, on the other hand, it was apparent early on that the fiscal and exchange rate policies were incompatibles and that it was only thanks to the massive capital inflows that the *tablita* could be maintained.[15]

In June 1979, with inflation standing at an annual rate of 34 percent, the government put an end to the system of a preannounced declining rate of devaluation and fixed the exchange rate at 39 pesos per dollar. Initially it was stated that the fixed rate would last until February 1980, when another preannounced schedule of devaluation was supposed to be designed. However, shortly before that time it was announced that the fixed rate would be maintained "forever."[16] It was expected that this move to a fixed rate would reinforce and accelerate the purchasing power parity type convergence of domestic to world inflation.

The use of the U.S. dollar as the benchmark currency in the formulation of the exchange rate policy introduced some unintended volatility into the Chilean economy. This was because during 1977–81 the value of the U.S. dollar varied significantly in relation to other currencies. For example, between 1977 and 1979 the dollar depreciated in real terms by almost 12 percent relative to the IMF MERM basket of currencies. This, of course, meant that during this period the Chilean peso was depreciating, in relation to this basket, at a rate higher than what the authorities had intended. Starting in February 1980 the dollar began appreciating against the major international currencies and so did the peso. In a sense, instead of having a fixed exchange rate, during the next 2½ years Chile had an exchange rate that *appreciated*, in nominal terms, relative to a basket of world currencies. This can be seen in Table 2–3, which contains indexes for Chile's nominal exchange rate with respect to the U.S. dollar, and with respect to a basket of eighteen currencies of Chile's most important trade partners. As may be seen, while between the third quarter of 1979 and the second quarter of 1982 the nominal exchange rate with respect to the dollar remained constant, the more comprehensive index of the nominal rate relative to the basket of currencies experienced a nominal appreciation that exceeded 31 percent.

Besides the adoption of a fixed exchange rate regime, two other important developments took place during 1979. First, an important step toward the liberalization of capital flows was taken, when in June of that year commercial banks were allowed to greatly increase their ratio of foreign liabilities to equity. This relaxation in the controls to capital flows — which was later complemented by further liberaliza-

Table 2-3. Index of Nominal Exchange Rates: 1979–83 (1979.3 = 100).

	Index of Nominal Exchange Rate Relative to U.S. Dollar	Index of Nominal Exchange Rate Relative to Basket of Currencies
1979.3 [a]	100.0	100.0
1979.4	100.0	95.9
1980.1	100.0	92.3
1980.2	100.0	90.8
1980.3	100.0	90.7
1980.4	100.0	88.1
1981.1	100.0	83.9
1981.2	100.0	76.4
1981.3	100.0	71.8
1981.4	100.0	72.1
1982.1	100.0	68.9
1982.2	100.0	68.7
1982.3 [b]	141.1	88.9
1982.4	177.6	109.9
1983.1	192.2	119.2
1983.2	193.2	116.2
1983.3	204.5	119.0
1983.4	218.7	126.2

Sources: Constructed by the authors using raw data from the IMF *International Financial Statistics.* The following countries were used for constructing the basket index (weights are in parentheses: United States (.23), Germany (.14), Japan (.10), Argentina (.10), United Kingdom (.07), Italy (.03), Netherlands (.05), Spain (.03), Brazil (.07), France (.03), Colombia (.01), Mexico (.01), Ecuador (.03), Peru (.02), Sweden (.01), Belgium (.02), Venezuela (.02), and Saudi Arabia (.03).

[a] In this quarter the exchange rate was fixed at 39 pesos per dollar.

[b] In this quarter the fixed exchange rate of 39 pesos per U.S. dollars was abandoned.

tions in 1980 and 1982—resulted in a dramatic increase in the level of foreign debt in the second half of 1979 and in the following two years. As discussed in detail in Chapter 3, most of these foreign funds were obtained by the private sector without government guarantee. The other important—in fact crucial—development of 1979 was the enactment of the Labor Law. This piece of legislation—which is analyzed in greater detail in Chapter 6—institutionalized real wage rigidity by

Table 2–4. Devaluation, Chilean Inflation, and U.S. Inflation: 1978–83 (percentage).

	(A) Annualized Rate of Devaluation with Respect to U.S. Dollar	(B) Annualized U.S. WPI Rate of Inflation	(C) Annualized U.S. CPI Rate of Inflation	(D) Annualized Rate of Inflation (CPI)
1978	21.4	9.6	9.1	37.2
1979	14.9	14.9	13.3	38.0
1980	0	12.3	12.4	31.2
1981	0	5.6	8.9	9.5
1982	88.3	1.5	3.9	20.7
1983	19.2	1.8	3.8	23.1

Sources: All data refer to December to December rates of change.
Columns A and D are from Table 2-1.
Columns B and C are from the IMF *International Financial Statistics.*

legally implementing a procedure by which wages of those workers subject to collective bargaining were fully indexed to past inflation.[17]

The Mystery of the Nonconvergent Rates of Inflation

Contrary to what was expected by the architects of the open economy stabilization plan, after the exchange rate was fixed in mid-1979, the domestic rate of inflation did not rapidly converge to its world counterpart. Table 2-4 contains data for 1978–83 on the behavior of the rate of nominal devaluation with respect to the U.S. dollar, of two measures of U.S. inflation, and of the Chilean rate of inflation. As can be seen, throughout this period the rate of domestic inflation exceeded the rate of the U.S. inflation (plus rate of devaluation). Using the change in the U.S. WPI as an indicator of international inflation, between 1978 and 1981 the accumulated divergence between Chile's and international inflation rates exceeded 120 percent.[18] In fact, the use of the exchange rate as a stabilization tool helped generate a steady real appreciation, or real overvaluation, of the peso, which, among other things, greatly hurt the degree of competitiveness of firms producing goods in the tradable sector, including nontraditional exports.

As shown in Chapter 3 this real appreciation became particularly important after June 1979.

Although the fixing of the exchange rate was not the only determinant of the real overvaluation of the peso—and, as pointed out in Chapter 3, probably not even the most important one—in 1980 many firms started to lobby for the abandonment of the fixed exchange rate policy. Of course, those firms whose final prices were more closely linked to the exchange rate led the effort toward persuading the government to readopt a more flexible exchange rate policy. However, some of the large conglomerates or *grupos*, which had heavily borrowed abroad and incurred high debts in foreign currency, staunchly opposed any changes in the exchange rate policy. As the degree of overvaluation became more serious, the view of these two groups became increasingly antagonistic as they tried to influence the behavior of the economic authorities. The failure for the law of one price to hold—and for domestic inflation to rapidly converge to the level of world inflation after the exchange rate was fixed—was initially considered as a major puzzle by the believers in the system, and a frantic search for possible explanations was launched.

Two explanations for the "divergent rates of inflation" puzzle became popular. The first one—which was favored by the government authorities—simply denied the fact that the law of one price failed to hold. It was argued that if appropriate indexes for Chile's "relevant external inflation" were used, the law of one price did in fact hold. For example, in his 1981 report, then-Minister of Finance Sergio de Castro stated that if the international inflation was correctly measured, "the relevant external inflation...added to the domestic devaluation, exceeded domestic inflation" (de Castro 1981: 26). Of course, a problem with this explanation is that it was not clear how these "appropriate" indexes should be constructed. In fact, if instead of using U.S. data one uses a weighted average of Chile's trade partners' WPIs as an index of international inflation, and a weighted average of bilateral nominal exchange rates to construct an index of devaluation of the peso, the law of one price still failed to hold by a substantial margin. In this case between 1977 and 1981 the sum of accumulated rate of devaluation plus international inflation amounts to 99 percent, well below the accumulated rate of domestic inflation of 171 percent.

The second explanation for the lack of rapid convergence of domestic and international inflation rates was more sophisticated. It was argued that although the law of one price tended to hold for tradable goods, the domestic and foreign inflation rates diverged because of an *equilibrium* increase in the relative price of Chilean nontradable goods.[19] The proponents of this view correctly pointed out that this change in relative prices was the consequence of the increase in the level of aggregate expenditure, which, in turn, was possible thanks to the higher degree of foreign borrowing.[20] Although this argument correctly identified the rapid growth of capital inflows as a source of relative price changes, it failed to recognize that this relative price change was only temporary and was creating a serious long-run macroeconomic disequilibrium. As explained in detail in Chapter 3, the reason for this was that the increase in the rate of capital inflows did not represent a long-run macroeconomic sustainable situation and eventually had to decline—as indeed it did in 1982. A second shortcoming of this "sophisticated" explanation was that it ignored the possible roles of other factors. The most important of these neglected factors was the backward wage indexation scheme.

Wage Indexation, Devaluation, and Stabilization

Under conditions of decreasing inflation, a wage indexation mechanism that adjusts wages to past inflation will result in a secular increase in real wages and will generate a real overvaluation. In this case, even if the law of one price holds for tradable goods, the convergence of domestic to international inflation can be quite slow. This fact can be illustrated using the following simple model of inflation in a two-sector economy with a fixed (or preannounced) exchange rate and a backward wage indexation mechanism:

$$\hat{P}_t = \alpha\hat{P}_{Tt} + (1-\alpha)\hat{P}_{Nt} \tag{2.1}$$

$$\hat{P}_{Tt} = \hat{E}_t + \hat{P}_{Tt}^* \tag{2.2}$$

$$D^N[(P_N/P_T)_t, Z_t] = S^N((W/P_N)_t) \tag{2.3}$$

$$\hat{W}_t = k\hat{P}_{t-1} \tag{2.4}$$

$\hat{P}_t$ is the percentage rate of change of the domestic price level; $\hat{P}_{Tt}$ is the percentage rate of change of the price of tradables expressed in domestic currency; $\hat{P}_{Nt}$ is the rate of change of nontradable goods prices; $\hat{E}_t$ is the rate of devaluation, and $\hat{P}_{Tt}^*$ is the rate of change of the international price of tradables; D^N and S^N are the demand and supply functions for nontradable goods; W is the nominal wage rate, and $\hat{W}_t$ is its rate of change in period t; and finally, Z_t is aggregate real expenditure.[21] Equation (2.1) states that the rate of change of the overall price level is a weighted average of the rate of change of tradables and nontradables inflation, with α and $(1-\alpha)$ being the weights. Equation (2.2) is the law of one price for tradables. Equation (2.3) is the equilibrium condition for the market for nontradable goods. Demand depends negatively on relative prices and positively on aggregate real expenditure. Supply of nontradables, on the other hand, depends negatively on the product wage rate. Equation (2.4) is the rule of wage indexation and states that in every period nominal wages are adjusted in a percentage k of past inflation. If, as was the case in Chile, there is full backward indexation, $k=1$ and $\hat{W}_t = \hat{P}_{t-1}$.

From the nontradables market equilibrium condition we can obtain the following expression for the rate of change in the price of nontradables:

$$\hat{P}_{N_t} = \left(\frac{\eta}{\eta+\epsilon}\right)\hat{P}_{Tt} + \left(\frac{\epsilon}{\eta+\epsilon}\right)\hat{W}_t - \left(\frac{\delta}{\eta+\epsilon}\right)\hat{Z}_t \qquad (2.5)$$

where η and δ are the price and real expenditure demand elasticities for nontradables (that is, $\eta<0$, $\delta>0$) and where ϵ is the supply elasticity of nontradables with respect to the product wage ($\epsilon<0$). Combining (2.5) with the definition of inflation (2.1), the following is obtained:

$$\hat{P}_t = \left(\frac{\alpha\epsilon+\eta}{\eta+\epsilon}\right)\hat{P}_{Tt} + \left(\frac{(1-\alpha)\epsilon}{\eta+\epsilon}\right)\hat{W}_t - \left(\frac{(1-\alpha)\delta}{\eta+\epsilon}\right)\hat{Z}_t \qquad (2.6)$$

Assuming, as was the case in Chile since mid-1979, that there is a fixed exchange rate ($\hat{E}_t = 0$) and that there is 100 percent backward indexation ($k=1$), and further assuming in order to simplify the exposition that there are no demand pressures ($\hat{Z}_t = 0$), the following equation for the inflation rate is obtained:[22]

$$\hat{P}_t = \left(\frac{\alpha\epsilon+\eta}{\eta+\epsilon}\right)\hat{P}_{Tt}^* + \frac{(1-\alpha)\epsilon}{\eta+\epsilon}\hat{P}_{t-1} \qquad (2.7)$$

This, of course, is a first-order difference equation, whose solution indicates that (as long as there are no demand pressures) the domestic rate of inflation will slowly converge through time to the international rate of inflation $\hat{P}_{Tt}^*$. The speed at which both rates of inflation will actually converge will depend on the magnitude of the coefficient $(1-\alpha)\epsilon/(\eta+\epsilon)$. Notice, however, that if there are positive demand pressures for nontradables — stemming for example from an increase in borrowing from abroad — $\hat{Z}_t > 0$ and the convergence of both rates of inflation will be much slower and can even fail to take place for a long period of time.

The slow convergence of the domestic to international rate of inflation in the presence of lagged wage indexation illustrated in equation (2.7) has two important consequences: First, under declining inflation real wages will generally increase through time, and second, there will be a real appreciation of the domestic currency. Combining equations (2.4) and (2.7) we find that the change in the real wage can be written as

$$\hat{W}_t - \hat{P}_t = (\hat{P}_{t-1} - \hat{P}_{Tt}^*)\left(\frac{\alpha\epsilon + \eta}{\eta + \epsilon}\right) \tag{2.8}$$

As can be seen from this expression, as long as lagged inflation exceeds international inflation (that is, $\hat{P}_{t-1} > \hat{P}_{Tt}^*$), as will usually be the case in a declining inflation environment, real wages will increase through time. Since in this example the increase in real wages is completely unrelated to increases in productivity, it would put considerable strain on the degree of profitability of the tradable goods sector.

Defining the real exchange rate (e) in the standard way:

$$e_t^* = \frac{E_t P_{Tt}^*}{P_t} \tag{2.9}$$

we find that its rate of change is equal (maintaining the assumption of fixed nominal exchange rate) to

$$\hat{e}_t = \frac{\epsilon(1-\alpha)}{\eta + \epsilon}(\hat{P}_{Tt}^* - \hat{P}_{t-1}) \tag{2.10}$$

This expression indicates that under a fixed exchange rate regime with backward indexation, as long as the international rate of inflation is below the lagged domestic rate of inflation, there will be a real exchange rate appreciation.

As suggested by this model, after the adoption of the fixed rate, and the legalization of the wage indexation scheme in 1979, both a steep increase in Chile's real wage and a substantial real appreciation of the peso were observed. Whereas between 1979 and 1981 the real wage rate increased by 31 percent, during the same period the real exchange rate experienced a real appreciation (that is, real overvaluation) of almost 30 percent.[23]

Passive Macroeconomics and the Automatic Adjustment

After the peso was fixed to the U.S. dollar in 1979, monetary policy became increasingly passive. Within the strict context of the simple monetary approach to the balance of payments, the authorities argued that in a small open economy with fixed exchange rates monetary policy was completely ineffective in the short run.[24] The Minister of Finance, Sergio de Castro, stated in 1981 that since the fiscal deficit was under control and the country had a fixed exchange rate system, there was no need for the Central Bank to engage in any kind of active monetary policy; the plan was that from that time onward, the Central Bank would follow a "neutral policy" where its stock of domestic credit would remain unchanged in nominal terms. According to this program, increases in the demand for money would have to be fully satisfied through the accumulation of international reserves that, in turn, would be a reflection of higher international loans.[25] During the second part of 1980 and most of 1981 the Central Bank tried to follow this neutral policy, with a large proportion of the increase in monetary aggregates during this period being the result of the evergrowing foreign debt.

In 1981, after almost two years of having a fixed exchange rate — and partially thanks to the steep appreciation of the dollar in the international financial market — the domestic rate of inflation began to converge to the level of international inflation. In that year the rate of change of the CPI was 9 percent.[26] At this time, however, the degree of real overvaluation of the peso had reached considerable proportions, and it became increasingly apparent that the situation was not sustainable. As shown in Chapter 3, generalized expectations of devaluation began to settle in, and in late 1981 and early 1982 a massive speculation against the peso erupted. In part as a result of these heightened expectations of devaluation interest rates skyrocketed, and numerous firms faced the prospect of bankruptcy. Surprisingly, even on the face of a major macroeconomic disequilibrium, the government decided to stick to "neutral policy," refusing to take an active stance on monetary and exchange rate policies. It was forcefully pointed out that without any intervention by the monetary authorities the economy would adjust automatically. Based on the most basic textbook interpretation of the law of one price, the economic authorities repeatedly argued that the only effect of nominal devaluations was to generate an equivalent domestic inflation, without affecting relative prices or the real exchange rate.[27]

The role the authorities assigned to the "automatic adjustment" macroeconomic mechanism is clearly captured by the following quote from the chief policymaker, Minister of Finance Sergio de Castro (de Castro 1981: 27).

> [T]he neutral monetary policy of the Central Bank implies that money is only created as a result of inflows of foreign exchange. If such inflows do not take place via a higher level of foreign loans, the private sector's desire to finance a high current account deficit will be simultaneously reflected in a loss of international reserves, and in an equivalent monetary contraction. This will raise the interest rate, generating a decline in expenditure and in the demand for imports, to the level required to finance a current account deficit compatible with the level of foreign borrowing that the country can sustain.

From here de Castro went on to say that devaluations were completely ineffective, since they would generate equiproportional inflation and would have no effect on the real exchange rate. He then stated that "the fixed exchange rate can be maintained, and will be maintained for many years" (de Castro 1981: 27).

This extraordinarily passive position regarding monetary and exchange rate policy ignored the fact that in most historical episodes where the initial real exchange rate was highly overvalued, nominal devaluations, if accompanied by appropriate macroeconomic policies, have been highly effective in generating relative price adjustments or real devaluations.[28] In the case of Chile in 1981 the problem was not that the devaluation would have been ineffective per se but that the 100 percent wage indexation scheme would have greatly reduced the effectiveness of a nominal exchange rate adjustment. It is well known that under fully indexed wages a nominal devaluation will be translated into higher wages. In 1981, then, a solution of the problem required both an abandonment of the ill-fated wage indexation law and an exchange rate adjustment. None of this was done by the government, and, although things got dramatically serious, it was insisted that without any need for intervention the process of "automatic adjustment" would restore macroeconomic equilibrium.

In a way the "automatic adjustment" mechanism almost worked. In late 1981 and early 1982, expecting the devaluation, the public started to actively speculate against the peso, massively purchasing foreign exchange. This plus the somewhat reduced level of foreign credits re-

Table 2-5. Rate of Change of Different Nominal Monetary
Aggregates: 1977–81 (quarterly).

	(A) Rate of Change of Base Money (%)	(B) Rate of Change of M1 (%)	(C) Rate of Change of M2 (%)	(D) Rate of Change of M3 (%)	(E) Rate of Inflation (%)
1977 Q1	33.1	45.1	58.3	58.4	19.4
Q2	23.2	22.9	28.7	30.1	18.9
Q3	7.7	14.4	16.6	18.6	12.7
Q4	13.0	11.8	13.7	13.8	12.0
1978 Q1	18.5	30.2	12.2	32.5	8.4
Q2	14.1	17.1	18.3	18.5	9.0
Q3	3.5	6.6	15.9	17.0	9.4
Q4	14.0	9.6	21.1	21.3	6.4
1979 Q1	12.7	21.9	24.3	26.2	5.7
Q2	10.1	9.9	9.0	10.6	7.4
Q3	4.8	7.2	13.3	14.8	10.4
Q4	12.3	11.3	11.2	11.8	8.6
1980 Q1	7.2	16.6	13.9	15.0	6.5
Q2	7.3	13.9	9.8	10.8	7.2
Q3	6.0	7.2	12.5	15.3	6.2
Q4	11.7	13.7	14.0	15.1	7.4
1981 Q1	9.0	10.5	14.0	17.0	4.2
Q2	−11.2	1.4	17.7	17.4	2.8
Q3	−3.7	−3.5	11.7	11.9	2.1
Q4	7.0	7.3	6.3	1.7	1.8

Source: Banco Central de Chile (1981, 1983, 1984).

sulted, as de Castro had pointed out, in a decline in the nominal level of base money in the second and third quarters of 1981 (see Table 2-5). This squeeze in liquidity and the generalized expectations of devaluation helped generate a steady increase in interest rates and a substantial decline in expenditure. The magnitude of this automatic adjustment was clearly insufficient, and the real overvaluation was not corrected. Also this adjustment mechanism was taking a high toll in terms of economic activity and employment. For example, during the first three months of 1982 industrial production experienced declines, with respect to the same months in the previous year, of 16 percent, 13 percent, and 12 percent. Also, in March 1982 the rate of open unemployment had climbed to 18.4 percent from 11 percent in March of 1981.

This unsustainable situation finally burst in 1982 after an abrupt drop in capital inflows. At that time the economy desperately needed a real devaluation and a macroeconomic readjustment. In June 1982 the government finally decided to abandon the "automatic adjustment" approach and to pursue a more active policy. The peso was devalued by 18 percent, the indexation clause of the labor law was amended, and the generalized wage indexation policy was abandoned. However, this was too little, and too late. At this point the loss of credibility in the government policies was almost complete, and the devaluation even accelerated the speculation against the peso, with the resulting large loss of international reserves in the following weeks. In addition, the international financial community reacted negatively to these measures, and the flow of foreign funds towards Chile was further reduced. The June devaluation was followed by a brief experiment with flexible rates and by a dual rates system. In November of that year surcharges of up to 30 percent were imposed on a number of import categories. In December 1982 a new Minister of Finance—the third since de Castro had resigned almost a year before—declared the inconvertibility of the peso and imposed severe exchange controls. In March 1983 a (temporary) general hike in import tariffs to a uniform 20 percent level was decreed. In twelve months—between June of 1982 and June 1983—the Chilean peso was devalued by 99 percent and inflation reached 32.7 percent. In this way the fixed exchange rate system, which according to some government officials should have lasted for decades—and which others even wanted to establish in the constitution—came to an embarrassing end. Inflation, on the other hand, was back to its long-term historical average.

THE COSTS OF DISINFLATION

The stabilization program almost succeeded. It reduced inflation from more than 600 percent to a one-digit level in little more than seven years. However, this goal was achieved at substantial costs in terms of unemployment, reduced production, and complete collapse of the financial sector (see Chapter 3). What is worse, the curbing of inflation was short-lived; between 1982 and 1984 inflation wandered around 25 percent, not far from the historical average.

It is possible to argue that until late 1979, and in spite of the recession generated by the "shock" anti-inflationary plan of April 1975, the stabilization program had been quite successful. Inflationary expectations had been broken, the fiscal deficit was under control, and the rate of inflation had been reduced to its historical average of around 30 percent per year.[29] Until June 1979 the preannounced rate of devaluation had generated only a small real appreciation when measured relative to the U.S. dollar. Moreover, partially due to the depreciation of the U.S. dollar in the international market, the exchange rate did not appreciate in real terms relative to a basket of currencies, between January 1978 and June 1979. In the fateful year of 1979, however, a series of ill-conceived and mutually inconsistent policy measures were taken, including the pegging of the peso to the U.S. dollar, the legalization of a rigid backward indexation scheme, and the relaxation of controls for capital movements. All these policies conspired to generate a severe disequilibrium situation in the external sector, which, as has been pointed out, was reflected by the massive real overvaluation of the peso. The maintenance of this overvalued exchange rate for a long time, and more seriously the insistance on relying on an automatic scheme to solve the macroeconomic disequilibrium, deepened significantly what otherwise should have been a serious but not devastating crisis generated from adverse foreign shocks.

There is little doubt that the manipulation of the exchange rate and ultimate pegging of the peso to the dollar when inflation was still running at a 30 percent annual rate was an ill-made policy decision. It is also true that pointing exclusively at the exchange rate policy — as many popular accounts of the Chilean experiments had — as the only cause of the failure of the liberalization reform is a gross oversimplification. The complexities of the Chilean case go well beyond a particular policy. Even though there is little doubt that the exchange rate played an important role in the events of 1973–83, it was, as emphasized in Chapter 8, only one of the elements that determined the final outcome of the Chilean experiment. It possibly was not even the most important one.

NOTES

1. Official consumer price indexes have a number of shortcomings, especially for 1971–78. For this reason in this study we use the indexes as

corrected by Yañez (1978) and Cortázar and Marshall (1980). At times we also use the GDP deflator, which is free of measurement problems.

2. Since during the UP there were fifteen different exchange rates, it is difficult to measure the extent of the devaluation. However, the official imports rate was devalued by more than 1000 percent. Initially the military government reduced the number of exchange rates to three. Later in 1975 all rates were unified into a single exchange rate.

3. See Chapter 4 for further details on the deregulation of privatization processes.

4. The lack of results in the stabilization program became somewhat of a political embarrassment, since in late 1973 a senior government official had stated that in one year the rate of inflation would reach zero!

5. On the fiscal reform see Minister Cauas's speech as reproduced in Mendez (1979: 119) and the analysis in Guzman (1975). Although the fiscal reform greatly improved the efficiency of Chile's taxation system, there still remained some highly distortive taxes. In particular taxes on labor — including social security taxes — remained quite high until the social security reform of 1980. See Chapters 4 and 6.

6. See also Harberger (1981b). Other experts — for example Alejandro Foxley — also agree that there wasn't a monetary crunch in Chile. See Cline and Weintraub (1981: 233). The main reason that in 1975 we observed a reduction in the fiscal deficit, while credit creation by the Central Bank continued (see Table 2-2), was that government enterprises — which are not part of the fiscal sector — still ran huge deficits. See Harberger (1982) and Foxley (1981, discussion). On the monetary policy followed during 1975–77 see also Barandiaran (1977).

7. See Bardón, Carrasco, and Vial (1985) for a long discussion on the precoup monetarist diagnosis. As Bardón et al. point out, this pre-coup document became, in a way, the original draft for the Pinochet economic program.

8. Chile had successfully used this type of crawling peg exchange rate system during the 1960s. See Ffrench-Davis (1981).

9. The maintenance of a high real exchange rate was thought, from the beginning, to be an important element in the trade liberalization strategy (see Bardón, Carrasco, and Vial 1985). This objective was later frustrated as a result of the preannounced and fixed exchange rate policy and of the opening of the capital account. See below and Chapter 3 for further discussions.

10. Expectations have played an important role in the analysis of hyperinflation processes. See, for example, Sargent (1983) and Dornbusch and Fischer (1986). Under rational expectations what matters is the public's expected path of future behavior of the determinants of inflation. In the Chilean case the public used the rate of devaluation as

a signal on the expected rate of money creation. During 1976, even though the fiscal deficit was under control, the rapid accumulation of international reserves became an important source of money creation. See Chapter 3.

11. At this time, and as a result of the 1975 stabilization program and of a partial recovery of the price of copper, the accumulation of reserves became the main source of money creation. This revaluation was also aimed at slowing down this reserves accumulation process. In fact, as discussed in Chapter 3, at this time the control of reserves accumulation became an important concern of the authorities.

12. Historically, of course, this was not the first time that the manipulation of the exchange rate was used as a tool in an attempt to bring down a substantial inflation. For example, the failed stabilization attempt of February/April 1923 during the German hyperinflation relied on fixing the exchange rate (Dornbusch and Fischer 1986). What was new in the Chilean case, however, was that rather than fixing the value of the peso, a declining rate of devaluation was announced. Barandiaran (1977), in fact, suggested in November 1977 the adoption of a *tablita*-type scheme.

13. For a discussion on the analytical aspects of the MABP see the essays collected in Frenkel and Johnson (1976). For an analysis on the role of the MABP in the Latin American stabilization programs of the 1970s see Barleta, Blejer, and Landau (1984).

14. On the Argentinian case see Fernández (1985) and Calvo (1986a). On Uruguay see Hanson (1985) and Hanson and de Melo (1983, 1985). For a comparison of Argentina, Chile, and Uruguay see Corbo, de Melo, and Tybout (1986).

15. See Cumby and van Wijnbergen (1983) for an analysis of how the persistence of the fiscal deficit in Argentina greatly affected the outcome of the devaluation crisis of 1981. See also Conolly and Gonzales (1986).

16. In June 1979 the previously preannounced path of the exchange rate still had six more months to go. In order to (partially) hold to its commitments, just before fixing the exchange rate, the government implemented a devaluation that brought the price of the dollar to the level it would have had in December of that year, if the *tablita* had not been abandoned.

17. As is discussed at length in Chapter 6, the wage indexation system for all workers was started in 1974 and was applied in a somewhat flexible way until 1982. The Labor Law of 1979, on the other hand, was very rigid. See Chapter 6 for further details.

18. The use of U.S. price indexes to proxy international inflation is not completely correct. However, as pointed out below, even if weighted average rates of inflation for Chile's trade partners are used, a large

divergence between the domestic and international rates of inflation is observed.

19. See, for example, de la Cuadra (1980). According to this view domestic inflation $\hat{P}_t$ is a weighted average of the rate of growth of nontradable and tradable prices: $\hat{P}_t = \beta\hat{P}_{Nt} + (1-\beta)\hat{P}_{Tt}$. If the law of one price holds for tradables, $\hat{P}_{Tt} = \hat{E}_t + \hat{P}_{Tt}^*$, where $\hat{E}_t$ is the rate of devaluation and $\hat{P}_{Tt}^*$ is international inflation for tradables, domestic inflation can be rewritten as $\hat{P}_t = (\hat{P}_{Tt}^* + \hat{E}_t) + \beta(\hat{P}_{Nt} - \hat{P}_{Tt})$. If there are no relative price changes (that is, $\hat{P}_{Nt} = \hat{P}_{Tt}$), the domestic rate of inflation will be equal to international inflation plus devaluation ($\hat{P}_t = \hat{P}_{Tt}^* + \hat{E}_t$). If, however, there is an increase in the relative price of nontradables ($\hat{P}_{Nt} - \hat{P}_{Tt}) > 0$, then $\hat{P}_t > (\hat{P}_{Tt}^* + \hat{E}_t)$.

20. Surprisingly, however, after recognizing the "Dutch-Disease" nature of capital inflow liberalization, then–Central Bank President Sergio de la Cuadra (1980) argued that the nominal exchange rate should be revalued.

21. In order to simplify the exposition we have assumed that Z_t is exogenous. A more appropriate assumption would link Z to permanent income. In that case it would be possible to introduce the distinction between permanent and transitory disturbances on the real exchange rate.

22. In Chapter 3, however, the assumption that $\hat{Z}_t = 0$ is lifted when the role of capital inflows is discussed in detail.

23. Notice that this model, and in particular equation (2.8), explains the dynamics of real wages without referring to their *level*. In Chapter 6 we discuss in some detail the movement of the sustainable long-run equilibrium level of real wages during this period.

24. See, for example, Bardón and Bacigalupo (1980). Corbo (1982), however, used a sterilization empirical model to analyze this issue and concluded that during all of this period the Central Bank was able to sterilize.

25. See, for example, de Castro (1981).

26. An important consequence of this drastic drop in inflation in 1981 was that real wages experienced an important jump. This was the result of nominal wages being adjusted by lagged inflation.

27. See de la Cuadra (1981) and de Castro (1981). Corbo (1982), in an econometric study, argued that nominal devaluations would have no effect on the real exchange rate under the existing economic conditions in Chile. However, for opposite results using a similar model and additional data points, see Corbo (1986c).

28. For a discussion on numerous devaluation episodes see S. Edwards (1987).

29. See, however, S. Edwards (1985a, 1985b) for a more detailed discussion on the costs of the 1975 plan.

3 FINANCIAL LIBERALIZATION, INTEREST RATES, AND THE REAL EXCHANGE RATE

During the 1960s and early 1970s Chile's financial market was under-developed and highly distorted; it was in fact a textbook case of "financial repression." The degree of financial intermediation was low, real interest rates were negative, reserves requirements were extremely high, and credit was rationed and allocated using arbitrary inefficient criteria. By late 1973 and as a result of the *Unidad Popular*'s nationalization process, the government either owned or controlled most banks.[1]

The liberalization of the domestic financial sector and the creation of a dynamic capital market was an early priority of the military government. The fundamental goals of this reform were to free domestic interest rates, allow the market to allocate credit, and to encourage the creation of new banks and financial institutions. Along the lines of the financial liberalization literature—pioneered by Edward Shaw and Ronald McKinnon from Stanford University—it was expected that as a result of these reforms the volume of financial intermediation would increase, credit would be efficiently allocated, the volume of domestic savings would rise, and, consequently, growth perspectives would improve. The crucial role assigned by the authorities to the financial reform was aptly summarized by Minister Cauas in his 1974 report (Mendez 1979: 92):

The development of the capital market has special importance in increasing the rate of savings. . . . This is achieved through financial intermediatiaries. . . . The necessity to increase substantially the rate of internal savings and to guarantee the best use of investment resources are indispensible requirements for the acceleration of economic growth. For this reason, special emphasis has been placed on the development of the capital market.

In this chapter some of the most important aspects of the financial liberalization reforms are analyzed: the most salient institutional characteristics of the reforms of the domestic capital market and of the opening of the capital account; the evolution of financial intermediation; the behavior of interest rates during the period; the effects of the financial reforms on the accumulation of a gigantic foreign debt, with special emphasis on the effects of the opening of the capital account on the real exchange rate; and some of the most important aspects of the financial crisis of 1981–82.

THE REFORM OF THE FINANCIAL MARKET

The liberalization of the domestic financial market started in early 1974 when reserves requirements were lowered, and new nonbank financial institutions — the so-called *financieras* — were permitted to operate. In May of that year the Central Bank allowed *financieras* to freely determine interest rates in short-term financial operations, and more than a year later, in October 1975, interest rates charged and paid by commercial banks were also freed. The freeing of interest rates represented a major change in a country where for more than 20 years financial operations had been tightly controlled, and it meant a move from negative to positive (and very high) real interest rates.

In April 1975 the government began a process of privatization of banks nationalized during the Allende period. A number of these banks were bought by private conglomerates (that is, the *grupos*), both old and newly formed, that saw the generalized privatization process pushed by the government as an excellent opportunity to rapidly expand.[2] In Chapter 4 we discuss in more detail the privatization process and the way in which the *grupos* operated. Besides encouraging the creation of new financial institutions and freeing interest rates, the government also implemented a process that greatly reduced banks' reserves requirements from more than 100 percent in 1973 to 42 percent in 1979, and to a final level of 10 percent in late 1980.

During the 1973–81 period the liberalization of the domestic financial market moved much faster than the liberalization of controls on capital movements in and out of the country. In fact, during the first years of the military rule the capital account was tightly controlled. Although the degree of controls became less stringent through time, until 1982 financial capital could not flow freely in or out of the country. During the early period, restrictions on banks intermediation of external funds were particularly severe.

Initially, since international banks were quite reticent to lending to Chile, there were no problems regarding capital inflows. Quite on the contrary during the initial period the prospect of massive capital flight was quite worrisome. Starting in 1976, however, and as the economic conditions improved, the authorities began to worry about the control of capital movements *into* the country. This preoccupation stemmed from the fact that starting in 1976 increases in international reserves, generated mainly by capital inflows, became an important source of base money creation, hampering the anti-inflationary effort.

Capital movements were controlled through an array of mechanisms. First, all capital moving into the country had to be registered with the Central Bank. Foreign lenders who wanted to have an assurance that they would have access to foreign exchange in the future faced, according to Article 14 of the Exchange Law, additional restrictions in the form of minimum maturities and maximum interest rates. For example, until quite late into the experiment loans with maturities below twenty-four months were forbidden, and those with maturities from twenty-four to sixty-six months were subject to non–interest yielding reserves requirements ranging from 10 percent to 25 percent of the value of the loan. Given the steepness of these deposits, until 1982 the overwhelming majority of loans and maturities exceeded sixty-six months. In fact, the average maturity for Article 14 loans was fifty-four months in 1979, sixty-four months in 1980, and sixty months in 1981. Unlike Argentina and Uruguay, Chile forbade short-run capital movements until the desperate days of the 1982 crisis.[3]

Restrictions on banks intermediation of foreign funds constituted the second major tool for controlling the level of capital inflows. These restrictions operated in two ways: First, there was a limit on the level of banks' foreign liabilities; second, and more important, there was a maximum amount by which banks could increase their foreign liabilities each month. Until December of 1978 foreign currency (gross) liabilities could not exceed 1.6 times the bank's equity. At that time this limit was increased to 1.8 times the bank's equity.

In June 1979 a major step toward liberalizing the capital account was taken when the restriction on banks' maximum ratio of foreign liabilities to equity was eliminated, and the *level* of foreign liabilities became subject to banks' overall maximum debt/equity ratio of twenty applicable to banks. The elimination of this restriction in mid-1979 had a major impact on capital inflows, with Article 14 loans increasing by almost 100 percent during that year. However, banks were still subject to a severe restriction on the maximum *increase* in the level of foreign liabilities permitted per month. In late 1979 the maximum monthly increase in bank's (gross) foreign liabilities was "the largest of 5% of equity or U.S. \$2 million." At this time this restriction on the maximum monthly increase in foreign liabilities became binding, as banks could obtain from abroad large sums that could be brought only slowly into the country. In April 1980 this flow restriction was eliminated, and banks could increase their foreign liabilities as fast as they wanted. This measure generated an astonishing increase in banks foreign liabilities. For example, and as is documented in detail below, banks' foreign credits imported via Article 14 jumped in 1980 by more than three times!

FINANCIAL INTERMEDIATION

An important result of the reforms of the financial sector was that both the number of financial institutions and the volume of intermediation greatly increased. For example, in 1981 there were twenty-six national banks, nineteen foreign banks, and fifteen *financieras*, a number significantly higher than the eighteen national banks and one foreign bank in operation in September 1973. On the other hand, between 1973 and 1981 the real volume of total credit to the private sector increased by more than 1,100 percent! In Table 3–1 some indicators of the evolution of the financial sector are presented. As can be seen, the volume of financial intermediation — as measured by credit to the private sector in real terms, the ratio of money to GDP, and the ratio

Table 3-1. The Behavior of the Financial Sector: Selected Indicators, 1970–81.

Year	(A) Credit to the Private Sector in Real Terms (1975 = 100)	(B) M2/GDP (%)	(C) Ratio of Monetary Base to M2 (%)
1970	63.2	8.8%	55.7%
1971	91.2	13.1%	63.2%
1972	93.2	13.6%	71.9%
1973	77.2	10.7%	69.9%
1974	88.2	5.4%	58.4%
1975	100.0	5.6%	49.7%
1976	136.8	5.9%	64.8%
1977	270.0	8.3%	66.2%
1978	444.3	10.4%	55.7%
1979	585.0	12.0%	46.4%
1980	817.2	13.2%	41.1%
1981	983.7	21.2%	28.9%[a]

Sources: Column A from Ramos (1984); column B from Banco Central de Chile (1981, 1983, 1984); column C from International Monetary Fund (IMF).

[a] This reduction of the ratio of monetary base to M2 is related to changes in regulations on reserves requirements on central government's deposits (*cuenta única fiscal*).

of reserve money to total money—experienced a spectacular increase during the first ten years of the military government.

In spite of the rapid growth and increased sophistication of the domestic capital market, most financial operations in domestic currency had very short maturities, with thirty days being most common. In 1982, for example, only 22 percent of total time deposits in domestic currency had a maturity that exceeded one year. On the loans side, maturities were slightly higher; in 1982, 55 percent of total credit had maturities below one year.

During the 1976–80 period the volume of real credit increased, but the level of transactions in the stock market also grew substantially, with stock prices experiencing a steep increase (see Table 3-2). Much of the activity in the stock market consisted of transactions conducted by

Table 3-2. Real Stock Prices and Volume of Transactions: 1976–83.

	Index of Real Value of Transactions in Stock Exchange (1976 = 100)	Real Index of Stock Prices (1976 = 100)
1976	100.0	100.0
1977	202.1	184.4
1978	310.8	364.8
1979	713.9	421.6
1980	1300.7	780.8
1981	1623.9	625.7
1982	3964.4	475.9
1983	2385.6	305.3

Source: Nominal values were taken from information provided by Bolsa de Comercio de Santiago. The real figures reported in the table were constructed deflating the values by a corrected consumer price index.

newly formed mutual funds, which became increasingly active during the period. However, in spite of its rapid growth in the early 1980s the stock market was still small in relative terms. Moreover, during the complete 1973–83 period the new issues of stocks were very limited.

There is no doubt that, at least in terms of increasing the degree of financial intermediation, the liberalization reform was a success. However, from the beginning it was apparent that the capital market liberalization reform was facing three major problems. First, and as discussed in detail below, interest rates were very high. Second, in spite of the very significant growth in the degree of *financial* intermediation, domestic savings did not increase, as the proponents of the reforms had expected (see Table 3–3). In fact, as was pointed out in Chapter 1, domestic savings were at one of their lowest historical levels. Third, and perhaps more important, the rapid growth of the financial sector took place in an environment with no supervision on behalf of the monetary authorities. As a result many banks accumulated an unprecedented volume of bad loans, which eventually led to the deep financial crisis of 1982.

Table 3-3. Investment and Savings in Chile: 1970–83 (percentages).

Year	(Gross Domestic Investment/GDP)	Gross Capital Formation on Fixed Capital/GDP	Depreciation/GDP	(Net Domestic Savings/GDP)	(Gross Domestic Savings/GDP)	(Foreign Savings/GDP)
1970	23.4%	20.4%	11.0%	10.6%	21.6%	1.7%
1971	20.8	18.3	11.9	6.0	17.8	2.9
1972	15.2	14.8	10.4	-0.1	10.4	4.8
1973	14.3	14.7	19.2	-9.7	9.5	4.8
1974	25.8	17.4	11.8	13.5	25.3	0.5
1975	14.0	15.4	15.7	-7.2	8.5	5.6
1976	13.6	12.7	14.1	1.4	15.4	-1.9
1977	14.4	13.3	11.7	-1.0	10.7	3.7
1978	16.5	14.5	10.5	1.1	11.6	4.8
1979	19.6	15.6	11.0	2.7	13.7	5.9
1980	23.9	17.6	11.4	4.1	15.5	8.5
1981	27.6	19.5	8.7	-1.2	7.5	14.5
1982	11.1	15.0	N.A.	-8.6	N.A.	9.2
1983	9.3	12.9	N.A.	-6.8	N.A.	5.4

Source: Banco Central de Chile (1981, 1983, 1984).

Financial Intermediation and Savings

The low level of domestic savings can be explained by a number of interrelated factors. The first one is related to the behavior of asset prices. In the late 1970s asset prices experienced a sharp increase generating an important hike in perceived wealth and consumption; naturally this phenomenon was reflected in a decline in private domestic savings.[4] The increased asset prices and perceived wealth stemmed from the growing optimism on the future perspectives of the economy that accompanied the "boom" years. The high rates of growth of output, the abundance of foreign capital, and the modernization of the economy were the base for this increase in perceived wealth. The extent of this asset appreciation is clearly illustrated by the evolution of the index of real stock prices presented in Table 3-2. To a large extent, this appreciation represented a "bubble" that eventually burst, generating major costs.[5]

The low level of domestic savings was also related to the privatization policy pursued by the government. As noted and as is reported in detail in Chapter 4, starting in 1974, to reduce the importance of the public sector, a process of privatization of government-owned firms was implemented, with firms' being auctioned to private (domestic and foreign) bidders. In general, the government used the proceeds from these sales to finance current expenditures. From a practical point of view, the private savings used to acquire these firms were matched by *negative* government savings. Finally, two other important factors affected the degree of intermediation and savings. First, the increase in foreign indebtedness, reported in detail below, also contributed to the increase in financial intermediation without a corresponding increase in *domestic* savings. Second, after 1975 the government channeled increasing fractions of its savings through the financial sector, increasing the degree of intermediation without having any effect on aggregate savings.

Financial Sector Regulation

Undoubtedly, the most serious institutional problem related to the reform of the domestic capital market was the lack of effective supervision and regulation. For example, as early as 1974 it was well known by everyone involved—including, of course, the "regulators"—that the large conglomerates (the *grupos*) were finding ways not to comply with the rules directed toward avoiding excessive ownership concentration in the financial sector (see Chapter 4). The laxitude of the supervision system was first reflected in 1974 and early 1975 when a number of informal financial institutions started to operate with the implicit approval of the government and with absolutely no control. Also, many *grupo*-owned banks concentrated large fractions of their loan portfolios on "related firms," which were either owned or controlled by that particular conglomerate. As is explained in more detail in Chapter 4, the basic scheme followed by many of these *grupos* was to use the financial resources obtained through the newly acquired banks to grow fast, mainly through the acquisition of firms that were being privatized; later some of these funds were also used to expand the level of operations of these and other firms. At the same time banks embarked on a frantic race where they tried to grow as fast as possible. As explained below, many of the loans to related firms did not represent, from a purely financial point of view, sound banking practices.[6]

In late 1976 and early 1977 as a serious financial crisis erupted, it became painfully clear that the supervision and regulation schemes for the financial sector were inadequate. A number of minor informal and formal *financieras* went bankrupt. More seriously, however, and mainly due to the large number of "bad loans" made to *grupo*-owned firms, a major bank—the Banco Osorno, owned by the Fluxa *grupo*—ran into serious trouble and had to submit to government intervention.[7]

As a result of this crisis some measures that were supposed to strengthen the financial sector's structure were taken. First, informal institutions were closed. Second, the required minimum equity of formal *financieras* was increased to 75 percent of that of banks. Third, the government established a compulsory deposit insurance scheme that, in theory, covered up to the equivalent of US$3,000 for each depositor; in practice, however, and given the government behavior during the Banco Osorno crisis where all depositors were paid off, the public expected that this insurance would cover any amount. In fact, this generalized implicit guarantee for deposits generated a classic case of moral hazard, where depositors—both large and small—had no incentives to distinguish between those banks that had been weakened by their bad loans from those few institutions that had a solid financial base. However, after the Banco Osorno crisis nothing serious was done to reduce the degree of interrelation between the banks and the *grupos*. In fact, after this date the percentage of loans directed by each bank to the *grupos'* firms grew significantly, reaching in some case almost 50 percent of total loans (see Chapter 4). As it turned out, and not surprisingly perhaps, this lack of regulation played a critical role in the financial crisis of 1981–82, and in the overall collapse of the Chilean experiment.

INTEREST RATES, THE "BOOM," AND EXPECTED DEVALUATION

Interest rate behavior constitutes one of the most fascinating features of the recent Chilean experience. During most of the experiment both nominal and real interest rates were very high. Table 3–4 contains quarterly data on deposit nominal interest rates, inflation, international interest rates (LIBOR), and the rate of devaluation for 1977 through 1983. As can be seen from these data, even after the capital account was significantly opened and the exchange rate was pegged against the dollar in June 1979, there was still a very substantial differential between the domestic borrowing rates and the foreign (LIBOR) rate. Only a small fraction of this differential can be explained by the premium over LIBOR charged by the international financial community to Chilean borrowers. The premiums averaged 1.55 percentage points in 1978; 0.99 percentage points in 1979; 0.99 percentage points in 1980; 0.89 percentage points in 1981; and 0.97 percentage points in 1982.[8] The data on nominal interest rates presented in Table 3–4 refer to average deposit rates of the banking system. Table 3–5 shows very wide spreads between deposit and lending rates, partially reflecting the inefficiency of the Chilean banking system, which had much higher operation costs per unit of deposits than banks of comparable size in the United States and other industrialized countries.[9]

Until mid-1979, when the process of opening the capital account was accelerated, ex-post real interest rates were also high. As can be seen from Table 3–6 the real borrowing interest rate averaged 8.8 percent per annum in 1977, 18.9 percent per annum in 1978, and 13.2 percent per annum during the first half of 1979. The (partial) opening of the capital account and the resulting large inflows of foreign capital quickly affected real interest rates; between the third quarter of 1979

Table 3-4.   Interest Rates, Rate of Devaluation, and Inflation: 1977–83 (quarterly data) (percentages).

	(A) Annualized Nominal Deposit Interest Rate	(B) Annualized Rate of Devaluation	(B) LIBOR Interest Rate	(C) Annualized Rate of Inflation
1977 Q1	124.6%	71.4%	6.3%	103.2%
Q2	83.6	23.4	6.8	100.0
Q3	70.8	71.9	7.0	61.2
Q4	99.8	85.5	7.8	57.4
1978 Q1	70.7	57.4	8.0	37.9
Q2	55.6	33.1	8.5	41.2
Q3	55.5	19.7	9.3	43.0
Q4	70.0	11.2	11.5	28.1
1979 Q1	47.3	14.3	11.8	24.9
Q2	44.1	18.7	11.8	32.9
Q3	42.7	33.8	12.3	48.8
Q4	46.1	0	15.5	39.2
1980 Q1	52.0	0	16.3	28.5
Q2	32.7	0	14.0	32.0
Q3	31.8	0	11.5	27.0
Q4	34.2	0	17.8	33.0
1981 Q1	45.0	0	19.0	18.0
Q2	40.9	0	20.5	11.6
Q3	38.8	0	20.5	8.5
Q4	38.5	0	16.0	7.4
1982 Q1	38.9	0	15.6	7.0
Q2	32.4	14.3	16.2	4.2
Q3	37.8	245.1	12.1	26.1
Q4	73.2	152.0	9.5	55.8
1983 Q1	33.1	36.9	9.5	18.7
Q2	28.9	1.3	9.7	25.4
Q3	25.0	26.2	10.5	26.8
Q4	24.9	30.8	9.9	26.5

Sources: Constructed from data obtained from Banco Central de Chile, the IMF International Financial Statistics and Cortazar and Marshall (1980). The annualized rate of devaluation was computed relative to the U.S. dollar as $(1 + \text{actual devaluation})^4$. The interest rate on deposit denominated in domestic currency (column A) refers to thirty days' deposits.

Table 3-5.   Annualized spreads between Deposit and Lending Interest Rates: 1979–83 (percentages).

	1st Quarter	2nd Quarter	3rd Quarter	4th Quarter
1979	20.0%	16.4%	39.3%	14.0%
1980	9.8	10.9	9.2	7.8
1981	7.2	9.7	12.1	15.4
1982	16.2	15.3	26.3	15.0
1983	17.0	15.2	14.2	12.8

Source: Calculated from data presented in Banco Central de Chile, *Boletín Mensual* (various issues).

Table 3-6.   Ex-Post Real Annualized Interest Rates: 1977–83 (real deposit rates; percent per annum).

	1st Quarter	2nd Quarter	3rd Quarter	4th Quarter	Average
1977	10.5%	−8.2%	6.0%	26.9%	8.8%
1978	23.8	10.2	8.7	32.7	18.9
1979	17.9	8.4	−4.1	5.0	6.8
1980	18.3	0.5	3.8	1.0	5.9
1981	22.8	26.3	27.9	29.0	26.5
1982	29.8	27.6	9.3	11.2	19.5
1983	12.1	8.6	−1.4	−1.2	4.5

Source: Constructed by the authors from raw data obtained from Banco Central de Chile (1981, 1983, 1984) and Cortázar and Marshall (1980). The ex-post real rates were constructed as $r = (1+i)/(1+\pi) - 1$ where r is the ex-post real rate, i is the annualized nominal rate, and π is the actual annualized rate of inflation.

and the fourth quarter of 1980 borrowing real rates declined significantly, averaging only 4.1 percent per annum. Toward the end of 1980 the situation drastically changed. In December of that year the real borrowing rate climbed to 15 percent per annum, while the real lending rate exceeded 20 percent per annum. Things became even worse in 1981 when in spite of the fact that capital inflows reached a record high, averaging US $1.1 billion per quarter, the real ex-post borrowing rate increased to an annual average of 27 percent, and the real ex-post lending interest rate averaged 37 percent. In the first half of 1982, immediately preceding the devaluation of the peso, the real borrowing rate averaged 37 percent, while the real lending rate reached the remarkable figure of 43 percent.

The bizarre behavior of interest rates during the military rule in Chile responded to a number of complex and interrelated factors. However, two major elements can be singled out as being the most important determinants of interest rates dynamics. The first is the ever-expanding demand for credit, which, in turn, responded to a number of factors, including the behavior of the *grupos* and the substantially higher levels of expenditure originated by the optimistic views on the future of the economy. The second element relates to the expectations of devaluation that increased steadily after the first quarter of 1980. Whereas the continuous increases in the demand for credit mainly explain the behavior of the real interest rate, the expectations of devaluation affected both the nominal interest rate and the ex-post real rate. Other factors that also played a role in interest rates behavior were the existence of transaction costs and, especially in 1981, the passive monetary policy pursued by the central bank.

The Demand for Credit

Very early during the liberalization attempt the demand for credit experienced important increases, which exceeded the expansion of the supply for credit. Initially this higher demand stemmed, mainly, from the *grupos*, which, after acquiring some of the newly privatized banks started using funds obtained through them to finance the purchase, modernization, and expansion of other firms that were being privatized.[10] At this early point there was also a strong credit demand, by all sorts of firms, to finance working capital. One of the consequences of the *Unidad Popular* government was that most firms were highly decapitalized and in great need of fresh working capital to finance the accumulation of inventories. Also, a nontrivial fraction of the demand for credit during this period had its origin on efforts made by different firms to avoid bankruptcy as a result of the 1975 recession.[11]

Harberger (1985) has argued that this initial demand for credit by the *grupos* soon became an evergrowing "false demand" consisting of the rolling-over of bad loans.[12] Many of the firms acquired by the *grupos* did not turn out to be profitable and increasingly resorted to additional borrowing from the banking sector in order to stay afloat. Instead of recognizing the "bad" nature of the loans, banks continued to roll them over, compounding the problem until in late 1981 the situation was completely out of control. The reluctance of banks to put an end to this scheme and make effective the collaterals obtained from the borrowing firms was partially based on the fact that by late 1981 and 1982 the book value of collaterals greatly exceeded their market value, implying that banks would in fact have to write off a fraction of these loans. Everywhere, of course, banks are very reluctant to write off bad loans, since it invariantly implies that total credit has to be reduced by a very high multiple of the amount written off.[13] The actual importance of the *grupos* in the generation of an upward pressure on the demand for credit is reflected, for example, by the fact that up to December 1982 Chile's second largest bank had directly granted more than 40 percent of all its loans to the *grupos*. The six largest conglomerates, on the other hand, had received, only through the banks each of them directly controlled, almost 15 percent of total credit.[14] Of course, rolling over these bad loans for a considerably long period of time was possible only because of the lax attitude that the authorities had regarding banking supervision.

In mid-1979 a fairly generalized feeling of prosperity and of very bright future economic perspectives began to invade the Chilean population. Based on the rapid rates of growth of the previous two years and on the abundance of foreign financing, and fueled by an implacable government propaganda and by the adulation of foreign bankers and pundits, the Chilean public started to form very optimistic expectations of the future growth path of the economy. In the eyes of the public, the rapid rates of growth of these years confirmed this optimism. During these "boom" years it was thought that Chile would grow at a long-run average of around 7 to 8 percent. In fact, the years 1980 and early 1981 were characterized by an euphoria *à la* Kindleberger (1978).[15]

This optimism resulted in a perception of substantially higher wealth — which, as noted, was reflected in dramatic rises of asset prices, including stocks and real estate — and was followed by major spending sprees by people belonging to most strata of society. The rise in expenditure (consumption and to a lesser extent investment) was largely financed through higher credit — denominated both in domestic and foreign currency — obtained from the banking sector. This higher demand for credit to finance higher expenditure had three major consequences: First, it exercised additional pressures on domestic interest rates, over and above those generated by the *grupo*-related "false demand" for credit; second, as is documented below, it resulted in very drastic increases in foreign indebtedness; and third, it helped create a dangerously fragile financial structure, where a high proportion of the banking sector loans were granted using highly inflated collateral prices.

During 1981 another important source was added to the increase in the demand for credit. The public perceived the deteriorating external environment as a transitory phenomenon and tried to adjust to it by intertemporally smoothing consumption through even higher external borrowing. Since, as shown below, domestic and foreign assets were very imperfect substitutes, this higher demand for credit exercised additional upward pressure on interest rates. In late 1981 and early 1982, as firm's financial conditions became exceedingly weak, they increased their demand for credit in order to avoid bankruptcy.

Expectations of Devaluation

Toward mid- to late-1980 the expectations of devaluation began to play an increasingly important role. Although the actual nominal exchange rate had been fixed at 39 pesos per dollar since June of 1979, the expectations of devaluations increased steadily as it became apparent that the real overvaluation was imposing a severe toll on the economy and was not sustainable. For example, Le Fort (1985) has determined using Bayesian methods that in May 1982 the public's perceived probability that the authorities would abandon the fixed rate system exceeded 90 percent. According to his computations, the expected rate of devaluation rose steadily from approximately 2 percent in July 1979 — one month after the parity was fixed — to more than 26 percent in May of 1982, just prior to the devaluation of that year (see Table 3-7).

In spite of the fact that during 1980, 1981, and the early months of 1982 there were still some controls on capital movements, as the expected rate of devaluation rose, so did the domestic nominal interest rate. As the expected devaluation became higher and higher, some firms and private individuals began substituting foreign credit for domestic credit, exercising additional pressures on domestic interest rates.

Table 3–7.   Expected Devaluation: 1979–82 (percentages).[a]

	March	May	September	December
1979	–	–	1.3%	1.1%
1980	1.0%	1.2%	1.7	9.8
1981	17.1	17.6	30.5	30.6
1982	32.7	26.3	–	–

Source: Le Fort (1985).
[a] These figures are computed as the perceived probability of abandoning the fixed rate times the conditional expected devaluation.

In a recent article S. Edwards (1986a) showed that, in addition to other factors, international interest rates plus expected devaluation play an important role in explaining nominal interest rate behavior in Chile. Based on the semi-open economy model of interest rate behavior in developing countries of S. Edwards and Khan (1985), the following result was obtained from the estimation of a reduced form equation for nominal interest rate, using OLS corrected by serial correlation on quarterly data for 1977 through 1982 (the numbers in parentheses are t-statistics):

$$i_t = 0.039 + 0.239\ (i_t^* + D_t^e) - 0.442\ \log m_{t-1}$$
$$(0.418)\quad (1.965)\qquad\qquad (-2.030)$$

$$-\ 0.153\ \log y_t - 0.378\ \pi_t + 0.090\ \text{dummy} \qquad (3.1)$$
$$(-0.175)\qquad\quad (-1.130)\quad (0.905)$$

$$R^2 = 0.905$$
$$D.W. = 1.932$$
$$N = 18$$
$$RHO = -0.389$$

where i_t is the domestic nominal interest rate; $(i_t^* + D_t^e)$ is the sum of the international (LIBOR) nominal rate plus the expected rate of devaluation; m_{t-1} is a measure of real money in period $t-1$, which proxies the availability of real liquidity in the economy; y_t is a measure of real income; π_t is actual inflation, which is used as a proxy for expected inflation; and "dummy" is a dummy variable that took a value of zero from 1977 to mid-1979 and a value of one then onward to allow for a distinction between the fixed and nonfixed exchange rates subperiods.[16]

These results are interesting. The fact that the coefficient of $(i_t^* + D_t^e)$ and of log m_{t-1} are significant at conventional levels and have the expected signs provides support to the hypothesis that during this period the behavior of the nominal interest rate in Chile was influenced both by open economy factors and internal real liquidity conditions. Particularly important is the finding of a significantly positive coefficient for the $(i_t^* + D_t^e)$ term. This means that higher expected rates of devaluation will be promptly passed on to higher nominal domestic rates of interest. For example, if the expected rate of devaluation increases from 2 percent in a given month to 26 percent in another month — as Le Fort's computations suggest — the *monthly* nominal rate of interest would increase by almost eight percentage points. Another important element in the explanation of the behavior of i_t pointed out by this equation are international foreign interest rates, which during 1980 and 1982 increased substantially. The coefficients of the constant and of the dummy variable confirm the hypothesis that domestic and foreign assets were not perfect substitutes during the period. Also, the significantly negative coefficient of the real liquidity variable (m_{t-1}) clearly points out that throughout the period nominal interest rates not only were affected by foreign factors but also responded to the behavior of the domestic money market.[17] The other coefficients in equation (3.1), however, are not estimated in a very precise fashion, suggesting that there are still some missing elements in the explanation of interest rate behavior in Chile.

The steady increase in the expected rate of devaluation between late 1980 and mid-1982 is especially important for understanding the dramatic increase in the ex-post real interest rates during this period. A key aspect of this problem, of course, is the difference between expected and actual rates of devaluation. While in a semi-open economy the nominal interest rate depends critically on the *expected* rate of devaluation, the actual rate of inflation — which is used to measure ex-post real interest rates, as those presented in Table 3-6 — depends mainly on the actual rate of devaluation. Since in spite of the growing expectations of devaluation the authorities maintained the fixed rate until June 1982, the actual rate of inflation was well below the expected rate of devaluation, and computed ex-post real interest rates turned out to be very high starting in late 1980.[18]

Summary

There are clear indications that the high nominal rates during most of the period responded mainly to a continuous increase in the demand for credit—which responded to a number of different factors and exceeded the expansion of credit supply—and, starting in early 1981, to very important increases in the expected rate of devaluation. Other factors also played some role in the behavior of interest rates, including the existence of transaction costs that impeded banks from taking positions on foreign currency (Sjaastad 1983); the increase in world interest rates; the increase in the country risk premium attached to Chile by the international financial community starting in mid-1981, following the bankruptcy of the *CRAV* grupo (S. Edwards 1985a; Arellano 1985); and the "automatic adjustment" macroeconomic strategy followed by the economic authorities in 1980 and 1981.

Although the formal modeling of Chile's interest rates has proven to be difficult and elusive, the appendix to this Chapter presents a model of interest rate determination in a semi-open economy that captures the more important highlights of the Chilean case. That model combines the demand for credit and expected devaluation factors with other elements to provide an explanation of the behavior of interest rates in a country like Chile.

THE LIBERALIZATION OF THE CAPITAL ACCOUNT, FOREIGN INDEBTEDNESS, AND THE REAL EXCHANGE RATE

In June 1979 the first significant steps toward opening the capital account were taken. However, as was explained above, the more important impediments for long-run and medium-run capital movements were not lifted until April 1980. The combination of reduced capital controls and a renewed eagerness to lend money to Chile on behalf of the international financial community resulted in a staggering increase in Chile's foreign debt. In Table 3–8 the evolution of Chile's foreign indebtedness is presented. Three things stand out from this table. First, the remarkably rapid increase in total foreign indebtedness, which almost tripled between 1978 and 1982. Second, the change in the relative importance of public and private debt. Whereas in 1973

Table 3-8.   Chile's Foreign Debt: 1973-82 (millions of U.S. $, end of period).

	Total Debt	Public Sector Debt	Private Sector Debt		
			Banking System	Rest	Total Private
1973	$ 3,667	$3,244	N.A.	N.A.	$ 423
1974	4,435	3,966	N.A.	N.A.	469
1975	4,854	4,068	$ 154	$ 632	786
1976	4,720	3,762	168	790	958
1977	5,201	3,917	309	975	1,284
1978	6,664	4,709	660	1,295	1,955
1979	8,484	5,063	1,968	1,453	3,421
1980	11,084	5,063	3,497	2,524	6,021
1981	15,542	5,542	6,516	3,561	10,077
1982	17,153	6,660	6,613	3,880	10,493

Source: Banco Central de Chile (1981, 1983, 1984).
N.A. = Not available.

private debt constituted less than 12 percent of total external debt, in 1981 it represented almost 65 percent. Between 1973 and 1981 private (nominal) foreign debt increased by more than twenty-three times. When expressed in constant dollars the increase is still more than eleven times, representing an average annual rate of real growth of almost 40 percent. Third, the figures in Table 3-8 highlight the rapid growth in the level of foreign indebtedness of the *private banking* system.

Of course, the increased role of private foreign indebtedness was not an accident. Quite on the contrary, it represented a deliberate government policy aimed at curbing public sector involvement in international financial transactions and at encouraging the private sector participation in the international financial sector. Consistent with the view that the government should not get actively involved in financial or productive deals, the vast majority of the private loans were obtained without *government guarantee*. In fact, it was thought at the time by the economic authorities and other observers that since most of the debt had been contracted by the private sector without any government guarantee, the very rapid increase in foreign debt did not represent a threat for the country as a whole: If a domestic private borrower could not pay its foreign obligations, that was a *private* problem, between it and the foreign creditor, which would be solved through a regular bankruptcy procedure.

The view that increases — even major increases — in private foreign indebtedness should not be looked at with concern is perhaps best reflected by the following quote from a paper delivered by Walter Robischek, then director of the IMF's Western Hemisphere Department, at a conference organized by the Chilean Central Bank (Banco Central de Chile 1981: 171):

> In the case of the private sector, I would argue that the difference between domestic and foreign debt is not significant. . .if it exists at all. . . . More generally, private firms can be expected to be careful in assessing the net return to be derived from borrowed funds, as compared with the net cost since their survival as enterprises is at stake.

In his 1981 Report of the Nation's Economic Conditions, Minister de Castro (1981: 23) even argued that private indebtedness from abroad should be actively encouraged since it represented higher foreign savings. According to de Castro, "[T]here is no doubt that the current account deficits. . .are highly beneficial for the country, and that we should make an effort to maintain them at the highest possible level and for the larger possible period of time."

As events showed later, the distinction between public and private debt was highly artificial, as in 1983 the Chilean government ended up nationalizing a very substantial proportion of the private nonguaranteed debt, independently of the fact that the original private borrower had gone bankrupt.

Although domestic banks greatly increased their degree of intermediation in foreign funds, they were not allowed to take the exchange risk, and all their loans financed with external funds had to be documented in foreign currency with the final borrower taking all the exchange rate risk. These regulations generated a highly segmented credit market, where only some agents had access to the "relatively cheap" credit denominated in foreign exchange. In fact, Zahler (1980) and Tybout (1985) have argued that these regulations initially resulted in large rents that were captured by those that access to the foreign funds (that is, the *grupos*).

The sudden and substantial increase in the level of capital inflows after capital controls were relaxed in June 1979 and April 1980 responded to two basic factors. First, as more and more market-oriented policies were adopted and the economy entered into the successful

years of the "boom," the perceived profitability of domestic investment over the longer run—as seen from abroad—increased. This, in
turn, provoked a portfolio disequilibrium in the international financial markets, where investors now wanted to hold a significantly higher
fraction of Chile's capital stock as part of their portfolios. In the case
of Chile this disequilibrium was quite evident since at least mid-1978,
when foreign banks were very eager to increase their exposure in Chile
but could not because of the capital controls. Immediately following
the liberalization, international investors tried to solve their portfolio
composition disequilibrium, increasing their acquisition of domestic
(that is, Chilean) securities. As a consequence capital inflows into the
country "jumped" in the way illustrated in Table 3–8 above. A very important characteristic of this mechanism, which is discussed in greater
detail in Chapter 7, is that after the relaxation of capital inflows there
will in fact be an overshooting in the level of capital inflows; immediately following the liberalization there will be a jump on capital inflows, which will then slowly decline to its new equilibrium level.

The second factor that explains the increase in capital inflows has
to do with the demand side and is related to the differential between
domestic interest rates and international rates adjusted by expected
devaluation. Unfortunately, since there are no reliable data on *long-
run* expected rates of devaluation, it is difficult to fully assess the importance of this factor. This data problem is particularly difficult, since
we need to have a good idea of the public's expected rate of devaluation for a period of five years or so into the future. The reason
for this, of course, is that given the regulations that governed capital
movements at the time, a Chilean firm or bank that wanted to decide
whether to borrow in pesos or in dollars would have had to compare
the *total* cost of obtaining a loan *of the same maturity* in pesos or in
dollars. Since between 1979 and 1981 the minimum required maturity
to freely import capital was sixty-six months, the expected devaluation that should be taken into account is one that relates to this period.[19] There is little doubt, as can be seen in Table 3–7, that even as
early as 1980 the expectations of devaluation for a sixty-six-month
period were significantly greater than zero. Once this maturity element is introduced, it becomes clear that the ex-ante long-term (that
is, sixty-six months) cost of foreign credit greatly exceeded the calcu-
lations based on the short term ex-post actual rate of devaluation.

Some researchers have attempted to evaluate empirically the importance of the differential between domestic and foreign rates of interest

in explaining the massive increase of capital inflows starting in 1979. Surprisingly, perhaps, the existing evidence suggests that for the 1979–81 period, capital inflows were not particularly sensitive to changes in interest rate differentials. Sjaastad (1983), for example, reports that between August 1979 and December 1980 there was a weak response of the rate of capital inflows to spread between domestic and foreign interest rates spread. Between January 1981 and March 1982 this relationship, however, basically disappeared. In addition, Corbo (1985a), in what is possibly the most ambitious attempt to econometrically explain the behavior of capital flows in Chile, failed to find a significant role for interest rates differentials. In an application of the Kouri and Porter (1974) model Corbo consistently found that the coefficient of the international interest rate plus rate of devaluation was negative and highly insignificant.[20]

The Liberalization of the Capital Account and the Real Exchange Rate

The increase in the availability of foreign funds that followed the opening of the capital account became a major cause, together with the backward wage indexation and the pegging of the exchange rate, of the persistent real overvaluation of the peso that took place since mid-1979. In fact, the increase in the level of capital flows into the country *required* a real appreciation of the peso. From an analytical perspective the reason for this is that, to the extent that a fraction of the increase in expenditure resulting from the importation of capital is spent on nontradable goods, an incipient excess demand for this type of goods will emerge; in order to restore equilibrium, nontradable goods' relative prices will have to increase, and a real appreciation will result.[21] This was indeed the case in Chile, where a large proportion of the newly imported foreign capital was used to finance a dramatic boom in the construction sector.

In Table 3–9 quarterly data on the behavior of the effective real exchange rate — constructed with respect to a basket of currencies — between 1977 and 1984 are presented. An increase in this index reflects a real depreciation, whereas a decline shows a real appreciation. A salient characteristic of these data is that during the first phase of the *tablita* period (that is, until June 1979) there was not a significant real appreciation of the peso. Moreover, according to this index, between

Table 3-9. Index of Real Effective Exchange Rate in Chile: 1977–83 (1975 = 100).

	First Quarter	Second Quarter	Third Quarter	Fourth Quarter
1977	83.6	78.5	81.8	89.5
1978	97.5	100.3	103.3	105.1
1979	106.3	105.8	109.4	102.5
1980	100.2	95.9	93.8	87.1
1981	82.1	75.2	71.3	72.8
1982	69.9	70.8	82.8	97.2
1983	103.2	96.6	95.9	97.1

Notes: This index has been constructed as the ratio of a weighted average of Wholesale Price Indexes (WPI) of Chile's ten major trading partners, expressed in pesos, to Chile's Consumer Price Index (CPI). For Chile the CPI as corrected by Cortazar and Marshall (1980) was used. It should be noted that alternative measures of the real exchange rate yield very similar results. For more details on the index see S. Edwards (1987).

the second quarter of 1978 and the third quarter of 1979 there is an effective real depreciation, which partially responded to the fact that the preannounced rate of devaluation had been set against the U.S. dollar and, at the time, the dollar was depreciating significantly in real terms against other major currencies. In fact, if we use a more simple measure of real exchange rate against the dollar only, during this period there is a small real appreciation.[22] Only in 1979, after the *tablita* scheme entered its second phase and the capital account was opened, did the real overvaluation accelerate. Between the third quarter of 1979 and the second quarter of 1982 the real appreciation amounted to 35 percent.[23] The fact that the real exchange rate did not experience a (significant) real appreciation during the first eighteen months of the *tablita* is very robust to the methodology used to calculate the real exchange rate. For example, using six alternative proxies for the domestic relative price of tradable to nontradable goods, Corbo (1982) found that between the fourth quarter of 1977 and the second quarter of 1979 there had been no significant change in this variable. This was the case in spite of the fact that he included import tariff reductions in his index of tradables prices. Moreover, according to three of these indexes there had been a real depreciation of approximately 4 percent during this period; the other three indexes indicated a real appreciation of 2 percent. Also, according to an elaborate index computed by economists in the think-tank CIEPLAN, between 1977 and 1979 Chile did not experience a real appreciation.

The way the rapid increase in capital inflows after June 1979 conspired with the nominal exchange rate and wage rate policies to generate the real overvaluation can be easily illustrated using the inflation model of Chapter 2. Assume now that due to the increasing greater availability of foreign funds, real expenditure increases through time (that is, $\hat{Z}_t > 0$). Then, the inflation equation (2.7) becomes

$$\hat{P}_t = \left(\frac{\alpha\epsilon+\eta}{\eta+\epsilon}\right)\hat{P}_{Tt}^* + \frac{(1-\alpha)\epsilon}{\eta+\epsilon}\hat{P}_{t-1} - \left(\frac{(1-\alpha)\delta}{\eta+\epsilon}\right)\hat{Z}_t \qquad (3.2)$$

and the equation for real exchange rate dynamics becomes

$$\hat{e}_t = \left(\frac{\epsilon(1-\alpha)}{\eta+\epsilon}\right)(\hat{P}_{Tt}^* - \hat{P}_{t-1}) + \left(\frac{(1-\alpha)\delta}{\eta+\epsilon}\right)\hat{Z}_t \qquad (3.3)$$

It is easy to see from these equations that as long as there is an increase in real expenditure, $\hat{Z}_t > 0$, the convergence of domestic to world inflation will be slower, and the degree of real overvaluation will greatly increase.[24] This is illustrated in Table 3–10, where the paths of $\hat{P}_t$ and $\hat{e}_t$ are compared for two hypothetical cases. In case A there are no capital inflows that generate real expenditure pressures (that is, $\hat{Z}_t = 0$), while in case B we assume that in each period, thanks to inflows of foreign funds, real expenditure increases by 10 percent (that is, $\hat{Z}_t = 10.0$). In both cases it is assumed that the initial domestic rate of inflation is equal to 30 percent and that international inflation is constant and equal to 8 percent. The assumptions regarding the different elasticities appear at the bottom of the table. The results obtained from this exercise are very revealing. First, they show that in the presence of capital inflows domestic inflation moves significantly slower toward international inflation than in the case of no capital inflows. Second, and more important, under capital inflows (case B) the degree of real overvaluation of the exchange rate can become very significant. In the hypothetic case with capital inflows, illustrated in Table 3–10, after three years the accumulated real overvaluation exceeds 20 percent.

In order to better assess empirically the extent of this relationship between capital inflows and the real exchange rate, a regression analysis was performed using quarterly data for the period between the first quarter of 1977 and the fourth quarter of 1982. In addition to the (lagged) rate of net capital flows, other possible determinants of the

Table 3-10. The Effect of Capital Inflows on Inflation and the Real Exchange Rate (an example).

Year	Case A: No Capital Inflows			Case B: Positive Capital Inflows		
	$\hat{P}_t$	$\hat{e}_t$	Index of Real Exchange Rate	$\hat{P}_t$	$\hat{e}_t$	Index of Real Exchange Rate
0	30.0%	—	100.0	30.0%	—	100.0
1	12.6	-4.6%	95.4	16.1	-11.2%	92.8
2	9.0	-1.0	94.4	13.2	-6.3	87.0
3	8.2	-0.2	94.2	12.6	-5.3	82.3

Notes: A negative value of $\hat{e}$ means real appreciation. Case A assumes $\hat{Z}_1 = \hat{Z}_2 = \hat{Z}_3 = 0$. Case B, on the other hand, assumes $\hat{Z}_1 = \hat{Z}_2 = \hat{Z}_3 = 10\%$. Both cases assume $\alpha = 0.5$, $\eta = -1.0$, $\delta = 1.2$, $\epsilon = -0.7$, $\hat{P}_{Tt}^* = 8\%$. The simulations use equations (3.2) and (3.3).

real exchange rate like the terms of trade and real growth were also included in the regressions. (Of course, by using lagged values of net capital inflows we avoid the simultaneity problem that could arise because of the endogeneity of this variable.) The following results were obtained where REER is the indexing of the real effective exchange rate and the numbers in parentheses are t-statistics:[25]

$$\log \text{REER}_t = 0.014 - 0.078 \ \log[\text{net capital flows}]_{t-1}$$
$$(3.458) \quad (-3.801)$$

$$+ \ 0.798 \ \log \text{REER}_{t-1} \qquad R^2 = 0.897$$
$$(10.376) \qquad\qquad D.W. = 1.887 \qquad (3.4)$$

$$\log \text{REER}_t = 0.016 - 0.076 \ \log[\text{net capital flows}]_{t-1}$$
$$(3.973) \quad (-3.521)$$

$$- \ 0.218 \ \log[\text{terms of trade}]_{t-1} + 0.271 \ [\text{growth}]_{t-1}$$
$$(-1.935) \qquad\qquad (1.250)$$

$$+ \ 0.005 \ [\text{devaluation dummy}]_t + 0.964 \ \log \text{RER}_{t-1}$$
$$(0.194) \qquad\qquad (7.889)$$

$$R^2 = 0.946$$
$$D.W. = 1.753 \qquad (3.5)$$

As may be seen, under both specifications, the coefficient of the lagged value of net capital inflows is significantly negative as expected. It can also be seen from the results reported in equation (3.5) that the coefficient of the terms of trade variable is negative as expected. The coefficient for real growth, however, turned out to be positive and insignificant, suggesting that the Ricardo–Balassa effect did not play an important role in determining the behavior of the real exchange rate in Chile during this period. Finally the coefficient of the lagged dependent variable was fairly high under both specifications, indicating that after a shock the real exchange rate moved only slowly toward its new equilibrium. This is, in some sense, not surprising given that these regressions were run using quarterly data. In sum, the results presented here provide support to the hypothesis that the real exchange rate has been negatively affected by the rate of capital inflows in Chile.

THE MIRACLE TURNS SOUR: THE FINANCIAL CRISIS OF 1981–82

In late 1981 the bubble originated with the euphoria of the boom years burst, and a major financial crisis erupted. Already in late 1980 and early 1981 fairly large segments of the population began to question whether the pace at which the economy, and in particular expenditure, had been growing was sustainable. The crisis atmosphere greatly increased in mid-1981 when a medium-size conglomerate, the CRAV *grupo*, could not pay its debts and went bankrupt. In spite of the optimistic government propaganda the public now seriously began questioning the strength of the financial sector. Undoubtedly, the failure of the CRAV *grupo* represented the turning point that marked the end of the euphoria (see Chapter 4).

In mid-1981, as interest rates continued climbing, asset prices began to fall and some non-*grupo* firms went bankrupt when they could no longer face foreign competition or pay the interest bill. Things became even more complicated in November of that year when two major banks — the *Banco Espanol* and *Banco de Talca* — ran into serious problems and had to be rescued by the government. The bankruptcies problem reached crisis proportion in 1982 when 810 failed, more than double the average of the previous five years.[26] The government, in the meantime, argued that there was no reason to worry, since the high interest rates were the reflection that the "automatic adjustment" process was operating as predicted. Moreover, Minister de Castro forcefully pointed out that given the circumstances bankruptcies were very healthy for the Chilean economy, since they would facilitate the process of adjustment. In his own words (1981: 23), "[I]t is important not to forget that bankruptcies are the appropriate channel through which an economy gets rid of inefficient investments. If the government interferes in this process...the period of inefficiencies is lengthened."

As the financial situation of most firms became dangerously weak and asset prices plummeted, bankers, *grupo* officials, and other debtors refused to realize their capital losses and began lobbying for a government solution. The government refused to intervene, citing, once again, the advantages of the "automatic adjustment." In an attempt to bring down interest rates *grupo* executives began desperately shuttling between Santiago and New York trying to obtain additional foreign funds. In the second half of 1981 international banks, taking an attitude that still puzzles most observers, agreed to pour vast amounts of resources into the sinking Chilean economy.

In 1982 the situation changed drastically as foreign banks suddenly decided that Chile was not a good risk any more. In the first half of that year net capital flows fell by almost 65 percent with respect to the second half of 1982.[27] Commercial banks were hit particularly hard, with their total importation of Article 14 loans dropping by 75 percent in that year. Of course, this decline in the level of capital inflows meant that total expenditure had to fall and that the macroeconomic process generated by the large inflows of capital in the previous years now had to be reversed. In order to maintain equilibrium, a real depreciation was required. The mechanism operating in this case is fully symmetric to the real appreciation effect of the increase in capital inflows discussed above. A serious problem at this point, however, was that the wage indexation scheme made the adjustment in relative prices (that is, the real depreciation) particularly difficult. As a way to get over this problem, some observers started calling for an abandonment of the fixed exchange rate policy.

It seemed however, that regarding the exchange rate policy, the *grupos* were in a no-win situation. On one hand, the real overvaluation of the peso was greatly hurting the profitability of their firms, which were largely oriented toward the export sector. In order to improve this profitability a necessary — but certainly not sufficient — condition was to engineer a real devaluation through the abandonment of the fixed rate policy.[28] On the other hand, the *grupos* had incurred in an extremely high foreign debt, and a devaluation — especially a large one — would have resulted in a significant increase in the peso value of that debt and in some cases would have meant insolvency. The two largest *grupos* decided to face this situation in opposite ways. One (the Cruzat grupo) tried to substitute foreign for domestic liabilities and lobbied extensively for a devaluation; another (the Vial *grupo*) gambled on the maintenance of the fixed rate and lobbied for an adjustment through a government imposed reduction in nominal wages.

The June 1982 devaluation came too late and did not provide any help to the struggling banks and firms. On the contrary, many debtors could not service their debts at the new exchange rate. Moreover, since the magnitude of the devaluation was generally perceived as insufficient, greater expectations of devaluation emerged, putting further pressure on domestic interest rates. As a result, and contrary to the government's previous announced policy of not favoring particular groups through economic legislation, a preferential lower exchange rate was established for those debtors with foreign liabilities. Interest rates continued to be high, in spite of some efforts made by the government, including the relaxation of the prohibition for short-term capital inflows. Banks continued to accumulate bad loans, and the financial structure of the major *grupos* steadily worsened. A major collapse of the financial system was avoided only by the continuous massive injection of funds to banks by the Central Bank.

In January 1983 the government stepped up its degree of intervention and liquidated two banks and nationalized others. The two major *grupos* were also intervened with, and the officials of one of them was charged with alleged fraud. At that time it was discovered, to the astonishment of some, that the proportion of loans banks had made to *grupo*-owned firms was extraordinary. For example almost 50 percent of the largest private bank (the Banco de Chile) loans had been granted to firms owned by that particular *grupo*. Perhaps the most controversial measure taken at this time was the nationalization of the liquidated banks foreign debt, which had been obtained without government guarantee. Responding to pressures by the international banks the Chilean government decided to take over this debt, guaranteeing now its payment.

Paradoxically, at the end of 1983, the financial sector was in some way at the same juncture as it had been ten years before. It had been nationalized and was tightly controlled by the state.

APPENDIX 3A
A MODEL FOR ANALYZING REAL INTEREST
RATE BEHAVIOR IN A SEMI-OPEN ECONOMY

This appendix sketches a simple model of interest rate determination in a small semi-open economy, developed with the Chilean case in mind. It is assumed that this economy has no trade restrictions but some restrictions to international capital movements. In particular, it is assumed that, as in the case of Chile until 1982, long-run capital movements are allowed, while short-run capital flows are forbidden. The nominal exchange rate is assumed fixed. The model has three main building blocks:

(a) *Determination of the Short-Run Real Interest Rate:* It is assumed that the short-run real interest rate clears the credit market. The demand for credit has the usual characteristics. The supply of credit, however, is composed of two sources: domestic credit and foreign credit. It is assumed that since net international capital flows (increases in international credit) are allowed only for long-run maturities, they will depend on the *long-run* interest differential adjusted by expectations of devaluation in a country risk premium. Given their different characteristics domestic and foreign credit are not perfect substitutes.

(b) *Long-Term Interest Rate Differentials:* It is assumed that due to institutional restrictions only long-term capital movements are allowed. As mentioned, these flows depend on, among other variables, an *adjusted* long-term interest rate differential, where the adjustment is due to long-term expectations of devaluation, a country risk premium, and transaction costs. If the long-term domestic interest rate exceeds the long-term foreign rate, *plus* expectations of devaluation, *plus* the country risk premium, *plus* a risk premium, a positive (net) capital flow will occur, having a positive effect on the total supply of credit. The domestic long-term interest rate is related to the domestic short-term interest rate through the term structure of interest rates. The existence of the risk premia reflect the non–perfect substitutability assumption. It is also assumed that there is a maximum ratio of foreign debt to GNP, after which a foreign borrowing ceiling is reached. This ceiling is an endogenous variable.

(c) *Term Structure of Interest Rate:* The long-term interest rate de-
     pends on the present short-term rate, the expected future short-
     term rates, and a liquidity premium. Then, an increase in the
     short-term rate (with future expected short-term rates constant)
     will generate an increase in the long-term rate, producing a posi-
     tive long-term interest rate differential. This, in turn, will induce
     a capital inflow from abroad.

NOTATION

r	Short-term real interest rate
C^d	Real quantity of credit demanded
C^s	Real quantity of credit supplied
π^e	Expected inflation
y^P	Real permanent income
y	Real income
F	Real foreign capital inflows
d	"Adjusted" interest rate differential
i	Short-term nominal interest rate
π^*	Foreign inflation
δ	Discount factor
$E_t(\ )$	Expectation formed on all available information
D^e	Long-term expectations of devaluation (this expectation refers to the minimum maturities at which capital can be imported)
i_L	Long-term nominal interest rate
R^e	Country risk premium
T	Transaction costs
CA	Current account
I	Ratio of investment to GNP
i_L^*	Foreign long-term interest rate
k	Increase in domestic credit
S	Exchange rate
IR	Stock of international reserves
P	Risk premium
L	Foreign debt

THE MODEL

In this section the model is presented. The way the model works is
illustrated using a diagrammatical analysis. The model is given by

equations (3A.1) through (3A.10), where the signs in parentheses are the assumed signs of the respective partial derivatives:

Demand for real credit:

$$C_t^d = f(\underset{(-)}{r_t}, y_t^P, \pi^e, r_{t+i}^e) \tag{3A.1}$$

Real supply of total credit:

$$C_t^S = C_{t-1} + F_t + k_t \tag{3A.2}$$

Net foreign capital flows:

$$F_t = F(\underset{(+)}{d_{t-1}}, \ldots) \tag{3A.3}$$

Short-term nominal rate:

$$i_t = r_t + \pi_t^e \tag{3A.4}$$

Expected inflation:

$$\pi^e = E_t(\pi_{t+k}) \tag{3A.5}$$

Long-term nominal interest rate:

$$i_L = i_t + \sum_{j=1} \gamma^j i_{t+j}^e \tag{3A.6}$$

Adjusted long-term interest rate differential:

$$d_t = i_L - [i_L^* + D^e + R^e + T + P_t] \tag{3A.7}$$

Foreign debt:

$$L_t = \sum_{i=0}^{t} F_i (1+\delta)^{t-1} \tag{3A.8}$$

Expectations of devaluation:

$$D_t^e = f(\underset{(+)}{L_t/y_t}, \underset{(+)}{(\pi^e - \pi^{*e})}, \underset{(+)}{CA_t}, \underset{(-)}{I_t^e}, \ldots) \tag{3A.9}$$

Country risk premium:

$$R^e = g(\underset{(+)}{L_t/Y_t}, \underset{(+)}{CA}, \underset{(-)}{I_t}, \underset{(-)}{IR_t}, \ldots) \tag{3A.10}$$

The short-term real interest rate r is determined by the credit market clearing conditions (equation (3A.1) equals equation (3A.2)). In order to simplify the diagrammatic exposition we have assumed that the supply for domestic credit does not depend on the real interest rate. However, relaxing this assumption does not affect in any substantial way the discussion presented here. For a *given* π^e, equation (3A.4) determines the short-term nominal interest rate i_t. Given i_t and the expected future short-run nominal rates, equation (3A.6) determines the long-term domestic nominal rate i_L. According to equation (3A.7) this long-term rate i_L, together with i_L^*, D^e, R^e, P, and T, determine the adjusted long-term interest rate differential, which, under full equilibrium, is assumed to be zero.

The initial equilibrium in this model is summarized in Figure 3A–1. In quadrant I the demand and supply of credit determine the short-term real rate r. For a given inflationary expectation π^e, the nominal rate i is determined in quadrant II. Schedule DD in quadrant III relates to short-term nominal interest rate i with the adjusted interest rate differential d, *for given values of i_L^*, i_{t+j}^e, D^e, R^e, P, and T*. The slope of this schedule indicates that a higher i will result, with given i_L^*, i_{t+j}^e, D^e, R_e, and T, in a larger interest rate differential. On the other hand, higher values of i_L^*, D^e, or R^e will result in a downward shift of the DD schedule.

Finally, in quadrant IV schedule FF relates the interest rate differential d and the supply of credit for given values of C_{t-1} and k. The slope of this schedule indicates that, for given k, a higher interest rate differential will result in a higher supply of real credit. The reason for this is that a higher d will induce a larger foreign capital inflow.

THE WORKING OF THE MODEL

This section illustrates how this model works. Two cases are investigated: (A) an increase in the demand for real credit stemming from increased consumption due to higher perceived real wealth and (B) an increase in expected devaluation. In order to maintain the analysis at a simple level these disturbances are analyzed one at a time, as if they were the only shock to the economy. Also, for expository purposes we assume that the supply for credit is inelastic, although it *shifts* in response to changes in capital inflows.

Figure 3A–1.   Interest Rate Determination in a Semi-Open Economy.

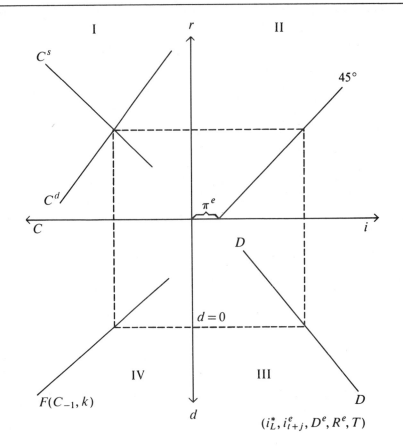

Case A: Increase in the Demand for Credit

Assume that in period t there is an exogenous increase in the demand for real credit and that in that period the supply of domestic credit remains constant (that is, $k = 0$). This case can be illustrated using Figure 3A–2: The demand for credit schedule shifts up to C_1^d, generating an initial increase in the short-term real rate in quadrant I. If inflationary expectations remain constant, the short-term nominal interest rate rises to i_1 in quadrant II.

Figure 3A-2. An Increase in Credit Demand and Real Interest Rates.

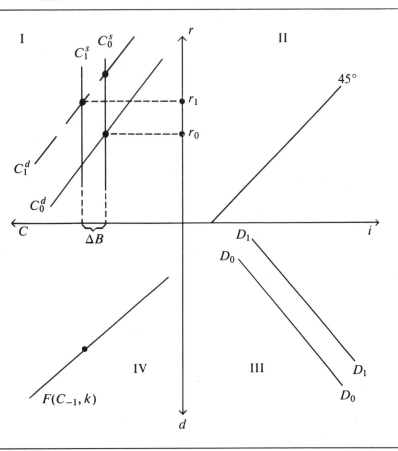

This increase in i generates, for given i_L^*, i_{t+j}^e, D^e, and R, a positive long-term interest differential $d_1 > 0$, which will induce an inflow of capital ΔB, which will increase the liquidity in the economy. However, since the capital inflows will result in a higher level of foreign debt, the country risk premium and maybe the expectations of devaluation will increase, generating a shift in the DD curve in quadrant III to $D_1 D_1$. In this case the new equilibrium long-term interest rate differential will be associated with a smaller inflow of foreign capital, and the new short-term real interest rate r_1 will be higher. This indeed seems to have been the case in Chile toward the second part of 1981.

Case *B*: An Increase in the Expectations of Devaluation

Assume now that the expectations of devaluation D^e increase. This will generate, through equation (3A.7), an initial *negative* long-term interest rate differential, which will be reflected by a downward shift of schedule *DD* in Figure 3A-3 to D_1D_1. As a consequence of this

Figure 3A-3. An Increase in Expectations of Devaluation and Real Interest Rates.

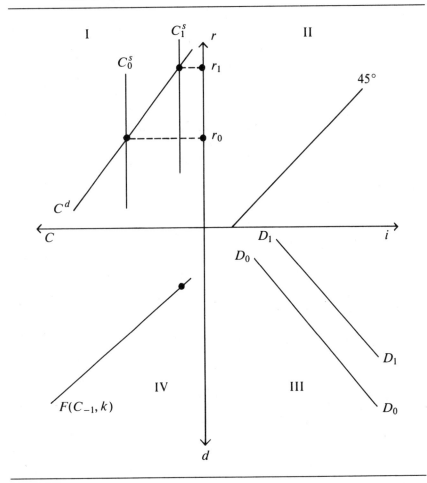

reduction in d, the net capital inflow from abroad will decline, generating a decrease in the supply of real credit to C_1 in Figure 3A–3. This, in turn, will result in a higher r and *for a given* π_1^e in a higher short-term nominal interest rate i_1. In the second run of effects, this higher i induces through a positive d, additional capital inflows, which increase liquidity but not enough as to reestablish old r. New equilibrium real rate will be r_2. Notice that this analysis will hold only if the expectation of devaluation is not associated with higher expected inflation. If, however, a higher D^e is related to a higher π^e, the final result will depend on the relative magnitudes of these two effects. It is important to note that increases in i_L^*, or R, and decreases in i_{t+j}^e will have the same effects on the real short-run interest rate as higher devaluation expectations.

Despite its simplicity, this model is able to capture the main characteristics of the Chilean experience during 1979–83. For example, according to the model, the combination of various factors — (1) an increase in the demand for real credit, (2) higher expectations of devaluations, (3) higher-risk premium assigned to the country by the international financial community, (4) a reduction in the expectations of domestic inflation, and (5) a higher world interest rate — will result in a large increase in the equilibrium domestic short-term real interest rate.

NOTES

1. On financial repression see, for example, the classical book by McKinnon (1973). By 1973 the degree of monetization of the Chilean economy was very low by international standards.
2. Initially the government tried to implement regulations to avoid excessive concentration of bank ownership. The private sector rapidly evaded these rules by setting innumerable interconnected holding companies, with each of them owning a small fraction of the bank's equity (see Arellano 1985). The role and behavior of these *grupos* is analyzed in more detail in Chapter 4.
3. An exception, of course, was trade financing. In 1982 as a way to speed up the "automatic adjustment" process the maturity restriction was lifted. At the time, however, the international financial community had very little interest in lending to Chile.
4. The expectations of future economic performance will affect savings via a Metzlerian mechanism where savings depend on the gap between de-

sired and actual wealth. The improvement in expectations on output growth are translated into higher perceived wealth and, thus, in a reduction of savings. For a discussion of the Chilean case see Harberger (1982), Barandiarán, Montt, and Pollack (1982), S. Edwards (1985), and Arellano (1985). It should be noted, however, that during this period Chileans greatly increase their consumption of durables (see Chapter 5). To the extent that this accumulation of durables represents partial savings, the national accounts figures reported in Table 3–3 underestimate real savings.

5. A *bubble* is defined as the difference of actual change in the price of a particular asset and the price change that responds to fundamentals. Recently a number of papers dealing with rational bubbles have appeared. See, for example, Singleton (1986) and the literature cited there. The appreciation of asset prices plays a crucial role in Barandiarán's (1983) perceptive analysis of Chile's financial crisis.

6. An interesting question is to explain analytically the behavior of the *grupos* using modern industrial organization theory. Although the theory on conglomerates is not well developed, some of the work on learning by doing and on predatory pricing can be adapted to explain the behavior of *grupos* in LDCs. Leff (1978) provides a number of perceptive observations on the subject.

7. Harberger (1985) in his interpretation of the Chilean experiment points out that the failure of Banco Osorno was one of the most important negative events in the period.

8. These figures refer to loans received by the banking sector; see Banco Central de Chile, *Boletín Mensual* (various issues). It should be noticed that due to restrictions to capital movements, foreign funds came in for only medium to long periods of time. See S. Edwards (1984b) for an empirical analysis of the determinants of the spread over LIBOR for a group of developing countries in the period 1976–80. Since domestic and foreign securities were imperfect substitutes, there is no reason to expect strict equality between both rates.

9. Arellano (1985) also makes this point.

10. An interesting debate that took place in Chile in 1977 is whether it was a mistake having privatized the banks before privatizing the manufacturing firms. See, for example, the interview with Minister Sergio de Castro in *Que Pasa* (April 14, 1977): 14.

11. In Chile the writing off of bad loans would have resulted in a reduction of the stock of credit equal to approximately forty times the value of the bad loans.

12. As is explained in Chapter 4 *CORFO* required 20 to 40 percent as downpayment in these sales of banks and firms. Most of the new *grupos* had to borrow heavily to come up with this downpayment.

13. Sjaastad and Cortez (1978) have argued that during the early period the high rates could be partially explained by the financial costs resulting from the existence of high reserve requirements under conditions of very high inflation. This, however, is only a possible explanation for the early period, since reserves requirements subsequently were drastically reduced to a final level of 10 precent, whereas interest rates remained, by and large, quite high.

14. This figure, which was computed from data provided by the *Superintendencia de Bancos*, refers only to loans each *grupo* received from its own banks. There was, of course, a significant amount of cross loans, where banks controlled by *grupo A* lend money to firms owned by *grupo B*. It is not possible to quantify the importance of those loans.

15. Barandiarán (1983) was perhaps the first to point out that Chile was following the pattern of a somewhat typical financial crisis as described by Kindleberger. The role of increased perceived wealth in the explanation of the low level of savings and of the high interest rates has also been emphasized by Harberger (1983a), S. Edwards (1985a, 1985b), and Arellano (1985).

16. This reduced form equation can be derived from combining a closed economy expression for interest rate determination with an open economy equation. In this model the degree of financial openness of the economy is not imposed exogenously but can be obtained from the actual data. In the current case it is the nominal borrowing rate; i^* is LIBOR; D^e is a proxy for the expected rate of devaluation constructed as the *tablita* rate between January 1978 and June 1979 and as the degree of accumulated real overvaluation after June 1979. It should be noted that one problem with this proxy is that the expected rate of devaluation should be over the long run. See the third section below and the appendix to this chapter. y is quarterly GNP as constructed by the Universidad de Chile; m is the M1 definition of money; and π is the actual rate of inflation, which under rational expectations is the appropriate proxy for the expected rate of devaluation. When alternative measures of real liquidity were used, similar results were obtained. See S. Edwards and Khan (1985) and S. Edwards (1985c) for discussions on the model and S. Edwards (1986a) for a description of the data.

17. Hanson and de Melo (1985) reached a similar conclusion in their analysis of the case of Uruguay.

18. Of course, to the extent that the public expected a *real* devaluation the ex-ante real interest rate also increased.

19. Rigorously, a risk-neutral firm or bank, in order to decide whether to borrow in pesos or in dollars will compare $1 + i_k$ with $(1 + i_k^*)E(S_k)/S$, where i_k is the interest rate charged on a peso denominated loan that matures in k periods from now (that is a loan of maturity k); i_k^* is the

interest rate on a dollar denominated loan also of maturity k; S is the nominal exchange rate — measured as pesos per dollar — in the current period; and $E(S_k)$ is the value of the exchange rate that is expected to prevail k periods from now. If $(1+i_k)$ exceeds $(1+i_k^*)E(S_k)/S$, then the firm will prefer to borrow in dollars. While it is true that in late 1979 people expected the exchange rate to remain fixed for a short period, there is no doubt that the expectations of devaluation during the relevant sixty-six-month period were significantly greater than zero. See Le Fort (1985).

20. In Corbo's (1986b) regressions the t-statistic for this coefficient was never greater (in absolute value) than 0.7. Our own attempts to explain econometrically the behavior of the net rate of capital flows in Chile during 1977–81 did not produce significant results. The regressions indicate that the rate of capital was not significantly sensible during the period to uncovered interest rate differentials. Morandé (1986) has recently used causality analysis to show that in Chile the inflow of capital preceded the real appreciation of the peso.

21. This follows from the traditional "transfer problem" in international economics. See Dornbusch (1985), Harberger (1982), S. Edwards (1984c), and S. Edwards (1985b). Condon, Corbo, and de Melo (1986), and Barandiarán, Montt, and Pollack (1982). See also Obstfeld (1986).

22. Between 1976 and 1979 the U.S. real exchange rate, as computed using the IFS MERM weights, depreciated by almost 12 percent. In a world where the major currencies float, if a small country determines exchange rate its policy (that is, fixes the parity) with respect to one major currency, it will fluctuate relative to the other currencies (see S. Edwards 1987).

23. It should be noticed that although the real exchange rate appreciated significantly between mid-1979 and mid-1982, its absolute value was still higher than in 1973. However, as is discussed in Chapter 5, as a result of the liberalization of trade and of the deterioration in the terms of trade, the long-run sustainable equilibrium real exchange rate had increased.

24. Of course, if $\hat{Z}_t$ is sufficiently high, convergence of $\hat{P}$ to $\hat{P}_T^*$ can even fail.

25. $D.W.$ is the Durbin-Watson statistic; R^2 is the coefficient of determination. These regressions were run correcting for the existence of first-order autocorrelation. Note that since lagged right-hand side variables are used, no simultaneity problems arise from the estimation reported here. The devaluation dummy in equation (3.5) takes a value of 1 in June 1979 and March 1982 and 0 otherwise. On the relationship between real exchange rates and its real determinants see S. Edwards (1987).

26. The number of bankruptcies per year follow: 1975, 81 firms; 1976, 131 firms; 1977, 224 firms; 1978, 312 firms; 1979, 344 firms; 1980, 415 firms;

1981, 431 firms; 1982, 810 firms. These data were obtained from the Frankel, Froot and Mizala-Salces (1986).

27. Also, starting in early 1982, and partially as a result of the expectations of devaluation and loss of credibility, a significant capital flight took place. See Arellano and Ramos (1986).

28. There is little doubt that, given the degree of overvaluation of the peso, a nominal devaluation accompanied with the appropriate macro policies and with a simultaneous abandonment of the wage indexation mechanism would have resulted in a real devaluation.

4 PRIVATIZATION AND DEREGULATION

From early on the theme that unified the military's policies was the desire to reduce the role of the government in economic matters. The Junta's views on the subject were aptly reflected in their Declaration of Principles of March 1974, where it was stated that the "state should only assume direct responsibility for those functions which the [people]...are unable to deal with adequately" (Mendez 1979: 30). This stance against government intervention in economic matters was a reaction to the failed populist policies of the previous thirty years or so and in particular against the increased importance of the government during the *Unidad Popular*. Initially, however, the military were not sure on how far they wanted to push this issue.[1] At first it was unclear whether they planned to implement a traditional market-oriented system or whether they would opt for a less orthodox type of economic organization. In fact, in light of the sweeping free market reforms implemented later, it is puzzling to find that in the 1974 Declaration of Principles there is a paragraph devoted to the possible Yugoslavia style management system for firms: "The statute governing the organization of enterprises, [and] the development and integration of labor...will establish methods of effective participation of workers in enterprises in which they serve" (Mendez 1979: 41).

The evolution of the government's view toward a stronger free market program was directly related to the gain in influence of the group

93

of economists popularly known as the "Chicago boys." During the first year senior military were assigned to all of the key economic and financial positions in the government, with civilian businesspeople and economists having advisory roles, and occupying lower-level administrative posts.[2] By late 1974, however, a mainly civilian team took over the most important government posts related to the economics sector, and in April of 1975 Jorge Cauas became the "superminister" in charge of the stabilization program. In late 1976, when then Minister of Economics Sergio de Castro replaced Cauas as Minister of Finance, the Chicago boys had greatly increased their influence and already had control of almost every key economic post in the government, including the Ministry of Economics, the Central Bank, the Budget Office, and the National Planning Office.[3] During 1977 the drive toward widening the free market policies made important progress as, among other things, Chile withdrew from the Andean Pact and began the final stage of the international trade reform — which eventually reduced tariffs to a uniform 10 percent level. In the next few years the Chicago boys became even more powerful as they took over the Labor Ministry, the Mining Ministry, and other key positions in the Education and Public Health ministries.

An interesting question, which in a way is beyond the scope of this book, is why the military, which traditionally had not participated in politics and, if anything, had a populist position regarding economic policy, embraced the free market approach with such enthusiasm. An important element — but certainly not the only one — in explaining this increased influence of free market proponents is that at the time of the coup the Chicago boys already had elaborated a full-fledged coherent economic program, based on a sharp reduction of the government's importance in economic affairs.[4] On the other hand, the possible alternative sources of economic advice (that is, other non–*Unidad Popular* groups) either had no coherent program or offered plans that were not convincing to Pinochet and other senior generals. For example, traditional businesspeople did not have a consistent and innovative long-term project, and their short term policies — tried briefly during 1974 under Ministers Léniz and Saez — made no dents on inflation. Interestingly enough, the Christian Democrats — who basically constituted the only other possible group that the military would trust politically — could not offer a coherent program that was convincing to the government. This was partly because some of the most prominent economists from the right wings of that party had at the time joined the ranks of the Chicago boys.[5] As time passed, and the Chicago boys' policies seemed to work, the military greatly increased their endorsement of the program, until in 1981 it was not possible to make a distinction between the military's program and the Chicago boys' long-term national project.

The reduction in the government's role in economic activity was to be achieved through two main mechanisms: privatization of a number of state enterprises, either nationalized or expropriated during the Allende regime or previously owned by the government, and deregulation of key markets and sectors. In terms of the deregulation process it is possible to distinguish two phases. The first consisted of the more basic reforms — including freeing prices, returning firms confiscated by the *Unidad Popular* to their owners, privatizing some public firms, and liberalizing the financial market and international trade. Many of these reforms had in fact been contemplated for a number of years by advocates of a development strategy based in price incentives and had been quite clearly delineated in the program that the Chicago boys had prepared during the *Unidad Popular* years. The second phase, which started approximately in mid-1979, consisted of more radical reforms aimed at transforming Chile's social as well as economic structure. These reforms, which came to be known as "the seven modernizations," were implemented once the military and the economists that supported them had a firmer grip on power and affected the labor market, education, health services, agriculture, and the administrative organization of the country.

THE PRIVATIZATION PROCESS

Starting in 1939, with the creation of the *Corporacion de Fomento de la Producción* (CORFO), state-owned enterprises began to play a key role in the production process. In particular, the state attained an important role in the production of steel, sugar, coal, agriculture products, fertilizers, copper processing, and electricity and in the provision of services such as public transportation and communications. As discussed in Chapter 1, the government's role was greatly increased in the early 1970s when the *Unidad Popular* undertook a massive process of nationalization, expropriation, and confiscation of firms and banks. In 1973 CORFO was a gigantic holding company that had expanded from owning forty-six firms and no banks in 1970 to controlling

488 firms and nineteen banks.[6] More than half of these firms (259) were not legally owned by CORFO; they had been confiscated — the word used at the time was *intervened* — during the *Unidad Popular* government, and CORFO controlled their productive and financial operations without actually owning them.[7]

After the coup the military very quickly returned to their owners those firms that had been intervened by the *Unidad Popular*. In 1974, 202 firms were returned to their stockholders, and by 1977 only eight "problem" firms had not been reinstated to their original owners. In 1974 a program for privatizing the banks and most of the firms that had been nationalized (rather than intervened) during the *Unidad Popular* period was implemented. Also, and in accordance with the goal of reducing the government's role, some of the firms that had been originally founded by CORFO and had traditionally been under its control were privatized.

Commercial banks — which had been nationalized during the *Unidad Popular* through the government's acquisition of shares from small and medium stockholders — were privatized first. According to newly implemented legislation, private citizens could not buy more than 3 percent of a bank's stock, while firms and holding companies could not own more than 5 percent of the stock of a particular bank. The purpose of these regulations was to avoid "excessive" ownership concentration. However, the private sector found ways to get around these rules, and very quickly different groups gained control of the newly privatized banks through the acquisitions of large packages of shares by innumerable interrelated holding companies. What is in a way astonishing is that this was not a mystery to regulators, who in fact knew that their measures to avoid ownership concentrating were consistently and systematically being violated.

Between 1975 and 1978 a large group of firms, including some that had traditionally been under government control, were also privatized. In this case the government did not worry about ownership concentration, and contrary to the banks' case, it auctioned all the shares it owned in one package. Table 4–1 includes the data on trajectory of firms privatization. Both in the case of banks and firms sales the government provided some financing, typically consisting of peso-denominated loans at 10 percent in real terms for two years in the case of banking and ten years for most firms.[8]

By 1978 all banks but one and most firms had been privatized, and by 1980 CORFO controlled only twenty-three firms, eleven of which

Table 4–1.   The Trajectory of Privatization.

Year	Number of "Intervened" Firms Returned to Stockholders	Number of Firms Sold
1974	202	49
1975	39	28
1976	10	22
1977	6	7
1978	2	8
1979	–	8
1980	–	6
1981	–	3
1982	–	4
Total	259	135

Source: CORFO (various issues).

were in the process of being sold to the private sector. In addition there were seventeen other government-owned firms that were not controlled by CORFO, including the gigantic national copper firm CODELCO, which the military decided to maintain under government control for "strategic" reasons.

There has been some discussion regarding the prices at which these firms and banks were sold. A number of observers have, in fact, argued that on average these firms' buyers—most of which were *grupos*—obtained a substantial subsidy from the government. Vergara (1981), for example, has argued that the amount of the subsidy ranged from 23 to 37 percent of the book value of auctioned banks and firms. Dahse (1979), on the other hand, calculated that in the case of forty-five major privatized firms, the average subsidy was approximately equal to 40 percent of book value. It is interesting to note, however, that not in all cases were sale prices below book value. For example, prices paid for a number of export sector firms and banks were significantly above their book value.[9] This, of course, is consistent with the fact that the *grupos* and others that participated in the auctions expected that as a result of the liberalization policies these two areas would be highly profitable, as in fact they were at least for some time.

Although there are a number of problems with using book value to compute the magnitude of the subsidy, there is little doubt that the timing chosen to sell them — basically in the midst of the recession — resulted in lower prices than what the government could have obtained had it postponed the privatization process.[10] To some extent, however, the timing chosen for these privatizations responded to the decision taken in 1975 to cut down fast on the fiscal deficit; a majority of these firms were experiencing negative cash flows, which were being financed by the government. The buyers, of course, thought that they could turn around these firms by improving the management systems and by investing in new and more modern equipment.

PRIVATIZATION, CONCENTRATION, AND THE *GRUPOS*

The military privatization process played an important role in the creation and expansion of the *grupos*, or large conglomerates that controlled banks and a varied array of major firms in many different sectors of the economy. Although these types of conglomerates had existed in Chile for a long time, the military experiment allowed a dynamic new style of *grupos* to emerge and expand.[11]

There were a number of important differences between the new *grupos* that emerged after 1973 and the old conglomerates of the 1950s and 1960s. First, while the old *grupos* were mainly family concerns, most of the new *grupos* relied less on family-type connections and were formed by small groups of capitalists and entrepreneurs. Second, the traditional *grupos* were financially conservative and operated with very low debt/equity ratios. The new *grupos*, on the contrary, were very aggressive and even temerary, operating on the basis of very high leverage. In fact, some of the new *grupos* were outright intrepid and started operations with very little equity, basing their phenomenal growth on the use of financial resources obtained through the financial intermediaries they controlled (that is, banks, *financieras*, mutual funds, insurance companies, and privately managed pensions funds) to build small empires. Third, whereas the old conglomerates were managerially conservative and sometimes even resembled small family businesses, the new *grupos* were very modern and technocratical. In fact, these new *grupos* revolutionized the way that firms and banks were managed in Chile by using highly trained professionals. These new managers, trained in Chilean and foreign business schools, became, in a way, a sign of the revolution that took place in Chilean business sector. They were young, arrogant, and highly paid; they in fact became a symbol of the changing times. And fourth, contrary to the old conglomerates that were mainly concerned with short-run to medium-run profitability, the new *grupos* were much more long-run oriented in their goals and strategies. In that sense, the larger new *grupos* had a very clear ideological position regarding the effects of the government's policies, recognizing that although some of them could hurt them in the short run—as was, for example, the case of the tariff reduction reform—they were the most adequate policies in the long-run for providing a stable free market type environment.

All the major *grupos* were organized around one or more banks, which were used to channel credit to the firms owned or controlled by *grupos*. In 1979, for example, the *grupos* directly controlled ten major banks, whose equity represented more than 80 percent of all private banks equity. As the privatization process proceeded the *grupos* acquired more and more firms. Although the government in some cases provided ten-year loans, the *grupos* had to borrow heavily in the domestic and international capital markets to finance the downpayment. As many of these firms were in relatively bad financial shape the *grupos* also had to borrow to finance heavy investment and retooling programs.

Most *grupos* bought firms in those areas they expected to flourish as a consequence of the liberalization policies and got involved in the export and financial sectors. In the financial sector they not only acquired banks but created *financieras*, new mutual funds, and insurance companies. After the social security system was reformed in 1980, they also invested heavily in the privately administered pension funds. In the exports sector they got heavily involved in timber, mining, paper, and fishing. They expected that as a result of the trade reform and high real exchange rate, profitability in this sector would be very high. In fact, the *grupos* interest in these fields was reflected in the relatively high prices paid in the privatization auctions for firms in these areas. For example, Dahse (1979) reports that firms in the paper, fishing, and forestry sectors, as well as banks, were among the few sold at prices above their book values. As the real exchange rate appreciated after mid-1979, however, exports profitability declined substantially, and profitability was greatly squeezed.

As a consequence of the mechanism used in the privatization process—namely, selling firms to a single buyer rather than selling packages of shares to many buyers—an important increase in the degree of ownership concentration took place.[12] For example, in 1979 the ten largest groups controlled 135 of the 250 largest private corporations. Moreover, these *grupos* controlled almost 70 percent of all corporations traded in the stock exchange.[13]

Also, as a consequence of the structural reforms introduced by the liberalization policies, the degree of market concentration of the manufacturing sector greatly increased. De Melo and Urata (1984) investigated the concentration issue using detailed data at the establishment level from Chile's manufacturing censuses of 1967 and 1979. They found that between these two years the degree of market concentration in the manufacturing sector increased substantially — at a faster pace than in other countries. Using Herfindahl concentration indexes for forty-five industries in the manufacturing sector they found that in 1979 the degree of market concentration had increased quite sharply over that in 1967.[14] In 1979 it took a significantly smaller number of equivalent (equal-size) firms to generate the same percentage of total output than in 1967. In a way this increase in the degree of concentration of production was an unavoidable result of the trade reform, since, as it is discussed in greater detail in Chapter 5, many marginal firms could not survive the increase in the higher degree of competition from abroad and exited the market. In other cases, in order to survive, reduce costs, and improve the level of efficiency, firms merged, increasing their share in production. However, the existence of foreign competition by itself meant that this higher market concentration in most cases could not be translated into a monopolistic pricing behavior. In fact, de Melo and Urata (1984) show that this increase in the degree of concentration was not associated with higher profit ratios.

The *grupos* were quite successful in increasing productivity and efficiency in most of their firms. However, as it turned out, and due to a number of factors, some of the firms acquired by them and even some of their new investments were not profitable. Some other firms, while initially successful, experienced a decline in profitability as the real exchange rate appreciated and interest rates increased. In late 1980 a number of *grupo*-related firms started to face serious financial trouble. However, in almost every case, and mainly for reasons of image, the *grupos* decided to pretend that everything was fine. The troubled firms were kept afloat thanks to the rolling over of what basically were bad loans. There were other reasons, in addition to image or signaling, for this decision of avoiding bankruptcy. First, as mentioned in Chapter 3, a bankruptcy meant declaring those loans "not performing" at the *grupo*'s banks' level, with the consequent negative effect on the banks' equity and thus the maximum legal amount of credit they could grant. Second, and more important, as the financial crisis generalized, the *grupos* began to expect that the government would at some point intervene, rescuing the ailing firms.[15]

The *grupos'* financial fragility became apparent in April 1981 when partially as a consequence of an amateurish speculation in the international sugar market a medium-size conglomerate—the Crav *grupo*—went bankrupt.[16] In fact the Crav affair clearly revealed to the public—and more importantly to foreign bankers—that the *grupos* had really been built on extraordinarily weak basis and that any negative shock, no matter how insignificant, could provoke extremely serious problems. There is little doubt that the Crav scandal was an important turning point; in a way it marked the end of the boom. After the Crav affair the public's—as well as international bankers'—doubts on the viability of the experiment began to mount. These doubts were quickly compounded by the government's passive attitude; as time passed the expectations of devaluation began to increase, interest rates climbed faster, and firms' troubles multiplied.

As pointed out, a result of the banks' refusal to recognize the nonperforming (or even defaulted) nature of the increasing proportion of "bad loans" was that they were rolled over, exercising considerable upward pressure on the demand for credit and on the interest rate. In late 1982 the porportion of credit that banks had granted to the firms directly related to the controlling *grupo* became alarmingly high. In fact, some of the banks had granted almost half of their loans to the controlling *grupo* (see Table 4–2). In early 1983 the financial situation was clearly unsustainable, and the government decided to intervene the main *grupos*, nationalizing a number of banks and liquidating others. In mid-1986, after three difficult years, the *grupos* or what was left of them were trying to recoup and were planning, as in the old days, to participate in the upcoming privatization auctions announced by the government.

THE DEREGULATION PROCESS AND THE SEVEN MODERNIZATIONS

The import substitution growth strategy of the 1940s through 1960s was accompanied by a major involvement of the government in all

Table 4-2.   *Grupo*-Related Loans: Selected Banks, 1982.[a]

Bank	Grupo-*Loans* as Percentage of Total Loans
Banco BHC	27.4%
Banco de Chile	18.6
Banco Santiago	42.3
Banco H.F.N.	18.5
Banco Credito	11.9
Banco SudAmericano	22.8

Source: Superintendencia de Bancos (various issues).

[a] These data refer to December 1982 and corresponds *only* to those loans granted by each bank to the controlling *grupo* of that particular bank. During the later stages of the experiment there were substantial cross *grupo* loans.

types of economic decisions. This involvement took place both directly via government-owned enterprises and indirectly through an extensive set of rules and regulations. By mid-1973 the government directly fixed and monitored more than 3,000 retail prices, prices of all utilities, and all interest rates. It also set rules for the allocation of credit and determined which financial intermediaries were allowed to issue specific instruments. International trade and domestic commerce were also heavily regulated, as were all activities related with transportation and the provision of other services. Many salaries were set by the government, and as is explained in Chapter 6, the labor market was subject to extensive regulation. As is usually the case, many of the rules and regulations that had piled up through the years were the result of rent-seeking activities and had often become inconsistent and contradictory.

Very early the military government decided to reduce the extent of regulation. The first step consisted on freeing most retail prices. This was followed by the processes of liberalization of the domestic capital market and international trade. The main aspects of the liberalization of the capital market — both domestic and to the rest of the world — were discussed in Chapter 3, while international trade deregulation is the subject of Chapter 5.

As time passed the deregulation process became broader, encompassing the agriculture and transportation sectors. In agriculture, prices were allowed to fluctuate approximately with world prices, and existing restrictions on land sales by beneficiaries of the agrarian reform were lifted. In transportation, regulations that restricted entry and imposed a government monopoly on a number of areas were reformed (see Wisecarver 1985).

Throughout most of the military rule the labor market was treated in an asymmetric way relative to other sectors. While the deregulation process in most markets started quite early on, the labor market — and in particular unions' behavior — was tightly controlled until mid-1979. This was to a large extent the result of a political decision; the military wanted to maintain a tight lid on unions, a majority of which had supported the *Unidad Popular* government. But even in the absence of union activities and collective bargaining the government followed the tradition with respect to wage indexation and readjustments.

The Seven Modernizations

As noted above, it is possible to distinguish two phases in the deregulation process. The first — generally associated to the name of Minister de Castro — dealt with more traditional reforms and encompassed the freeing of retail prices, the liberalization of the domestic capital market, the privatization of some government-owned firms, and the reduction of import barriers. The second phase began in mid-1979 and has been associated to the names of Ministers Miguel Kast and Jose Piñera. It consisted of more fundamental reforms affecting labor relations, social security, education, health, and the administration of justice and was aimed at introducing more fundamental and structural changes in the Chilean society.

In January 1981 for the first time General Pinochet pointed out that these more profound reforms formed part of a global long-run program for transforming the Chilean society; he called them "the seven modernizations." He stated that in order to make further progress on the "social advance that Chile is experimenting," the government had developed a plan that would help to "materialize new social institutions" (Banco Central de Chile, *Boletín Mensual* (February 1981: 269–84)). The general went on to explain that the seven modernizations were (1) the Labor Law of 1979, (2) the social security law, (3) educational reform, (4) health services reform, (5) agriculture sector reform, (6) justice system reform, and (7) administrative and regionalization reform.

The labor law introduced revolutionary changes to Chile's labor relations. It regulated the creation and operation of unions, established rules for collective bargaining, and determined the legal characteristics of labor contracts. The most important aspect of this law was that it greatly reduced the union's power. This was done in several ways: First, union membership became voluntary; second, unions were restricted to individual firms and could not join forces in order to negotiate at the industry level, as they had traditionally done; and third, firms could now impose lock-outs and temporarily lay off workers. The collective bargaining process was also profoundly changed. After a union made its petition, management's counteroffer should include, *at least*, an increase in salaries according to past inflation (Article 26). If no accord was reached on the terms of the new contract, a strike could take place. Thirty days after the strike had started, individual union members were free to negotiate on a one-to-one basis with the management, which was still bound by the 100 percent backward indexation mechanism. If after sixty days still no agreement had been reached, workers had to reassume their jobs at the old contract terms — with wages fully adjusted by past inflation — or it was understood that they had resigned their job.

The government attached great significance to the approval of the labor law. Ironically, the authorities thought that the incorporation of the backward wage indexation change in the collective bargaining process was one of its most important achievements. The general, himself, proudly stated that the new labor law "assures workers an increase in remuneration of at least 100% of the increase of the cost of living."

After its first year the labor law was praised as a big success by the government. In 1980 more than 600,000 workers participated in collective bargaining negotiations, with only fifty-two strikes, which lasted on average twenty-three days, resulting from this process. Workers obtained average wage increases of 8 percent over past inflation. During its second year (1981) approximately the same number of strikes took place, and wage increases averaged 2.6 percent over past inflation. In mid-1981 the labor law faced its first major test when more than 8,000 workers from one of the government-owned copper mines (*El Teniente*) went on strike. After thirty days of tense — and sometimes violent — negotiations the workers returned to their jobs having only obtained the minimum adjustment established by the law: past inflation. For the company, however, this represented a major increase in real labor costs, since the price of copper had dropped by more than 20 percent since the previous year.

The "modernization" of the social security system enacted in 1980 replaced a virtually broke pay-as-you-go system by a capitalization system, based on workers' individual retirement accounts. The new legislation also eliminated a number of distortion and inequalities, with early retirement being strictly limited and with the amount of pensions directly determined by each individual's fund accumulated through the years. However, for those workers whose individual fund was too low, a minimum pension, partially financed by the government, was established.

Perhaps the most interesting difference between the new and the old social security systems was that the new pension funds were administered by private companies (the so-called *AFPs*) that charged a small commission for doing the job. Workers could choose freely to which of these pension funds they wanted to be associated with, and they could move to a different fund as often as they wanted. Each time they moved to a different *AFP*, they took with them their accumulated individual pension assets. The *AFPs*, on the other hand, were supposed to be closely regulated, and there were fairly strict guidelines regarding the instruments in which they could invest the workers' contributions. Perhaps not surprisingly, most of these *AFPs* were owned by the *grupos*.

The social security reform had a number of important immediate effects. Since in the new social security law all exemptions were eliminated and early retirement was severely restricted, it was possible to reduce social security taxes. For example, total social security contributions (employer plus employee contributions) for blue-collar workers declined from 50 percent of after-tax salaries in 1977 to 20 percent in 1982. These lower taxes, in turn, resulted in a once-and-for-all important increase in salaries for all workers who opted to switch to the new system.

Between 1979 and 1983 some progress was also made in the education and health modernizations. In education there was a decentralization of the government's role in the provision of primary and secondary education. Until 1979, when the so-called Education Directive was enacted, the central government directly ran all primary and secondary public schools. This, of course, was a major task that was accomplished by a variety of institutions, including a huge public construction company that built schools and a publicly owned catering firm that provided school lunches. As a result of the reform, the local governments (that is, municipalities) took over public schools, and many of the services indirectly related to the provision of education were now obtained, via open bidding systems, from private sector contractors.[17] Also, as a result of the educational reform subsidies granted to higher education were drastically reduced, university tuition was hiked, and a system of scholarships and loans was established. During 1981 some important steps toward reforming the public health system were taken. Until then all workers belonged to fairly inefficient health plans run by the state and funded by required workers contributions and by the government. The new reform, however, allowed private insurance companies (the *ISAPRES*) to collect workers health contributions and provide some type of health plan. Workers were free to remain in the old government-run system or to have their health *premia* deposited in the private companies, which generally required an additional contribution to enroll them in their plans.[18] Once again, most of the new health insurance companies were owned by the *grupos*.

The handling of the 1982 crisis required all the attention of government officials, slowing down the drive for structural reform. Moreover, starting in late 1982 the Chicago boys moved to a clearly defensive position, trying to "protect" the reforms already enacted from possible reversals. Other groups, including traditional businesspeople, tried, with relative success, to persuade the military to impose controls on imports and ceilings on interest rates and to provide subsidies to ailing firms. During 1984 the Chicago boys staged a tactical retreat, only to be called back by Pinochet to the highest ranks of the government in 1985. In early 1986 their power and influence among the senior ranks of the military remained very high.

NOTES

1. On the contrary, at the political level it was clear from early on that the military rejected the traditional liberal democratic system, even as a long-run permanent system for Chile. They called, instead for a "protected" democracy. See, for example, the Junta's Declaration of Principles.
2. The first Ministers of Finance and Economics were an admiral and an army general; the first president of the Central Bank was also an army general.

3. As mentioned in Chapter 1 *Chicago boys* was the generic name given to a group of economists, most of them trained at the University of Chicago or other U.S. institutions, who had a strong view against the role of government intervention in the economy. The more prominent members of this group were Sergio de Castro, who was both Minister of Economics and Finance, Jorge Cauas (Minister of Finance), Miguel Kast (Minister of Planning and then president of the Central Bank), Sergio de la Cuadra (president of the Central Bank and then Minister of Finance), Jose Piñera (Minister of Labor and the Minister of Mining), and Alvaro Bardón (president of the Central Bank).
4. Obviously, this is only one element in the explanation of this problem. A full analysis of the transition of the military thought regarding economic policy is well beyond the scope of this book. A good summary of that program can be found in Bardón, Carrasco, and Vial (1985).
5. On the other hand, the center-left Christian Democrats had a very coherent economic program that, however, was too tainted with socialist ideas to be palatable to the military. This group went on to form the opposition think-tank CIEPLAN, where much work on alternative economic policies has been carried out. See the bibliography to this book for the most important work by CIEPLAN economists.
6. See Chapter 1 for a brief discussion on the mechanisms used by the *Unidad Popular* to take control over different firms.
7. However, the government had for a long time owned the major commercial bank, Banco de Estado.
8. See Vergara (1981) for more details.
9. The computation of the value of the subsidy implied by these sales is particularly difficult, since the relatively small size of the stock market in the mid-1970s makes the market value of firms a highly deceiving figure.
10. See Dahse (1979).
11. See Lagos (1961) for a discussion on the traditional role of *grupos* in the Chilean economy. Leff (1978, 1979) presents a discussion on the role of *grupos* in developing countries, including South America and Southeast Asia.
12. It should be noted, however, that it is unclear whether an attempt to sell small packages of shares would have been successful.
13. See Dahse (1979).
14. The Herfindahl index of concentration is defined as $H = \Sigma s_i^2$, where S_i is the ith firm share in the industry's output.
15. Although there are no satisfactory theoretical models of conglomerate behavior in the LDCs, the *grupos'* attitude toward ailing units and bankruptcy can be explained by resorting to signaling models from the industrial organization literature. On these types of models see, for example, Milgrom and Roberts (1982).

16. On the Crav scandal see, for example, the stories in the weekly maga-
    zine *Hoy* (May 27, 1981): 11–13.
17. Interestingly enough, the Catholic Church expressed serious reserva-
    tions on the educational reform (*Hoy* (June 3, 1981)).
18. Since the required health premium was only equal to 4 percent of after
    tax salaries, they did not cover the required private insurance premiums.

5 THE LIBERALIZATION OF INTERNATIONAL TRADE

One of the central policies of the military government was the opening up of international trade. In five years all quantitative impediments to trade were eliminated, and import tariffs were reduced from an average of more than 100 percent to a uniform 10 percent level. The liberalization of international trade affected the Chilean economy in a profound way. Between 1974 and 1979 Chile was transformed from a highly closed economy, where international transactions were severely repressed, into an open economy whose foreign trade regime corresponded quite closely to the neoclassical ideal. As a consequence of this sweeping reform a number of firms that had traditionally been subsidized through high import tariffs had to close down, and others embarked on major reorganization processes that greatly increased their level of efficiency and productivity. Also, thanks to the reform a number of imported goods, until then out of reach to most Chileans, became accessible to blue-collar workers and the lower-middle classes. The trade reform was initially accompanied by a high real exchange rate that encouraged a frantic growth of nontraditional exports, which continued until 1980 when a combination of factors — including the overvaluation of the peso — inhibited further expansion. On the other hand, the combination of lower tariffs, higher perceived wealth, an overvalued exchange rate after 1979, and an abundance of foreign financing resulted in imports' growing at rates even faster than exports, thus generating a widening trade deficit.

In this chapter we discuss in detail several aspects of the international trade reform, including its effects on resource reallocation and the way in which the manufacturing sector adjusted to the lower level of protection. We emphasize the role of exchange rate policy and analyze the reform's effects on international trade, focusing in particular on the performance of noncopper exports and on the deluge of imports that took place in 1980–81.

THE REFORM

The liberalization of international trade had long been a pet project of a large number of Chilean economists including the "Chicago boys."[1] According to traditional economic theory and in line with a large amount of empirical support, it was expected that opening the economy to the rest of the world would result in a reallocation of resources toward those sectors in which Chile had a comparative advantage, increased efficiency, rising exports, higher employment over the longer run, faster growth and an improved income distribution.[2]

In the late 1930s and early 1940s Chile's foreign trade became increasingly distorted through the indiscriminatory imposition of tariffs, import quotas, and all sorts of regulations and controls. Initially, as in the great majority of Latin American countries, these trade restrictions were a fundamental element of an import substitution strategy aimed at encouraging industrialization through the development of infant industries. With time, however, the tariff structure more and more reflected benefits obtained by different pressure groups. By the late 1960s high and variable tariffs had become a permanent feature of the Chilean economy. In fact, Chile's protective structure had become one of the most distortive in the developing countries. Things worsened during the *Unidad Popular* period, as the government imposed layer after layer of regulations in an attempt to avoid a balance of payment crisis and the collapse of the external sector. Chile's long tradition of trade restrictions generated a number of negative effects, including a high degree of inefficiency in the manufacturing sector, the use of highly capital-intensive techniques, and stagnation of noncopper exports.[3]

At the time of the military coup import tariffs averaged 105 percent and were highly dispersed, with some goods subject to nominal tariffs of more than 700 percent and others fully exempted from import duties. In addition to tariffs, a battery of quantitative restrictions were applied, including outright import prohibition and prior import deposits of up to 10,000 percent (see de la Cuadra and Hachette 1986). These protective measures were complemented with a highly distortive multiple exchange rates system consisting of fifteen different rates.

In October 1973 then–Minister of Finance Admiral Gotuzzo stated that Chile's "best prospects for growth are in opening to international trade" (Mendez 1979: 63–64). Initially, however, the authorities had no clear idea on how far they wanted to go with this reform. In fact, not until late in 1977 – after Chile had withdrawn from the Andean Pact – was it determined that the final goal of the trade liberalization was the achievement of a uniform 10 percent import tariff.

In early 1974 the first set of trade liberalization measures was taken. The maximum tariff was reduced from 700 percent to 220 percent, and those duties between 50 percent and 220 percent were reduced by ten percentage points. This first round of tariff reduction had little effect on relative prices and foreign competition, since the great majority of these duties were redundant; even after they had been reduced, prices of imported goods remained at "prohibitive" levels. Still at this point the government was vague regarding the final protective level it wanted to achieve. In 1975, after additional rounds of tariff reductions, the government announced that by early 1978 nominal tariffs would range between 25 percent and 35 percent. In 1976, after all quantitative restriction had been abolished, the trade reform goals were revised; Minister de Castro argued that "[A] tariff schedule ranging from 10 to 35 percent is perfectly adequate for the Chilean economy since it provides reasonable levels of protection for the nation's industrial activity" (Mendez 1979: 209).

Throughout this period the import tariffs and foreign direct investment policies became increasingly at odds with those of the Andean Pact, and periodic arguments ensued between Chile and the other members of the Customs Union. In mid-1976 then–Economics Minister de Castro went as far as to suggest that the Andean Pact's tariff policies constituted a "threat to Chile's sovereign right to establish its own exchange rate policy" (Mendez 1979: 209).

In 1977 Chile withdrew from the Andean Pact, and in December of that year Minister de Castro announced that the final goal was now to reduce tariffs to a *uniform* rate of 10 percent by mid-1979. In explaining this new change in the tariff policy de Castro pointed out that the prevailing schedule with differentiated rates between 10 percent and 35 percent generated an unjustifiable discriminatory situation. In his speech he said, "[W]e have decided to eliminate the distortions generated by the discriminatory tariff structure and to establish a uniform tariff; in this way all activities producing for the domestic market will be on an equal footing regarding foreign competition" (Banco Central de Chile, *Boletín Mensual* (December 1977: 1960)).

In Table 5-1 we present data on the itinerary of nominal import tariff reduction between December 1973 and June 1979, including the dates when the tariff reductions took place, the maximum tariff rate, and the average rate. As may be seen the liberalization was somewhat

Table 5-1. The Itinerary of Tariff Liberalization.

Dates in Which Tariffs Were Lowered	*(1)* Rate of Maximum Tariff	*(2)* Percentage of Items Subject to Maximum Tariff	*(3)* Tariff Mode	*(4)* Percentage of Items	*(4)* Average Nominal Tariff
12/31/73	220%	8.0%	90%	12.4%	94.0%
3/1/74	200	8.2	80	12.4	90.0
3/27/74	160	17.1	70	13.0	80.0
6/5/74	140	14.4	60	13.0	67.0
1/16/75	120	8.2	55	13.0	52.0
8/13/75	90	1.6	40	20.3	44.0
2/9/76	80	0.5	35	24.0	38.0
6/7/76	65	0.5	30	21.2	33.0
12/23/76	65	0.5	20	26.2	27.0
1/8/77	55	0.5	20	24.7	24.0
5/2/77	45	0.6	20	25.8	22.4
8/29/77	35	1.6	20	26.3	19.8
12/3/77	25	22.9	15	37.0	15.7
6/78[a]	20	21.6	10	51.6	13.9
6/79[a]	10	99.5	10	99.5	10.1

Source: Ffrench-Davis (1981).
[a] During 1978 and the first half of 1979 the tariff schedule was reduced in a linear form.

abrupt, and already in June 1976 the average tariff was 33 percent, significantly below the average tariff in the majority of the developing countries. This achievement is particularly impressive, since at the time all quantitative import restrictions had also been eliminated. By June 1979 when the trade reform came to an end, all items, except automobiles, had a nominal import tariff of 10 percent.

The liberalization of international trade generated substantial changes in domestic relative prices that, together with changes in the cost of hiring labor and in the real exchange rate, greatly affected the ability of the Chilean economy to compete internationally. While as a consequence of the trade reform the manufacturing sector as a whole experienced a reduction of its domestic relative prices, the agriculture, forestry, and fishing sectors were subject to an increase in their relative prices. Naturally, the effect of the trade reform on the different manufacturing industries was not uniform. In Table 5–2 we present data on the evolution of the rate of effective protection for eighteen industries within the manufacturing sector.[4] As the reform progressed, both the level and dispersion of the effective rates of protection were reduced, until in June 1979 the average effective tariff was 13.6 percent, and the range between highest and lowest effective tariffs was only six percentage points.

While the liberalization reform reduced the average rate of effective protection in manufacturing, it increased the level of protection granted to agriculture value added. This was because traditionally, through the imposition of price controls on agriculture products and high import tariffs on inputs, most crops had a substantially negative rate of effective protection. In 1974, for example, the agricultural sector had an average rate of effective protection of −36 percent. As a result of the tariff reduction process and of a new agriculture pricing policy aimed at maintaining domestic agriculture prices approximately in line with world prices, this negative protection to the sector was eliminated and even became positive during the first years of the military regime.[5]

TARIFFS, THE REAL EXCHANGE RATE, AND NOMINAL EXCHANGE RATE POLICY, 1974–79

The liberalization of international trade had an important effect on the long-run equilibrium value of Chile's real exchange rate. Changes

Table 5-2. Effective Rates of Protection in Selected
Manufacturing Sectors (percentages).

Sector	1974	1976	1978	1979
Food stuff	161%	48%	16%	12%
Beverages	203	47	19	13
Tobacco	114	29	11	11
Textiles	239	74	28	14
Footwear	264	71	27	14
Timber products	157	45	16	15
Furniture	95	28	11	11
Paper products	184	62	22	17
Publishing	140	40	20	12
Leather products	181	46	21	13
Rubber products	49	54	26	15
Chemicals	80	45	16	13
Petroleum and coal	265	17	12	13
Nonmetallic minerals	128	55	20	14
Basic metals	127	64	25	17
Metallic industries	147	77	27	15
Nonelectrical machinery	96	58	19	13
Electrical machinery	96	58	19	13
Average	151.4	51.0	19.7	13.6
Standard deviation	60.4	15.70	5.3	1.7

Source: Aedo and Lagos (1984).

in other real factors, or "fundamentals"—such as the deterioration
in the terms of trade, the reduction in government expenditure, and
the opening of the capital account—modified the long run equilibrium real exchange rate as well. More specifically, as a result of the
tariff reform and of the worsening of the terms of trade a depreciation of the long-run real exchange rate was required to maintain external equilibrium. This new higher value of the real exchange rate
was first achieved via the maxi-devaluation of October of 1973 and
then maintained through the active use of an active crawling exchange
rate system, which lasted until January of 1978.[7]

The importance assigned by the government to a "high" real exchange rate was clearly articulated by the general himself in a 1976
speech (Mendez 1979: 195): "We shall continue to encourage nontra-

ditional exports.... The Minister of Finance will announce the manner in which the exchange rate shall be established in order to guarantee a viable and permanent value for foreign currency."[8] Moreover, the government publicly linked the lowering of tariffs with higher real exchange rates. For example, in December 1977 Minister de Castro pointed out (Banco Central de Chile, *Boletín Mensual* (December 1977: 1960–61)):

> [T]he lower are tariffs, the higher should the exchange rate be.... [A]s a compensation for the tariff reduction corresponding to the current month, we have decided to devalue by 4.3 percent.... For the following months the exchange rate adjustment will correspond to inflation in the preceding months plus an additional amount to compensate for the tariff reduction.

Table 5–3 contains quarterly data for 1973–78 on the nominal rate of devaluation with respect to the U.S. dollar, on the rate of domestic inflation, and on the real *effective* exchange rate (REER). This latter multilateral index captures the real movement of the peso relative to a group of Chile's ten major trade partners. A higher REER reflects a real depreciation, while a reduction captures a real appreciation of the domestic currency or a reduction in country's ability to compete internationally. As can be seen from this table the degree of real depreciation achieved during the first two and a half years of the regime was remarkable. At the end of 1976 the real effective exchange rate was almost 150 percent higher than in the third quarter of 1973. In June 1976 and again in March 1977 the peso was revalued as a way to break inflationary expectations (see Chapter 2). In the second half of 1977, to partially compensate for the effects of the new rounds of tariff reductions, the rate of nominal devaluation with respect to the U.S. dollar was once again increased. During 1978, in spite of the fact that the newly adopted *tablita* contemplated a rate of nominal devaluation with respect to the U.S. dollar below the ongoing inflation, the real effective exchange rate actually experienced a slight real depreciation. As noted in Chapter 2, this was in part a reflection of the fact that the rate of devaluation of the *tablita* was determined relative to a depreciating U.S. dollar.[9] In the second quarter of 1979, when the reform of international trade achieved its final goal of a 10 percent uniform tariff, the index of the real effective exchange rate was 160 percent higher than in the third quarter of 1973, when the first talks on trade reform had begun.

Table 5–3. Nominal Devaluation, Domestic Inflation, and Real Effective Exchange Rates: 1973–78.

		(A) Rate of Nominal Devaluation Relative to U.S. $ (%)	(B) Domestic Inflation (%)	(C) Index Real Effective Exchange Rate (1975 = 100)
1973	2	160.0%	71.9%	26.5
	3	30.8	57.7	40.3
	4	303.5	107.7	72.2
1974	1	40.8	60.2	71.3
	2	50.1	48.7	75.1
	3	40.8	39.2	76.6
	4	58.5	41.3	83.5
1975	1	72.2	64.0	99.1
	2	64.2	69.0	102.5
	3	35.2	32.7	100.4
	4	33.3	26.4	98.0
1976	1	30.4	26.4	104.1
	2	25.8	34.7	97.3
	3	5.8	28.2	85.5
	4	18.8	19.4	87.2
1977	1	7.9	23.9	83.6
	2	10.1	16.4	78.5
	3	17.9	13.8	81.8
	4	15.6	12.4	89.5
1978	1	8.2	7.8	97.5
	2	6.6	8.8	100.3
	3	3.8	11.1	103.3
	4	2.4	5.4	105.1

Sources: Column A from Banco Central de Chile (1981, 1983, 1984) and refers to *mercado cambiario*. For each quarter these data refer to the average for March, June, September, and December of each year. Column B from Cortazar and Marshall (1980) also end of period. Column C from S. Edwards and Ng (1985) and refers to period average. For data on the real effective exchange rate until 1983 see Table 3–9 in Chapter 3,

After mid-1979, the pegging of the exchange rate with indexed wages plus the opening of the capital account generated the already discussed overvaluation of the peso that drove the actual real exchange rate further and further apart from its new (that is, after tariff reform) long-run sustainable equilibrium. As this difference between actual and long-run equilibrium real exchange rate accumulated, the ability of domestic firms to compete internationally declined.

Terms of Trade, Labor Markets, and Competitiveness

The general tendency during the period was for the international terms of trade to worsen significantly, although international prices of specific imports and exports moved in different directions. As can be seen from Table 5-4, between 1973 and 1983 the external terms of trade deteriorated in almost 50 percent, with much (but not all) of the action coming from changes in the price of copper. As is discussed below, prices of some of the other major exports also experienced important changes throughout the period, as did the price of oil and other imports.

The initial reforms of the labor market—discussed in greater detail in Chapter 6—increased the ability of domestic firms to adjust to the lower level of protection and helped some of them compete

Table 5-4.   Terms of Trade and Copper Prices: 1973–83.

	External Terms of Trade (1973 = 100)	Nominal Price of Copper (U.S. $/lb.)	Index of Real Price of Copper (1973 = 100)
1973	100.0	$0.909	100.0
1974	105.7	0.933	97.2
1975	70.3	0.559	53.3
1976	75.7	0.636	58.0
1977	67.8	0.593	50.9
1978	67.7	0.619	49.3
1979	72.2	0.893	63.6
1980	69.2	0.992	61.6
1981	55.9	0.789	44.9
1982	50.4	0.672	36.3
1983	53.1	0.722	38.6

Sources: Column A is defined as the ratio of export to import prices and was obtained from the U.N. Economic Commission for Latin America. Columns B and C from Banco Central de Chile (1981, 1983, 1984).

internationally. In particular, the curtailment of unions activities and almost complete absence of labor conflicts, plus the greater flexibility for laying off workers, helped to reduce the effective cost of hiring labor. Also, the reduction of social security taxes, which amounted to almost 60 percent between 1974 and 1981, reduced quite significantly the cost of labor. On the other hand, the indexation mechanism used throughout the period and later institutionalized by the Labor Law of 1979 reduced the ability of firms to adjust to changes in market conditions.

ADJUSTMENT AND PRODUCTIVITY

The tariff reduction process, and the accompanying exchange rate policy, affected the structure of production and resource allocation in a profound way. Initially, the major beneficiaries of this process were nontraditional (or noncopper) exports that experienced a sharp increase, growing from 9.5 percent of total exports in 1971 to 35 percent in 1981. In Table 5-5 we include data on the relative shares of different sectors in Chile's GDP.

Surprisingly, perhaps, the tariff reform did not have a large effect on the manufacturing sector as a whole; its share in GDP was reduced from 24.3 percent in 1965-70 to 22.3 percent in 1980. However, the structure of production within manufacturing was significantly affected, with those industries that traditionally had had a very high level of protection — for example, textiles and leather goods — experiencing large output losses. As is reflected in Table 5-6, seven out of twenty manufacturing subsectors had a lower level of production in 1980 than in 1970. According to a survey conducted in 1978 by the Manufacturers Association (SOFOFA) more than 60 percent of total firms in the textile, clothing, and footwear industries and more than 75 percent of firms in the nonmetallic and basic metals sectors were severely affected by the increased import competition resulting from the tariff reform.[10]

Those industries that experienced an increase in production during the 1970s — beverages, paper products, and tobacco, among others — achieved this by greatly increasing their level of efficiency and productivity. This was done by reducing the number of workers, by closing of inefficient plants, and by implementing investment projects aimed at modernizing management and productive processes. As a result of

Table 5-5. Relative Shares of Different Sectors on GDP,
Selected Years: 1974-82 (percentages).

	1974	*1977*	*1979*	*1981*	*1982*
Agriculture and forestry	5.3%	9.3%	6.7%	5.8%	4.9%
Fishing	0.4	0.5	0.6	0.5	0.7
Mining	12.0	8.1	9.8	5.6	7.7
Manufacturing	29.5	21.7	21.2	22.3	18.9
Electricity, gas, and water	1.1	2.3	2.0	2.3	3.2
Construction	6.1	4.1	4.3	6.4	5.6
Trade	14.1	15.6	16.7	15.0	15.6
Transport and communications	5.7	5.3	5.2	4.9	4.6
Financial services	5.3	6.3	8.1	10.7	11.2
Real estate (housing)	3.7	7.1	7.4	7.8	9.4
Public administration	6.5	6.4	5.5	5.3	6.3
Education	3.8	4.6	4.1	4.8	5.4
Health	2.5	3.2	3.0	3.5	3.6
Other services	2.8	3.8	3.9	5.3	4.8
Minus: Imputed bank service charge	−2.4	−3.2	−4.0	−6.4	−6.5
Plus: Import duties	3.6	4.9	5.5	6.2	4.6
Gross domestic product	100.0	100.0	100.0	100.0	100.0

Source: Banco Central de Chile (1981, 1983, 1984).
Note: These ratios were computed using GDP computations at current prices.

the trade reforms and of the adjustment made by industrial firms, average labor productivity in manufacturing increased by 42 percent between 1971 and 1981. Moreover, in some specific cases, the increases in productivity were much greater, reaching figures that stretch the imagination. For example, Corbo and Sanchez (1985) report the case of a textile firm where average labor productivity increased by twenty-eight times! They also report the case of a *grupo*-owned electric appliances firm whose average labor productivity increased more than seven times. In Table 5-7 we present a more general picture on labor productivity changes. As may be seen in mining, manufacturing, construction, transportation, and communications productivity rose very sharply. For the economy as a whole labor productivity grew at an average annual rate of 4.3 percent per annum between 1976 and 1981,

Table 5-6. Index of Manufacturing Production: 1970, 1975, 1980 (1968 = 100).[a]

Sector	1970	1975	1980
Food	99.6	102.3	115.8
Beverages	91.1	87.2	152.9
Tobacco	97.7	120.8	155.8
Textiles	96.0	62.4	60.7
Footwear	104.8	86.8	84.4
Timber products	108.1	54.4	99.7
Furniture	113.4	61.8	127.7
Paper products	88.3	101.0	141.7
Publishing	109.5	55.6	65.9
Leather products	103.9	70.6	45.8
Rubber products	111.0	35.8	86.1
Chemicals	120.9	79.7	141.8
Derivatives of oil and rubber	105.4	110.9	136.7
Nonmetallic minerals	102.9	76.1	122.2
Metallic industries	108.7	119.8	160.5
Metallic industries except transport	98.6	59.7	99.9
Machinery	94.2	77.4	110.1
Electrical products	99.5	75.8	131.6
Transportation equipment	127.0	50.0	138.3
Rest of manufacturing	81.0	63.6	73.7
General index	104.0	81.2	115.0

Source: Instituto Nacional de Estadística, published in Banco Central de Chile, *Boletín Mensual* (various issues).

[a] Annual averages.

Table 5-7. Average Labor Productivity in Selected Sectors: 1971, 1978, 1981 (1971 = 100).

	1971	1978	1981
Agriculture	100.0	88.1	106.8
Mining	100.0	87.2	122.3
Manufacturing	100.0	108.4	141.6
Construction	100.0	122.8	155.6
Commerce	100.0	80.7	88.2
Transportation and communications	100.0	143.8	166.1

Source: Bardón, Carrasco, and Vial (1985).

almost twice as fast as the rate for 1965–70 (2.2 percent) and significantly higher than in countries such as Brazil, Mexico, the United States, Germany, Japan, and Korea during the same period.[11]

The tariff reform also affected relative prices and resource allocation within agriculture. For example, while traditional crops lost importance, investment related to export items such as fresh fruits increased very rapidly. Between 1972 and 1980 total acreage devoted to fruit production almost doubled. Also, investments in forestry increased, with the average yearly number of new trees planted in the late 1970s exceeding by almost four times the level of the late 1960s (see Banco Central de Chile 1981, 1983, 1984).

Tariff Reform and Employment

A subject extensively debated in Chile's popular press is the extent to which the process of tariff reduction "contributed" to the unemployment problem. There is little doubt that as a result of the tariff reform a number of contracting and even disappearing manufacturing firms laid off large numbers of workers. On the other hand, expanding firms from the exporting sectors increased employment, partially offsetting the negative effect. The net result, however, was an increase in unemployment generated by the trade reform. This negative effect was particularly marked in manufacturing where, as mentioned, firms worked their way out of the difficult situation created by increased foreign competition by trimming their payrolls and increasing productivity.[12]

There were two main ways in which the tariff liberalization generated short-run unemployment. First, there was a natural adjustment period where laid off workers took time to start searching for work in a different, expanding, sector. Second, in reality—contrary to the simplest textbook case—physical capital is fixed in its sector of origin, which made the expansion of production in a number of the exporting sectors somewhat sluggish at first. Only as additional investment took place through time was it possible to fully increase production and employment in these expanding sectors. However, the existence of wage rigidity and in particular of a minimum wage in real terms made the absorption of labor by the expanding industries more difficult.[13]

The proportion of total unemployment that can be attributed to the tariff reform is, however, relatively small when compared to the magnitude of the overall unemployment problem. S. Edwards (1982), for example, calculated that an upper bound for the unemployment effects of the trade reform was 3.5 percentage points of the labor force, or 129,000 people, with the bulk of this unemployment located in the food, beverages, tobacco, textiles, and leather products subsectors (57,000 people). More recently, de la Cuadra and Hachette (1986) have calculated that the trade reform generated a reduction of employment in the manufacturing sector of approximately 50,000 workers. Even though these are not negligible numbers, they clearly indicate that an explanation for the bulk of the unemployment should be sought elsewhere. That is, indeed, what we do in Chapter 6 where we analyze the unemployment problem in great detail.

RESPONSE OF EXPORTS AND IMPORTS

As expected, the trade reform resulted in a major increase in Chile's volume of international trade. Exports, and in particular noncopper exports, grew initially very fast. Imports, on the other hand, quickly responded to the reduction in tariffs and to the perceived increase in wealth, growing at an even faster pace, and thus generating a widening trade deficit.

Exports

As reflected in Table 5-8, the dollar value of total exports increased at an average rate of 15 percent per annum between 1973 and 1983; the *real* value of exports on the other hand grew at an average annual rate of growth of 12 percent.[14] Much more impressive, however, was the performance of the so-called nontraditional exports, which grew from a mere 9.5 percent of total exports in 1971 to more than 35 percent of exports in 1981. In real dollar terms, nontraditional exports grew at almost 20 percent per year between 1971 and 1981.

As can be seen from Table 5-8, exports of industrial goods exhibited great dynamism, jumping by more than ten times between 1971 and 1981. Initially (1974-76) this increase in manufactured exports was in part the result of the very depressed level of domestic demand and in part the result of the very high real exchange rate. Many firms that were unable to reach their break-even point by supplying the domestic market embarked on the search for new foreign markets. That

Table 5-8. The Evolution of Exports: 1971-83 (millions U.S. $).[a]

	1971	1975	1977	1979	1981	1983
1. Mining	$813.2	$1,075.4	$1,403.2	$2,253.9	$2,279.1	$2,296.6
Copper	701.8	890.4	1,187.4	1,799.6	1,692.1	1,835.7
2. Agriculture	29.4	86.1	159.5	264.5	365.4	327.5
Fresh fruits	13.4	37.8	63.6	123.3	198.6	220.5
3. Manufactured goods	119.6	390.6	627.6	1,245.0	1,286.0	1,211.4
Fish meal	29.8	29.2	86.5	152.6	202.0	307.1
Timber	7.0	25.2	70.4	164.7	158.5	116.4
Paper products	32.0	93.7	134.4	238.8	259.0	208.0
Chemicals	11.8	46.4	77.9	128.2	143.0	109.8
Metallic products and machinery	4.4	42.4	36.8	59.5	45.1	20.3
Basis metals industries	9.0	58.6	103.7	306.5	235.0	285.5
Total (1+2+3)	$962.2	$1,552.1	$2,190.3	$3,763.4	$3,930.7	$3,885.5

Source: Banco Central de Chile (1981, 1983, 1984).
[a]This table contains data on export shipments for the three main categories of exports—mining, agriculture, and manufactured goods. In each category we have included some specific items.

was the case, for example, of the metallic and machinery products sector, which, as can be seen in Table 5-8 increased its exports in 1975, only to decrease them in 1977 and the subsequent years. Later, however, as it became apparent that the government would stick to the trade reform and as entrepreneurs believed that the high level of the real exchange rate would continue, export-related investment projects started to develop, with those in the paper, agriculture, and forestry sectors being relatively more important. Many of these new investment projects reached more significant proportions after the relaxation of capital controls in mid-1979 allowed firms to finance expansion through the importation of foreign capital.[15]

In some cases — like timber and copper — the increase in exports was partially related to a more intensive utilization of quite massive investments that had been undertaken prior to the military regime. In other cases — mostly manufacturing exports — the new trade regime, and in particular the higher real exchange rate, made it profitable to use existing capacity more intensively and to implement investment projects that improved the quality of production and had a very high marginal return. Ironically perhaps, toward the early 1980s, as the real exchange rate was appreciating and thus reducing exports profitability, a number of relatively important new investment projects in the export sector matured and were incorporated to the production process.[16]

The evolution of international prices also played an important role in determining the behavior of exports during the period. In Table 5-9 we present price indexes for some of the more important Chilean noncopper exports for 1978-82. As may be seen, the surge in the dollar value of exports between 1978 and 1980 was partially a result of changes in exports international prices; likewise, the stagnation of export dollar values after 1980 reported in Table 5-8 was directly related to the decline in commodity export prices that accompanied the world recession.

Copper Exports

Historically the behavior of Chile's external sector — and of the economy as a whole for that matter — has been closely linked to the vagaries of the world copper market. The 1973-83 period was not an exception. (See Table 5-8 for total value of copper exports, and Table

Table 5-9.   Indexes of International Prices of Selected Chilean
Exports: 1978-83 (1980 = 100).

Export	1978	1979	1980	1981	1982	1983
Copper	62.3	90.6	100.0	79.4	67.6	72.7
Iron ore	71.2	86.0	100.0	90.4	96.2	88.0
Fish meal	81.3	78.3	100.0	92.7	70.1	89.7
Logs	48.9	85.4	100.0	80.0	77.0	72.1
Plywood	69.2	95.9	100.0	98.2	71.9	65.2
Newsprint	81.2	88.9	100.0	110.3	113.4	108.7
Pulp	55.1	79.9	100.0	92.3	75.3	64.9

Source: The IMF International Financial Statistics.
Note: These indexes correspond to U.S. $ prices on commodities exported by Chile but do not necessarily represent the exact price paid for Chilean exports. Copper price is in London; Iron ore in Brazil; Fish meal in Hamburg; Logs in the Philippines; Newsprint in New York; Pulp in Sweden; and Plywood in the Philippines.

5-4 for copper prices.) For example, the high price of copper that prevailed during 1974 created a false sense of prosperity, which was not warranted by the massive structural and financial problems that at that time plagued the economy. On the other hand, the sharp decline in the price of copper in 1975 and 1981-82 profoundly affected the economy by reducing the level of real income and fueling recessions — which, in the case of 1981-82 were greatly compounded by other external and internal difficulties, including the increase in world interest rates, the halt of capital inflows into Chile, and, most important, the macroeconomic policy inconsistencies discussed in Chapters 2 and 3.

In spite of the sharp reduction in the relative price of copper the military decided to increase production of the government-owned mines during the period. Between 1970 and 1979, for example, total copper output increased by more than 50 percent — from 692 to 1.061 thousand tons. The Chilean copper policy during the period has generated substantial controversy, since the authorities decided to ignore any monopolistic-type production-pricing strategy and opted instead for increasing output at the fastest possible way in an effort to maximize foreign exchange revenues. In fact, it has been argued by some observers that the decline in copper international prices during most of the period may not have been completely exogenous and in fact partially reflected Chile's decision to increase production at such a rapid pace.[17] However, econometric studies show that the price elasticity of demand for copper faced by Chile is very high and that the country had little, if anything to gain, by acting in a monopolistic fashion. (See, for example, Mardones, Marshall, and Silva (1984)).

Other important developments related to the copper sector during this period include the Mining Law of 1981 — brainchild of Jose Pinera — which established the legal aspects that would govern foreign investment in mining concerns. This law generated a heated controversy, since in order to attract elusive foreign investors, it contemplated a novel and sophisticated procedure, based on the computation of the net present value of output, for compensating foreign firms in case of expropriation. However, the low price of copper and the political instability that took over the country after 1982 have proven to be more powerful than the new legislation, and no major foreign investment has taken place in the copper sector.

Imports

As a result of the 1975 recession imports declined by more than U.S. $1 billion. After that, however, as the economy recovered, imports grew at a frantic pace, generating an increasingly widening trade deficit.[18]

Table 5-10 presents data on the value of imports by different categories for selective years. Possibly the most remarkable aspect of this table is the behavior of consumer goods imports, including automobiles, whose surge was particularly marked toward the latter years. By mid-1981 the imports of capital goods had also increased substantially; in fact in 1981 imports of machinery and equipment had reached a proportion of total imports that surpassed the value of that ratio for 1971.

The surge in imports not only increased competition, forcing domestic producers to lower their prices and improve the quality of their goods, but it literally changed the appearance of the Chilean economy. Suddenly, the country joined the ongoing western-world consumer revolution. Goods that people had much dreamed about became available at reasonable prices. Undoubtedly, consumers were the major beneficiaries of this availability of imported goods at low prices. Toward late 1980 however, it became apparent that imports were growing at an unsustainable rate. During 1981 imports grew even faster, and the overall macroeconomic disequilibrium was reflected in the trade deficit that reached the astonishing level of $2.5 billion U.S..

Table 5–10. Imports: Selected Years (millions U.S. $).

	1971	1975	1977	1979	1981	1983
1. Consumer goods	$ 245.3	$ 87.3	$ 526.5	$ 852.0	$1,830.0	$ 517.4
Automobiles	N.A.	3.5	108.3	117.3	371.8	31.2
2. Machinery and equipment	139.0	217.2	364.7	493.5	796.6	256.7
3. Transport equipment	57.9	160.6	154.5	382.4	617.9	73.5
4. Intermediate goods	720.4	872.1	1,384.0	2,486.5	3,130.4	2,119.4
Oil	109.7	257.0	447.0	888.7	940.8	572.4
5. Other	3.0	—	2.6	3.4	3.6	1.8
Total (1+2+3+4+5)	$1,165.6	$1,338.2	$2,414.3	$4,217.6	$6,378.5	$2,968.8

Source: Banco Central de Chile (1981, 1983, 1984).
Note: These data refer to imports registered. There is a slight discrepancy between imports registered and actual imports.

Why did imports grow so fast? The answer lies, as always, on a combination of income and price effects. Initially, after the large decline in 1975, the increase in imports was mainly a result of the recovery of the level of economic activity. Soon, however, imports also began to respond to the reduction in their relative price generated by the lowering of tariffs. In those early years, however, the high real exchange rate kept things somewhat in check. After 1978 the increase in perceived wealth and real permanent income — a phenomenon thoroughly discussed in Chapter 3 — added to the import surge. However, the use of actual price changes and of permanent income changes, in conjunction with historical estimates of income and price elasticities for Chile's demand for imports are not able to explain more than 60 percent of the increase in the real value of imports during the period. For example, using Khan's (1974) estimates of the long-run price and income elasticities for aggregate imports we can account for an increase in real imports of 26 percent between 1979 and 1981, significantly lower than the increase in almost 40 percent actually experimented by real imports during those two years.[19] This means, then, that in order to fully understand the behavior of imports toward the latter years we should look for less orthodox factors.

The main nontraditional element that explains the incredible surge of imports in 1981 is related to the public's expectations on future relative price changes. As was shown in Chapter 3, starting in late 1980 the expectations of devaluation experienced a quite significant increase. Of course, to the extent that these expectations of devaluation implied expectations of a change in the real exchange rate, it meant that the public expected that the price of importables would increase in the future. As the public became more and more convinced that the external situation — including the real exchange rate and the level of capital inflows — was unsustainable and that the government policies were inconsistent, the confidence in the maintenance of the overall announced external sector policy, including the tariff reform itself, began to erode. Indeed, in late 1981 an increasingly large number of people began to expect a collapse of the external sector that would lead not only to a devaluation but to a hike in import tariffs. These expectations of devaluation and higher import tariffs resulted in massive imports of durables. While in Argentina and Mexico the loss of credibility in government policies resulted in outright capital flight, in Chile it initially generated "capital flight" in the form of imports of television sets, washing machines, and automobiles. With hindsight, we know that these expectations were not far off the mark. In November 1982 import surcharges ranging from 4 to 28 percent were imposed on more than thirty items. Later in June 1983 import tariffs were uniformly raised to 20 percent, and in September 1984 they were temporarily hiked to 35 percent.[20]

OVERVALUATION AND THE EXTERNAL SECTOR

The steady process of real overvaluation of the peso greatly hurt the performance of noncopper exports. In 1981 the dollar value of non-traditional exports dropped by 15 percent, while traditional noncopper exports declined in 16 percent. In fact, for those firms in the Corbo and Sanchez (1985) study the overvaluation of the peso was one of the most severe blows received throughout the first ten years of the experiment.[21]

An interesting question is how firms in different sectors performed during the first part of the real overvaluation phase. Although comparative data on differential financial performance are somewhat limited, an analysis of the behavior of stock market returns can shed some light on the subject.[22] Table 5-11 contains data on indexes on real return and on systematic risk for four stock portfolios for 1978 and 1980: The first portfolio corresponds to ten firms whose main activity is related to the export sector; the second portfolio includes fourteen import competing firms; the third portfolio summarizes data for thirteen firms in the nontradable sector; finally, the fourth portfolio is the market portfolio and contains some firms not included in any of the previous portfolios. The *average return* refers to the ex-post real monthly return and includes dividends, splits, and capital gains. These averages are very high and reflect the already discussed (Chapter 3) bubble-type behavior of the stock market during part of this period. Notice, however, that in spite of the high average, the market portfolio return was highly volatile, with its standard deviation standing at 18.2 percent in 1978 and 10.8 percent in 1980.

Ths risk coefficients (betas) in Table 5-11 are measures of systematic or nondiversifiable risk and tell us the extent to which the returns of each specific portfolio vary in relation to the market portfolio. A beta of 1 indicates a perfect covariation, while a beta greater than 1 means that the particular portfolio's returns vary proportionally more

Table 5-11. Returns and Financial Risk in Exportables, Importables, and Nontradable Sectors: 1978–80.

	1978		1980	
	Average Real Return	Portfolio's Systematic Risk Coefficient (Beta)	Average Real Return	Portfolio's Systematic Risk Coefficient (Beta)
Portfolio of export-oriented firms	5.5%	0.966	2.0%	0.952
Portfolio of import-competing firms	5.7%	0.841	3.3%	0.780
Portfolio of nontradable firms	5.3%	1.196	3.5%	1.081
Market portfolio	5.3%	1.000	3.6%	1.000

Sources: These indexes were computed using raw data obtained from *Bolsa de Comercio de Santiago* (various issues).

Notes: The average return refers to monthly real return. The standard deviation for the market portfolio was 18.2 percent in 1978 and 10.8 percent in 1980. The betas were computed for two different periods, since F-statistics show that they had not been stable through time. The 1978 betas use monthly data for 1977 and 1978; the betas for 1980 used monthly data for 1979 and 1980.

than the market and conversely for a beta smaller than 1. The betas in Table 5-11 indicate that the nontradable portfolio was slightly more risky than the market, whereas the importable and exportable were somewhat less risky. In addition, these data show that the nontradable portfolio experienced some reduction in its degree of risk between 1978 and 1981.

The data in Table 5-11 are interesting and show that between 1978 and 1980 there was a significant change in the relative returns. More important for our purpose, however, these data show that between 1978 and 1980 the average return fell for the market as a whole and for each individual portfolio. Whereas in the earlier year the nontradable sector had the lowest relative return—with the highest risk coefficient—in 1980 the nontradable sector had the highest relative rate of return of the three portfolios, with a relatively lower level of risk. Regarding the trade-oriented portfolios, the data in Table 5-11 indicate that the decline in average return was higher for export-oriented firms.[23] This change in relative returns reported in Table 5–11 — and in particular the increase in nontradables returns relative to both traded sector-oriented portfolios — is consistent with what is expected in an economy where there is a move in relative prices against the traded sector, as was the case in Chile during the period of steady real appreciation.

In the preceding chapters we have already discussed the different ways in which most firms tried to survive the critical period of the 1981–82 recession. Of course export-oriented firms were not an exception; when greatly affected by the real appreciation, the rising real wages, and exorbitantly high real interest rates, they resorted to heavy borrowing from the financial sector in order to stay afloat. The consequences of these strategies are well known by now.

SUMMARY

The tariff reform was in many ways a success. It resulted in very important improvements of efficiency and productivity in the manufacturing sector, and, until 1979, it also had a very positive effect on nontraditional exports, which diversified and grew very fast. Also, thanks to the reform a number of goods, until then out of reach to most Chileans, became accessible to blue-collar workers and the lower-middle classes. For the first time the poorer layers of the population could afford consumer durables, such as television sets, washing machines, and even automobiles. These important positive aspects of the trade reform have been somewhat overshadowed by the disequilibrium of the external sector that began to mount in late 1979 as a result of the already discussed policy mistakes and inconsistencies.

NOTES

1. Before the Pinochet government there were a number of timid attempts to liberalize international trade. The most noteworthy of those attempts took place in 1961 and 1969. See de la Cuadra and Hachette (1986) and Ffrench-Davis (1973).
2. The reallocation of resources, efficiency, and income distribution effects follow from standard economic theory. The faster growth proposition is based on the export-led growth approach as exposed in Krueger (1978).

132   MONETARISM AND LIBERALIZATION

Of course, trade liberalization has long been advocated throughout the world by economists of very different persuasion. See, for example, Little, Scitovsky, and Scott (1970), Bhagwati and Srinivasan (1979), Díaz-Alejandro (1970), and Krueger (1978, 1983).

3. On the effects of Chile's commercial policy see, for example, the study by Corbo and Meller (1981).

4. The effective rate of protection is a measure of the relative degree of inefficiency of domestic production relative to international production. A positive value means that domestic value added for that particular activity exceeds value added at international prices. The effective tariff for good i (τ_i) is computed in the form $\tau_i = (t_i - \Sigma a_{ij} t_j)/(1 - \Sigma a_{ij})$, where t_i is the nominal tariff, a_{ij} is the input/output coefficient between input j and good i, and t_j is the nominal tariff on input j. Notice that if the good and *all* inputs have the same nominal tariff, then the effective and nominal rates of protection are the same ($\tau_i = t_i$). It should be noted that from a general equilibrium perspective the usefulness of the concept of effective rates of protection is quite limited. See Bhagwati and Srinivasan (1980).

5. On the degree of effective protection in Chile's agriculture sector prior to the reform, see, for example, Varas (1975).

6. Although in a general equilibrium setting it is not necessarily the case that a tariff removal results in a real depreciation, this is the case in most plausible conditions such as Chile. On this see S. Edwards (1987).

7. The initial maxi-devaluation responded, in part, to the need to avoid an almost imminent balance of payments crisis. As the tariff process proceeded the crawling peg tried to (approximately) maintain the high level of the real exchange rate.

8. In fact, the exchange rate played a crucial role in the government's explanation of the negative effects of protectionism during the previous decades. According to de Castro, for example (Mendez 1979: 201),

> The relatively forced industrialization of the country was obtained through various mechanisms. One of these was the foreign exchange rate policy. From 1939 on, the exchange rate was maintained artificially low. . . . The exporting sector lost all possibility to export because. . . [with a low] exchange rate. . .they could not manage to cover their local production costs.

9. As was pointed out in Chapter 2, the real effective depreciation between mid-1977 and mid-1979 was to some extent the result of Chile's decision to conduct exchange rate policy using the U.S. dollar as the reference currency and of the real devaluation of the dollar in the financial market. As the dollar depreciated so did (to some extent) the peso. Of course, as we discussd in Chapter 3, in mid-1980, when the dollar began its appreciation period the peso also appreciated with respect to a broad basket of currencies.

10. Using a twelve-firm sample Corbo and Sanchez (1985) found that the reduction of tariffs was a major shock for import-competing firms. For export-oriented firms, however, it was initially a boon, since the exchange rate was higher and tariffs on imported inputs had gone down. See also Frankel, Froot, and Mizala-Salces (1986).

11. See Meller, Livacich, and Arrau (1984). In that article these authors question the methodology used to compute Chile's real GDP.

12. See S. Edwards (1982) and Cortes and Sjaastad (1981) for a discussion on the employment effects of the trade reform.

13. The reason for this is that, in an economy where imports are capital intensive as in Chile, to the extent that capital is sector specific in the short run, a tariff reduction will require a short-run reduction in the real wage of low skill labor in order to maintain the level of employment. If this reduction is precluded by a minimum wage, unemployment will result (see S. Edwards 1982).

14. Given changes in relative prices of different exports goods, even changes in aggregate export at constant prices may be misleading. Sjaastad (1982), however, calculated that the exports *quantum* increased by almost 50 percent between 1974 and 1980.

15. Notice, however, that as noted in Chapter 1 the aggregate investment ratio was depressed throughout most of the experiment. Contrary to the authorities expectations large foreign projects in the exports (or other) sectors never materialized.

16. See Arriagada (1986) and Corbo and Sanchez (1985) for interesting accounts on how firms adjusted and entered the exports business.

17. See, for example, "Will General Pinochet Sink the Copper Market?" (1984).

18. This trade deficit was partially financed by the rapid inflow of capital.

19. De Gregorio (1984) has estimated that imports of consumer durables have a very high income elasticity, ranging from 2.5 to 4.7.

20. See S. Edwards and van Wijnbergen (1986a) for a theoretical model where expected changes in tariffs affect the intertemporal consumption decisions. Arellano and Ramos (1986) have argued that actual financial capital flight started in early 1982.

21. See Galvez and Tyebout (1985) for a discussion on the effects of the real appreciation and other shocks on individual firms' performance.

22. A word of caution is needed here. Since, as discussed in Chapter 3, the volume of transactions in the stock market was rather limited during the period, the results that follow should be looked at with a slight degree of skepticism. However, S. Edwards (1981) found that in spite of the relatively small size of transactions the Chilean stock market was efficient.

23. This is somewhat puzzling, since during this period the import-competing firms were subject both to the first phase of the real apprecia-

tion and to the last stage in the import reduction process. Frankel, Froot and Mizala-Salces (1986) however, report that according to questionnaire answers, import-competing firms did not see their situation deeply hurt by the last round of the trade reforms.

6 UNEMPLOYMENT AND INCOME DISTRIBUTION

From the early years of the military rule unemployment became a serious and persistent problem.[1] Already in mid-1974 the rate of unemployment began to experience a steep increase, and in September of that year it reached 9.4 percent in the Greater Santiago area, signifiicantly higher than the 5.9 percent average of the 1960s. In his 1974 report Minister Cauas attributed this rise in unemployment to two factors (Mendez 1979: 99):

> The difficult employment situation is basically the result of two phenomena. On the one hand, during the previous regime many workers were hired in the Public Sector.... [T]he productivity of these workers was extremely low and, therefore, represented disguised unemployment, which is now openly apparent.... On the other hand, the lack of investment during the last three years prevented the creation of new sources of work.

At this time the government basically saw the increase in unemployment as a temporary problem and consequently decided to tackle it with temporary measures. In fact, in 1974 the authorities expected a reduction in unemployment for the following year. According to Cauas, "[T]he recovery of the levels of investment [in 1975]...will permit a reduction in unemployment" (Mendez 1979: 107). Nothing of the sort happened, and in December of 1975, in the midst of the recession, unemployment climbed to almost 20 percent in the greater Santiago area. Table 6-1 presents some general data related to unemployment and wages for 1970–82.

In late 1975 the government still considered unemployment a temporary problem that was only partially related to its policies. In his 1975 report Minister Cauas stated (Mendez 1979: 173–34):

> It is true that unemployment is high.... This is, however, by no means the result of the [1975 stabilization]...program. The restriction is a consequence of the depletion of fiscal resources, of the artificial creation of jobs, of the drop of the price of copper, of the rise in the price of petroleum...and the low level of investment.

As time passed and it became apparent that unemployment was not going to disappear overnight, the government recognized that the structural changes implemented by the liberalization reforms were to some extent related to the unemployment problem. In 1976 Cauas pointed out that "in the medium run there will be relatively high rates of unemployment" and that only in the "long run, and insofar as the process of resource allocation is consolidated and high rates of investment in highly productive sectors are achieved, will the traditional problem of unemployment be permanently solved" (Mendez 1979: 228).

The immediate and direct reduction of unemployment was not as high a priority to the government as the elimination of inflation and the freeing of key markets. According to the official view, unemployment reduction would follow once the economy adjusted to the new path of higher and sustained rates of growth consistent with a more efficient use of resources. Undoubtedly, the postponement of a solution to unemployment was possible only due to the dictatorial nature of the government, where traditional channels for manifesting dissatisfaction with the economic conditions had been severed. There were, however, some efforts to alleviate poverty and provide temporary support to the unemployed, like the Minimum Employment Program, discussed in greater detail below.

This chapter analyzes the behavior of employment, unemployment, wages, and income distribution during the military rule. Not surprisingly, the high and persistent rates of unemployment cannot be attributed to a sole cause. Our analysis indicates that unemployment was basically the result of four interrelated factors: First, the slow average rate of growth of economic activity between 1974 and 1981

Table 6-1. Unemployment and Wages in Chile: 1970–83.

Year	(1) Total Labor Force (Thousands)	(2) Total Unemployment (Thousands)	(3) Open Unemployment Rate (%)	(4) Minimum Employment Program (Thousands)	(5) Minimum Employment Program as % of Labor Force	(6) Index of Real Wages (1970 = 100)
1970	2,923.2	167.1	5.7%			100
1971	2,968.8	112.8	3.8			125.4
1972	3,000.8	93.0	3.1			124.0
1973	3,037.0	145.8	4.8			86.0
1974	3,066.8	282.1	9.2			90.2
1975	3,152.9	425.6	13.5	41.7	1.3%	88.7
1976	3,216.4	511.4	15.9	168.8	5.2	86.3
1977	3,259.7	462.9	14.2	187.1	5.7	96.6
1978	3,370.1	478.6	14.2	148.0	4.4	97.5
1979	3,480.7	480.3	13.8	128.4	3.7	98.7
1980	3,539.8	417.7	11.9	187.9	5.3	108.3
1981	3,669.3	400.0	10.9	171.2	4.7	115.7
1982	3,729.7	760.9	20.4	190.2	5.1	112.2
1983	3,797.5	706.3	18.6	391.6	10.3	N.A.

Sources: The labor force and unemployment figures (Columns 1, 2, and 3 refer to June of each year and were estimated by Castaneda (1983). Column 4 is based on Banco Central (1983: 212–13). Column 5 corresponds to column 4 divided by column 1. Column 6 was constructed using National Accounts data. (See A. Edwards 1984: 85 for further details.)

Notes: The Minimum Employment Program was a temporary palliative system created by the government in 1975 to alleviate the unemployment problem.

resulted in a sluggish rate of increase of employment creation; second, the reduction in government employment had a direct negative impact on employment growth; third, during this period there was an important increase in the labor force or total supply of labor; and fourth — and most important for explaining the *persistence* of unemployment — the existence of a number of rigidities precluded a smoother adjustment of the labor market to a number of shocks, including the structural reforms. In fact, in the absence of these rigidities the first three factors — slowdown in rate of jobs creation, reduction in government jobs, and faster growth in the labor force — could not explain the persistence in the rate of unemployment; in a perfectly flexible textbook-type labor market, higher supply and lower demand of labor would reduce wages but not generate unemployment.

The chapter examines the following topics: (1) the traditional role that government had in Chile's labor relations and the segmented structure of the Chilean labor market; (2) the supply of labor and the rate of participation of the labor force; (3) the behavior of employment, particularly the relation between economic activity and aggregate employment creation and the decline of the public sector as a source of jobs creation; (4) wages and indexation, including the Labor Law of 1979 and the Social Security Law of 1980; (5) an analytical interpretation for the persistence of unemployment based on a model of segmented labor markets and emphasizes the role of rigidities; and (6) the evolution of income distribution during the first ten years of the military rule. The chapter concludes with a summary.

GOVERNMENT INTERVENTION AND LABOR MARKET STRUCTURE

Government Intervention

The Chilean labor market has been characterized by tradition of government intervention in labor relations. Even during the military rule, and in spite of the major institutional market-oriented reforms, government involvement in the labor market was to some extent maintained.

Historically, the influence of the government has been present at different levels. First, public sector wages have had an important effect on all wages and salaries across the economy. Second, through labor legislation, the government has imposed generalized minimum wages, across-the-board wage adjustments and mandatory fringe benefits and bonuses that have to be paid by the private sector. Third, high social security taxes have increased the relative cost of labor in the economy. And fourth, the government also intervened in the labor market directly through its hiring policies and indirectly through the sectoral biases induced by the economic policies. Throughout the years, for example, the import substitution development strategy induced massive transfers of workers to the cities, some of which were absorbed by the new industries or by the public sector; the less fortunate, however, entered the ranks of the urban unemployed.

The government also played an important role in settling labor disputes. Until 1973 unions were allowed to organize across firms in a given industry and to negotiate wages at the industry level, thus exercising considerable monopolistic power. Consequently, in order to protect the "public interest" government intervention usually was called for in cases of collective bargaining settlements.

As a result of this system of government intervention some serious distortions emerged in the late 1960s and early 1970s. For example, some industries, which were highly protected from competition through import tariffs, export drawbacks, subsidies or tax exemptions, were able to accede to unions demands by increasing wages considerably above productivity gains. Also, unions were able to keep employment below competitive levels, inducing a bias toward the use of capital-intensive techniques.[2] In short, the unionized sector worked under noncompetitive conditions, most of them supported by the existing labor legislation. Government intervention in the labor market reached unprecedented proportions during the *Unidad Popular* period. Between 1970 and 1972, public sector employment grew at an average rate of 11.4 percent per year.[3] This, in fact, is one of the reasons that during the *Unidad Popular* government, in spite of the massive distortions prevailing in the labor market, the rate of unemployment dropped significantly.[4]

After the military coup, from 1974 to mid-1979, union power was greatly reduced, with strikes prohibited and with all activities related to unionism greatly curtailed. Some steps toward reforming the labor market were taken, including the reduction of social security taxes and the removal of the *ley de inamovilidad* that had made termination of labor contracts very expensive for employers. However, the backward wage indexation mechanism, applied since 1974, and a minimum wage that increased in real terms between 1974 and 1978, became increasingly more distortive.[5]

In 1975, as a way to provide a temporary solution to the unemployment problem, the government created the so-called minimum employment program (PEM), where unemployed performed, for a reduced number of hours a week and for a very low salary, some menial public works, like raking leaves in public parks. At first the government imposed severe restrictions on entry into the program. Slowly through time most of these restrictions were lifted, allowing a larger number of unemployed to take part in it.[6] In Table 6-1 we present data on the number of people enrolled in this program. As may be seen, in spite of the recovery and "boom" between 1977 and 1981 and of the reduction through time in the real PEM compensation relative to real wages in the rest of the economy, the proportion of the labor force covered by the program remained virtually constant. This was because, as noted, with time more and more people became eligible. Additional measures to deal with unemployment included a total reform of the unemployment insurance program that increased protection to manual workers against losses of income due to unemployment; a wage subsidy program adopted in 1975 that was a stimulus to unskilled unemployment; and a special training program implemented in early 1977 under which private employers were eligible for income tax credits for the cost of providing special training to their workers.

In 1979 a labor law was enacted that gave unions a greatly reduced role in the process of wage determination. This law — the brainchild of Labor Minister Jose Pinera — established a complex bargaining mechanism, which departed significantly from the traditional legislation; union affiliation within a firm became voluntary, and all negotiations were conducted at the firm level with multifirm bargaining being eliminated. Possibly, however, the most significant innovation, in terms of its immediate impact, was the introduction of a backward indexation clause into collective bargaining.[7] (Chapter 4 discusses some of the more interesting aspects of this law.)

Labor Market Structure and Segmentation

Historically the pervasive government intervention in the labor market plus the existence of powerful unions resulted in the emergence of a segmented structure of the Chilean labor market, which maintained its relative importance during the military rule. Traditionally, as in many developing countries, it has been possible to distinguish at least two segments in Chile's labor market. The first is the *protected* sector, where due to a number of institutional reasons, including the existence of labor unions and large multinational firms, wages are set exogenously above their market clearing level. The second sector is the *unprotected* or *free* segment, where wages are set competitively.[8] As is shown below, the existence of empirical evidence supports the hypothesis of labor market segmentation in Chile even for the years of the military rule. In fact, our explanation of Chile's unemployment "puzzle" provided below relies quite heavily on the existence of such a segmented structure. In applying this model to Chile it is useful to think that the segmented structure of differentiated wages was first (prior to 1973) imposed by unions and large firms and was later perpetuated by the mechanism of across-the-board backward indexation.

POPULATION AND LABOR FORCE PARTICIPATION

Table 6–2 presents some data related to the behavior of the supply of labor during the period. The table includes information on population, the rate of participation, and the labor force. As can be seen, during 1973–83 the labor force grew at 3 percent per annum, a pace significantly faster than that of the 1960s (1.6 percent per year). This faster growth in the labor force was the result both of demographic factors — a fairly high rate of growth of the population of age 12 years and older — and of a failure of the rate of participation to continue to decline at the pace of the 1960s (see column *C*).

This higher rate of growth of the labor force, combined with a lower rate of growth in the level of economic activity and therefore in aggregate labor demand, contributed to the creation of a situation of excess labor supply. For example, the difference in the average rate of growth of the labor force between 1960–70 and 1973–83 explains, on its own, an annual average increase in the unemployment rate of one half of a point, while the difference in the rate of growth in employment between the two decades can explain an annual average increase in the unemployment rate of almost 1 percent of a point.[9]

Table 6–2. Population, Rate of Participation, and Labor Force: 1970–83.

Year	(A) Population (Thousands)	(B) Population 12 Yrs. and More (Thousands)	(C) Rate of Partici- pation (%)	(D) Labor Force (Thousands)	(D) Labor Force Rate of Growth (%)
1970	9,368	6,456	45.4%	2,932	—
1971	9,534	6,623	44.8	2,968	1.2%
1972	9,697	6,799	44.1	3,001	1.1
1973	9,861	6,980	43.5	3,037	1.2
1974	10,026	7,161	42.8	3,067	1.0
1975	10,196	7,339	43.0	3,153	2.8
1976	10,372	7,515	42.8	3,216	2.0
1977	10,551	7,692	42.4	3,260	1.4
1978	10,733	7,867	42.8	3,370	3.4
1979	10,918	8,057	43.2	3,481	3.3
1980	10,104	8,207	43.1	3,540	1.7
1981	11,294	8,370	43.8	3,669	3.6
1982	11,487	8,527	43.7	3,730	1.7
1983	11,682	8,682	43.7	3,798	1.8
1960–70	N.A.	N.A.	N.A.	N.A.	1.6

Source: Instituto Nacional de Estadisticas as published in Banco Central de Chile, *Boletín Mensual*; Castaneda (1983).

THE BEHAVIOR OF EMPLOYMENT

During the first ten years of the military rule employment grew on average at a rate significantly lower than the average of the 1960s. For 1973–83 the average rate of growth of employment was only 0.7 percent per year, less than half of the 1960–70 average of 1.8 percent. However, the evolution of employment during the different phases of the military regime was not homogeneous, nor was the distribution of employment changes across sectors.

Economic Growth and Employment

In order to fully understand the evolution of employment it is useful to first investigate its interaction with the level of economic activity.

Table 6–3.   Chile: Labor Market Indicators (average rates of growth for each period).

(1)	(2)	(3)	(4)	(5)
				Elasticity
Period	Labor Force	Employment	GDP	(3)/(4)
1960–70	1.6	1.8	4.2	.43
1970–73	1.2	1.5	0.5	3.00
1973–76	1.9	−2.2	−3.1	.71
1976–81	2.7	3.9	7.9	.49
1981–83	1.7	−2.8	−7.6	.36
1973–83	2.3	0.7	1.3	.54

Source: Columns 2 and 3 calculated from Castaneda (1983); column 4 from Banco Central de Chile (1984).

An interesting pattern is obtained from the estimates of the ex-post output elasticities of employment. These elasticities reflect the actual change in employment associated to a 1 percent increase in aggregate output over a given time period. Table 6–3 presents data on these elasticities and on the average annual rates of growth of the labor force, employment, and aggregate output. As can be seen the ex-post elasticities for the 1960s and for 1973–83 are somewhat similar (0.43 and 0.54), suggesting that the bulk of the explanation for the reduction in the pace of increase in labor demand lays, in fact, on the slowdown of the level of economic activity for the decade.

But as we discussed earlier, the 1970–83 period was marked by big contrasts. From 1970 to 1973 the economy experienced a slow average rate of growth, while employment kept growing at almost the same pace of the preceding decade (see Table 6–3). The estimated employment-output elasticity for this period is 3.0, reflecting an extraordinary creation of jobs within the public sector and in the economy as a whole. Between 1973 and 1976, on the other hand, the economy experienced a severe contraction and so did employment. From 1976 to 1981 the level of economic activity recovered at a fast pace, and finally between 1981 and 1983 there was another even more severe recession.

It is interesting to note the difference in the relation between output decline and employment reduction between these two recessions. A 1 percent decline in output between 1973 and 1976 was associated with a 0.71 percent decline in employment, while the same change in output between 1981 and 1983 was associated with only a 0.36 percent decline in employment. This difference reflects the presence of "redundant" employment by 1973, which was the result of the hiring practices used throughout the 1970–73 period. Starting in 1974, as a consequence of the different reforms implemented by the military, competition forced employers to reduce costs and to change their hiring practices. During the 1981–83 recession employment reduction was mainly a response to the reduction in the level of production without the "redundant" labor force element playing any role.

The relatively faster rate of growth of labor supply coupled with the slowdown of the rate of increase in labor demand created a situation of excess supply for labor. A crucial question at this point, however, is why real wages did not decline sufficiently toward their new lower long-run equilibrium and reduce (or even eliminate) the excess supply of labor. In fact, Table 6–1 indicates that average wages did experience an important reduction after 1973. This, however, was in part reflecting a correction of the artificial increases in real wages in 1970–72. As is pointed out below, wages did not fall "sufficiently" because of the across-the-board indexation mechanism.

Sectoral Employment

Table 6–4 contains data on changes in sectoral employment for 1960 through 1982. As can be seen, between 1960 and 1970 there were about 45,000 jobs created per year on average. About half of those jobs were created in services and one-fourth in the industrial sector. The agricultural sector, on the other hand, showed a reduction of about 9,000 jobs per year (or 1.3 percent per annum). As a result of this trend, the economy was concentrating employment in the nontradables sector, with construction growing at the fastest rate (7.6 percent per year) and transportation growing rather slowly relative to the other nontradables (1.7 percent per year). Within the tradables sector employment was declining in agriculture and growing in the manufacturing sector; however, the overall tradables sector share in employment was falling.

During the *Unidad Popular* government (1970–73) there were again about 45,000 new jobs per year, but this time the growth in employment in services accelerated to 5.8 percent per year from 3.2 percent per year between 1960 and 1970. This higher employment in services corresponded, almost exclusively, to higher government employment. Moreover, the number of jobs created in services was larger than the abso-

Table 6-4. Employment by Sectors: 1960–82 Annual Average Rate of Growth and Number of Jobs Created per Period (thousands).[a]

	1960–70	1970–73	1973–76	1976–81	1981–82
Agriculture	−1.3%	−7.6%	1.3%	0.5%	−11.7%
	(−87.5)	(−127.7)	(19.5)	(11.6)	(−59.6)
Fishing	3.8%	3.8%	7.1%	2.5%	N.A.
	(5.5)	(2.1)	(−17.5)	(3.2)	(N.A.)
Mining	−0.5%	5.8%	−1.5%	−2.4%	−1.3%
	(−4.3)	(16.4)	(−4.6)	(−11.5)	(−9.7)
Manufacturing	2.9%	3.5%	−2.8%	2.6%	−32.2%
	(122.1)	(52.8)	(−45.5)	(67.4)	(−166.1)
Utilities	3.8%	9.9%	−1.8%	5.8%	−15.6%
	(11.6)	(7.3)	(−1.6)	(9.1)	(−4.1)
Construction	7.6%	−4.8%	−14.8%	7.7%	−52.9%
	(59.5)	(−26.1)	(−62.4)	(45.4)	(−90.0)
Commerce	4.2%	3.0%	−1.5%	7.7%	−23.1%
	(53.2)	(36.6)	(−16.7)	(158.6)	(−143.7)
Transportation and Communications	1.7%	3.5%	−2.9%	4.7%	−20.6%
	(61.6)	(17.1)	(−17.0)	(47.4)	(−45.1)
Financial services	3.5%	2.1%	3.1%	2.6%	−13.3%
	(15.3)	(3.4)	(5.4)	(8.3)	(−15.6)
Other services	3.2%	5.8%	0.4%	2.5%	19.2%
	(212.1)	(143.2)	(10.5)	(122.1)	(168.7)
Total	1.8%	1.5%	−1.3%	3.1%	−11.6%
	(449.1)	(125.1)	(−107.9)	(461.6)	(−365.2)

Source: Banco Central de Chile (1983).
[a] Figures for rates of growth correspond to annual averages.

lute change in employment for the economy. This occurred because the reduction in the number of jobs in the agricultural sector more than offset the employment creation in the other sectors. Throughout this period employment in agriculture declined at 7.6 percent per year. This affected not only the sectoral allocation of labor but also the geographical allocation of the labor force.

During 1973–76, and in part due to the shock stabilization program, employment experienced a major dip. Central government employment was reduced by approximately 100,000 jobs. Moreover, the government's commitment to reduce the public sector's size continued steadily through the military regime, and in 1982 there were only 130,000 government employees compared to 196,000 in 1960 and 308,000 in 1973.

During the late 1970s there was an important change in the pattern of employment growth. Employment in agriculture stopped declining, mainly as a result of the improvement in the relative prices of agricultural products, until at least mid-1979. Migration flows out of the agricultural sector, which had been around 11,000 per year between 1965 and 1970, were reduced by half to 5,500 per year between 1975 and 1981.[10] In the tradables sector employment grew relatively fast, in spite of the slowdown of employment growth in manufacturing. While in the 1960s, 7.7 percent of the new jobs were created in the tradables sector, between 1976 and 1981 that percentage was 12.8. The relatively slow rate of growth of employment in manufacturing was partially the result of the international trade reform. As was discussed in Chapter 5 most firms adjusted to the increased degree of foreign competition generated by the opening up of the economy by reducing their wage bills and by greatly increasing the level of productivity. Also, about half of the jobs created during this period were concentrated in "commerce" and the "transportation and communications" sector. The construction sector, on the other hand, showed a significant recovery toward the end of this period, but in terms of employment, the rate of growth was just comparable to the historical rates of the 1960s, and the number of jobs created between 1976 and 1981 did not offset the employment reduction of the 1970–73 period. However, and as was documented in Chapter 5, productivity in construction, as in most other sectors, increased dramatically.

WAGES AND INDEXATION

Aggregate real wages declined significantly during the initial years of the military rule. From 1976 onward average real wages increased steadily until in 1981 they stood 16 percent above their 1970 level (see Table 6–1). In this section we analyze the behavior of wages, placing particular emphasis on the roles of indexation and legally established minimum wages.

Wage Indexation

Starting in October of 1974, the military government mandated periodic across-the-board nominal wage increases of magnitudes somewhat related to past inflation, which represented the minimum increase in wages that employers had to pay. Initially, this wage indexation mechanism was quite flexible because the magnitudes of the required nominal wage adjustments were not exactly equal to the level of past inflation. In fact, as shown in Table 6-5, in many instances the mandated wage adjustment differed markedly from the accumulated past inflation. In the later years, however, the indexation rule came very close to a 100 percent indexation rule as the legally required increases in wages were almost exactly equal to past inflation. This downward rigidity in real wages was in some sense institutionalized with the implementation of the Labor Law of 1979.[11]

In October 1974 it was established that for the rest of 1974 and for 1975 there would be quarterly adjustment of nominal wages by (at least) the full amount of the change in the CPI during the second, third, and fourth months prior to the adjustment. By late 1975 and as part of the renewed efforts to reduce inflation, a new wage adjustment formula was enacted. Beginning with September 1975 the nominal wage increase was based in the sum of the inflation rates of the three months ending in the month of adjustment. Since at the time that the wage rate adjustment was decreed the last month's inflation was not known, it was estimated at one-half the preceding month's rate, with any shortfall being made up at the time of the next quarterly adjustment. The new formula shortened the lag of wage adjustments, offering greater protection against subsequent price increases, but its immediate effect was a substantial reduction of the real increment being mandated.

Wage policy in 1976 remained essentially unchanged, but as a consequence of the deceleration of the rate of inflation and of the indexation mechanism, real wage and salaries started to increase. In view of the declining inflation rate, the government decided to lengthen gradually the intervals between wage adjustments. Between March of 1978 and late 1979 wages were adjusted only three times each year — in March, July, and December. During 1980 there were only two official wage increases — in April and October. In August of 1981, when annualized domestic inflation had reached one-digit rates, a nominal wage adjustment of 14 percent was mandated. However, this wage increase, as well as those decreed in 1980, excluded those workers subject to collective bargaining, since their wages' 100 percent backward indexation was explicitly specified in the new law governing unions behavior.

In principle the 100 percent indexation formula applied by the government could result in increasing or declining real wages, depending

Table 6–5.   Wage Indexation: 1974–80 (percentages).

(1) Period	(2) Accumulated Inflation[a]	(3) End of Period Mandated Nominal Wage Increase
10/1/73–1/1/74	107.7%	50.0%[b,d]
1/1/74–5/1/74	87.1	61.1[b]
5/1/75–7/1/74	31.3	34.5
7/1/75–10/1/74	39.5	24.1
10/1/75–12/1/74	30.4	35.2
12/1/75–3/1/75	41.4	33.1
3/1/75–7/1/75	103.2	71.0
7/1/75–9/1/75	19.0	24.0
9/1/75–12/1/75	28.1	28.0
12/1/75–3/1/76	30.2	32.0
3/1/76–7/1/76	56.8	39.0
7/1/76–9/1/76	14.8	26.0
9/1/76–12/1/76	19.2	18.0
12/1/76–3/1/77	17.8	19.0
3/1/77–7/1/77	19.2	18.0
7/1/77–12/1/77	18.7	18.0
12/1/77–3/1/78	7.5	8.0
3/1/78–7/1/78	10.0	10.0
7/1/78–12/1/78	11.9	12.0
12/1/78–3/1/79	5.5	6.0
3/1/79–7/1/79	10.8	11.0
7/1/79 12/1/79	18.0	18.0
12/1/79–4/1/80	9.4	8.0
4/1/80–10/1/80	13.9	14.0[c]
10/1/80–8/1/81	14.3	14.0[c]
8/1/81–7/1/83	37.1	5.0[c,e]
7/1/83–1/1/84	11.8	15.0[c]

Source: Banco Central de Chile (1984) and A. Edwards (1985).

[a] Corresponds to the official CPI.

[b] Corresponds to increase in minimum wage.

[c] Not binding for workers subject to collective bargaining.

[d] Between October 1973 and January 1974 two bonuses were paid. Their nominal value was equal to the April 1973 taxable salary.

[e] The 23.4 percent loss in real income was partially offset by four bonuses of 30 percent, 15 percent, 15 percent, and 15 percent of current wages paid in September, October, November, and December 1983.

Figure 6–1.   Wage Indexation and Real Wages: The Sawtooth Effect.

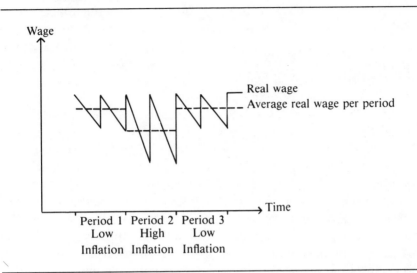

on the dynamics of the inflation rate. Under declining (increasing) inflation a 100 percent indexation formula results in increasing (declining) average real wages. This has been called the sawtooth effect and is described in Figure 6–1, where it is assumed that there are three inflationary periods with nominal wages constant at 100 and two wage readjustments per period. These wage readjustments reestablish the real wage to its initial level, but the average real wage for the period depends on the real wage deterioration due to inflation throughout the period.

Table 6–5 presents some data related to the indexation mechanism process between 1973 and 1983. In column 1 are given the dates that bracketed each official wage adjustment. Column 2 gives the official accumulated rate of inflation between these two dates. Column 3 contains data on the nominal wage adjustment decreed at the end of each period in column 1. This wage adjustment was effective for the next period. As can be seen from this table, until mid-1976 there were important divergences between accumulated past inflation and the mandated wage adjustment. For example, in July of 1975 a nominal wage adjustment of (at least) 71 percent was decreed. However inflation accumulated since the last adjustment had been more than 103 percent. In September 1976, on the other hand, a 26 percent adjustment was decreed, while the accumulated rate of inflation was only 14 percent. As can be seen, starting in December 1976 and until 1981 there is a very close link between mandated wage adjustments and accumulated past inflation. Naturally, since inflation was decreasing, this backward indexation mechanism exercised considerable upward pressure on real wages. For example, due to the indexation effect only, a worker's end of period real wage would have increased by 30.9 percent between June 1976 and August 1981.

The 1979 labor law established the mechanisms that would govern union behavior and collective bargaining. Among other things this law established a floor in real terms for union workers and expressly dictated that the wages would be subject to a 100 percent backward indexation mechanism. There were some important, indeed crucial, differences between the indexation mechanism applied until 1979 and the Pinera labor law. As noted, the former mechanism was flexible and was based on periodic decrees that were valid for short periods of time. This flexibility allowed the government to actually change the indexation rule several times, as the economic conditions changed. The Labor Law of 1979, on the contrary, was very rigid. Its Article 26 established that independently of the economic conditions, unionized workers nominal wages should be adjust by at least past inflation. Article 26 established: "The employer's response [to the union requests] could not contain a proposal for remunerations...lower, *in currency of the same purchasing power,* as those established in the previous work contract" [emphasis added]. This article then proceeded to establish that in order to compute the salary of the same purchasing power, past inflation as computed by the National Institute of Statistics should be used. Most other provisions of the law—including those on salaries for firms where unions could not strike—established that the mechanism of Article 26 was applicable to all workers.[12]

Minimum Wages

In January 1974 the existing minimum wages for blue- and white-collar workers were unified into a single rate, whose level was increased 50 percent above the minimum pay established in the previous quarter. From that period until 1978 the minimum wage was periodically adjusted, increasing in real terms. During 1974–79 the minimum wage was relatively higher than during the previous years, representing, on average, 54 percent of the wage rate for blue-collar workers in manufacturing. In March 1978 the minimum wage was incorporated into the public sector wage scale, and since then it followed the same path as general wage adjustments.

Although there is little doubt that the minimum wage added to the rigidities existing in the labor market, we will not distinguish here its effects from the effects of the overall indexation mechanism on the generation and persistence of unemployment. As discussed in Chapter 5, one of the ways in which the minimum wage played a role was by making the adjustment following the trade reform more difficult. A study by S. Edwards (1980b) calculates that the elimination of the minimum wage would have resulted in an increase in aggregate employment over the longer run of approximately 80,000 jobs.

Taxes on Labor

In 1980 the social security system was reformed. As noted in Chapter 4 this meant moving from a traditional — and basically bankrupt — pay-as-you-go system to a capitalization system, where workers had their own individual retirement accounts that were administered by privately owned companies — many of them in fact owned by *grupos*. Traditionally social security taxes had been very high, introducing important distortions in the labor market. In 1974, for example, total taxes on blue-collar workers, as a proportion of net wages, amounted to 56.9 percent.[13]

An important goal of the government, and a measure directed toward reducing unemployment, was to reduce these taxes on labor. This was done slowly through time. In 1977 the social security tax had been reduced to the still extraordinary figure of 48.3 percent, and by 1979 it was 36.3 percent. The 1980 social security reform further reduced the tax on labor. Under the new individual capitalization system, in 1981 the average tax had been reduced to 24.4 percent, and in 1983 it was 20.8 percent on average.

THE UNEMPLOYMENT "PUZZLE": A SUGGESTED INTERPRETATION

The preceding sections described the behavior of employment, unemployment, and wages during the first ten years of the military rule.

This section argues that the persistent and high rates of unemployment can be explained once it is recognized that Chile's labor market is characterized by segmentation, which greatly reduced flexibility and inhibited the economy to adjust efficiently to various shocks. Furthermore, it is shown that this segmented markets representation is able to trace quite closely the evolution of employment, unemployment, and wages.

Segmented Labor Markets

A number of studies on labor markets in developing countries have taken the segmented labor market demand structure as a working hypothesis. Harris and Todaro (1970) and Harberger (1971) explain the persistence of unemployment by wage differentials institutionally imposed in a protected segment of the market.[14] Employed workers in the protected segment acquire rents. Therefore protected sector jobs are preferred to other jobs in the economy, and this generates an excess supply of labor to the protected segment. Under general assumptions, some labor force participants will stay unemployed rather than taking a nonprotected segment job.

In the Chilean case there is little doubt that until 1974 unions were the main force behind labor segmentation. Those firms that had strong unions traditionally paid wages above the market wage. Although the unions' power was greatly reduced after the military took over, the "unionized" sector continued to pay real wages that exceeded the market level. Of course, this is because the across-the-board indexation mechanism introduced important rigidities in the relative wage structures. In addition, at that time the newly emerging *grupos* became another important element behind segmentation. In fact during the period *grupos* acted in a way similar to that suggested by Harberger (1971: 162):

> [P]rotected sector wages...can be held above the market clearing level by minimum wage laws, by collective bargaining agreements, or (as is often the case with large...concerns operating in less-developed countries) *by the policy of the hiring company itself* [emphasis added].

In a 1980 survey that covered twelve large *grupo*-related firms, S. Edwards (1980b) found that these corporations indeed paid salaries that significantly exceeded the wages they could have paid for labor of equivalent skills.[15] For example, in 1977 when the open rate of unemployment was 12 percent and the PEM program covered 6 percent of the labor force, these firms paid wages to their lowest skilled workers that averaged 2.6 times above the minimum wage. This ratio was, on average, 2.1 in 1978 and 2.2 in 1979. Additional support for the labor market segmentation hypothesis is provided by A. Edwards (1984), who used a 15,000 observation data set to estimate earning functions for different sectors for 1974–80. After dividing the data set into three segments—protected, covered by the minimum wage, and uncovered—she found that the Mincer-type earning functions across these segments were statistically different, providing important support to the hypothesis of labor market segmentation.[16]

The Structure of Chile's Labor Market and Unemployment

One way to reconcile the evolution of the unemployment rate and real wages during 1973–83 is to think about the Chilean labor market as a two-segment market. One segment, which we have called "protected," comprises all workers in those sectors where wages have been protected from changing market conditions by virtue of the indexation mechanism and the minimum wage laws. These include mining, manufacturing, construction, utilities, commerce, transportation and communications, financial services, and government. The "free" segment, on the other hand, comprises employment in those sectors where wages are set freely, either because they are not covered by the minimum wage or indexation legislation or because employment is of temporary nature. We have included here agriculture, fishing, social, personal, and domestic services.[17] The main feature of this labor structure is that all those workers whose reservation wage is between the free segment wage and the protected segment wage and who are not employed in the protected segment are in fact unemployed. Although these workers would not take a job in the free market segment—because its wage is below their reservation wage—they would like to be employed in the protected sector. In a way they are *quasi-voluntarily unemployed*. Figure 6–2 summarizes the changes in the distribution of the labor force across these two segments. As can be seen, employment in the protected sector became significantly less important, in relative terms, after 1973.

Figure 6-2.   Chile: Labor Force Distribution (percentages).

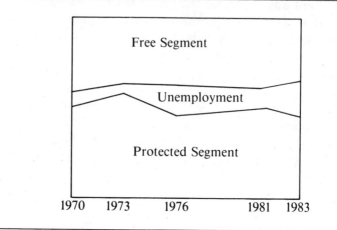

The Model

The wage differential between the protected and free segments creates quasi-voluntary unemployment among workers willing to take a protected segment job but not willing to become part of the free sector labor supply at the free sector wage. Figure 6–3 illustrates the working of this model. In panel *a* we have the protected segment demand for labor D_p and an exogenously determined (real) wage rate W_p. Employment in this segment is equal to the distance $O_p E_p$. Panel *b* depicts the equilibrium in the free segment. The supply to this segment is a fraction of the total labor supply at each wage rate. Possibly the simplest way to analyze this case is by assuming that employers in the protected segment hire workers using a criterion unrelated to supply prices. That is to say, if employment in the protected segment is a fraction β of the labor supply, we expect the labor supply to the free segment to be a fraction $1-\beta$ of the original labor supply at each wage. Using the above assumption, supply of labor to the free segment is given by S_f in panel *a*.2. Distance *AB*, of course, is equal to protected employment $O_p E_p$ in panel *a*.1. Given the demand for labor in the free segment D_f, the wage rate in this segment is W_f and employment is distance $O_f E_f$. The most interesting feature of this model is that distance $E_f Q$ in panel *a*.2 captures the amount of unemployment. These workers are unemployed in the sense that although

Figure 6–3.   Segmented Labor Market.

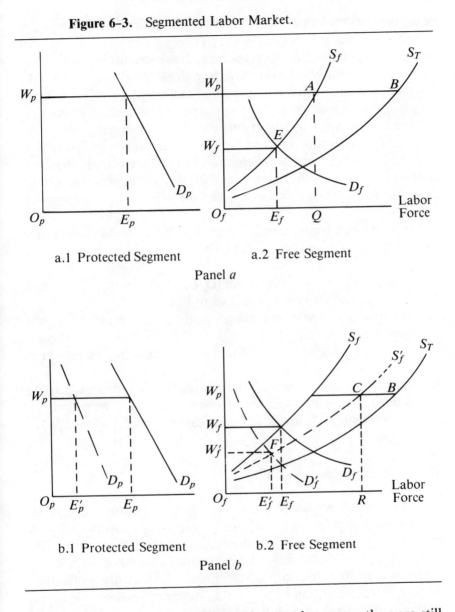

a.1 Protected Segment   a.2 Free Segment

Panel *a*

b.1 Protected Segment   b.2 Free Segment

Panel *b*

their reservation wage is above the free market wage, they are still willing to work at the protected market wage W_p. In a sense, then, these workers are quasi-voluntary unemployed.

Panel *b* in Figure 6–3 captures the effects of a recession on wages, employment, and unemployment. This type of aggregate shock is similar to the 1975 recession in Chile and is reflected by a leftward shift of the demand for labor in both sectors. Since by assumption the wage rate in the protected segment is exogenously determined, it does not change. Employment in that segment, however, drops to distance $O_p E_p'$. Consequently, we now have to redraw the supply of labor to the free segment (which is equal to a fraction $\beta' < \beta$ of total labor supply). The new labor supply to the free segment is S_f', where now distance CB is equal to employment in the protected segment. As a result of the recession, demand for labor in the free segment falls to D_f', and a new equilibrium is determined in this segment by the interaction of the new supply curve S_f' and the new demand curve D_f'. The new free segment wage rate is W_f', and the new level of employment is $O_f E_f'$.

As can be seen from panel b in Figure 6–3 this model predicts that as a result of the recession the following things will happen:

1. Total employment will fall from $(O_p E_p + O_f E_f)$ to $(O_p E_p' + O_f E_f')$.
2. Free segment's wages will decline to W_f'.
3. Measured *average* wages will generally decline because free segment wages decline. The change in the distribution of employment across segments would ultimately determine the change in measured average wages.
4. Most important, however, the model clearly indicates that the number of unemployed and the rate of unemployment will go up. In Figure 6–3, unemployment goes up from $E_f Q$ to $E_f' R$.

Segmentation in Chile

In order to make this simple model operational in our interpretation, it is necessary to define in a more precise way what do we mean by the protected and free segments in the context of the Chilean case. This is done in Table 6–6, where we have distributed the labor force in two segments according to sector of employment. Given the availability of data, this distribution is, of course, an approximation. However, as discussed in detail in A. Edwards (1986a), it turns out to be a good and reasonable one.

The allocation of the labor force to the two segments was approximated with employment classified in ten sectors of economic activity. Unfortunately, the data available on wages cannot be matched directly with employment by sectors. In particular, we do not have reliable estimates for wages in agriculture. For this reason, we used a

Table 6-6. Chile's Labor Market Indicators: 1970-83.

	1970	1973	1976	1981	1983
Labor force (thousands)[a]	2,932.2	3,037.0	3,216.4	3,669.3	3,797.5
Employment (thousands)[a]					
Total	2,776.1	2,891.2	2,705.0	3,269.0	3,091.2
Protected	1,558.8	1,766.3	1,489.8	1,826.2	1,726.7
Free	1,207.3	1,124.9	1,215.2	1,443.0	1,364.5
Output (GDP)					
Mill—1977 pesos					
Total	283.1	287.8	261.9	383.6	327.2
Protected	220.4	228.4	202.2	304.2	257.1
Free	52.9	51.1	57.9	68.8	64.9
Productivity (pesos per worker)					
Total	102.3	99.5	96.8	117.3	105.8
Protected	141.4	129.3	135.7	166.6	148.9
Free	43.8	45.5	47.7	49.4	47.6

Annual Average Rates of Growth	1970-73	1973-76	1976-81	1981-83
Labor Force	1.2	1.9	2.6	1.7
Employment	1.4	−2.2	3.8	−2.8
Protected	4.2	−5.7	4.1	−2.8
Free	−2.4	2.7	3.4	−2.8

Source: Labor force and Total Employment, Castaneda (1983); Productivity, Banco Central de Chile (1984).

Note: The protected segment includes the traditionally unionized sectors of economic activity and the government. The free segment includes agriculture, fishing, social, personal, and domestic services. For a more detailed explanation see A. Edwards (1986a).

[a] Figures correspond to June of each year.

wage series for each segment that was representative of a particular type of skill within the segment—reducing the effect of changes in the combination of employment. Wages of domestic service employees were used to study wage variations within the free segment, and wages of blue-collar workers in manufacturing were used to study wage variations within the protected segment. These series are presented in Table 6-7.

From the blue-collar workers' wages series it can be seen that monthly wages (estimates for May of each year) throughout the period

Table 6-7.   Real Wages (May each year) (in December 1978 pesos).

Year	(1) Blue Collar	(2) Minimum Wage	(3) Domestic Service	(4) (3)/(1)	(5) (2)/(3)
1970	3,920.2	1,978.0	1,853.0	.47	1.07
1971	4,385.0	2,553.2	2,017.9	.46	1.27
1972	4,238.3	2,380.9	2,114.1	.50	1.13
1973	3,486.1	1,909.1	1,859.4	.53	1.03
1974	3,277.1	2,334.9	1,567.0	.48	1.49
1975	2,466.7	1,586.6	1,231.9	.50	1.29
1976	2,693.4	1,858.5	1,262.6	.47	1.47
1977	2,834.6	2,173.9	1,588.8	.56	1.37
1978	3,178.2	2,584.4	1,985.6	.62	1.38
1979	3,642.7	2,510.9	2,265.0	.62	1.11
1980	3,476.9	2,557.8	2,333.1	.67	1.10
1981	4,371.3	2,367.7	2,489.3	.57	.95
1982	4,300.0	2,603.9	2,800.1	.65	.92
1983	3,540.4	1,987.7	2,202.9	.62	.90

Source: A. Edwards (1986a). Constructed from raw data obtained from Banco Central de Chile (1981) and World Bank (1980).

showed a cyclical behavior with no significant trend. This is not too surprising given the evolution of real income for the Chilean economy. Wages in 1973, 1979, 1980, and 1983 were very close to the average of 3,558 pesos for the fourteen-year period. The years 1971–72 and 1981–82 are characterized by substantial real wage increases of between 25 and 30 percent above the average. During the 1974–77 period, on the contrary, wages are about 30 percent below the trend.

The path of the minimum wage relative to domestic service wages (column 5 in Table 6–7) is, to a large extent, a reflection of the effort of the authorities to maintain the real purchasing power of wages through the indexation mechanism. This effort, nevertheless, had negative implications for the unemployment problem.

The ratio of domestic service wages to blue-collar wages (column 4) highlights in the context of our model how the two segments of the labor market adjusted to these changes. For example, between 1973 and 1976 labor demand declined in the protected segment, but we see wages in the free segment declining relative to the protected segment.

This is consistent with what our model would predict. If wages are higher and relatively inflexible in the protected segment and demand is reduced there, we will expect an increase in unemployment and also an increase in labor supply to the free segment that will tend to depress the free segment real wage.

Although this model has the advantage of being very schematic and appropriate for analyzing some of the important questions regarding the Chilean experience, it is too aggregated to be of much help in understanding the more intricate effects of the trade liberalization on the labor market. In each segment, we have added up all employment, without making any attempt to decompose it in different labor categories. Some additional analysis will be necessary in some of the subperiods studied below.

1973–76

We first concentrate on 1973–76, a period where unemployment grew very drastically. Partly as a result of the government's effort to reduce its size, labor demand within the protected segment—which includes government—declined by 276,500 (5.6 percent per year), where 100,000 of this reduced job vacancies can be identified with the employment reduction within the public sector. The rest of the demand decline (176,000) was the result of the effects of the world recession and especially of the drastic stabilization policy implemented by the government in 1975. At the same time, labor supply continued to increase, adding 179,400 workers throughout the period. As a result labor supply to the free segment increased, inducing a reduction in the wage rate there. According to available figures, the agricultural sector was the one that absorbed most of the additional employment within the free segment. Table 6-6 summarizes the changes in the key variables for the labor market situation in 1973, 1976, 1981, and 1983.

In our view the employment policies of the public sector play an important role in understanding the high unemployment rates observed in Chile since 1974. Previous papers have provided a somewhat casual discussion of this problem. Tockman (1984), for example, estimated the public sector employment level for the period 1970–82 if the trend observed in the 1960s for public employment had been maintained. Using these estimates he concluded that the reduction in public sector employment between 1973 and 1976 explains less than 10 percent of the increase in the unemployment rate for the same period. Meller (1984) pointed out the cyclical pattern of the public sector employment and has argued that if 1973 is used as the base of comparison for the later evolution of public sector employment, the reduction in the employment level within the public sector between 1973 and 1976 explains about 30 percent of the increment of the unemployment rate for the same period (about 3 percent of the labor force). This is exactly what the model used in this section emphasizes. The change in the employment policy between 1973 and 1976 operates on a labor market that had already been adjusted to the structure of labor demand of the 1970–73 years — that is, to a higher level of protected segment demand for labor.

Figure 6–4 illustrates, within the context of our segmented labor market model, the changes in the labor market situation between 1973 and 1976. Labor supply to the economy and therefore to the protected segment increased by about 200,000 individuals, while demand in the protected segment declined by 276,500. The excess supply of labor to the protected segment does not entirely become part of the free segment labor supply, since only a fraction of the unemployed would be willing to take a job at the free segment wage. In the free segment, employment actually increased, and the wage rate, measured by the evolution of domestic service wages, declined relative to other wages. These changes could be consistent with a growing free segment labor demand, but it is assumed that demand in the free segment declined at the original wage and that the level of employment in the same sector increased due to the effect of the growing labor supply on the free segment real wage. As a result, unemployment increased from about 150,000 in 1973 to over 500,000 in 1976. According to Table 6–7, wages did experience a substantial decline, but, as our model suggests, this decline was more pronounced within the free segment, while it was in the protected segment that the policy of employment reduction had a direct impact. Clearly, a larger reduction in real wages within the protected segment would have diminished the decline in employment there and reduced the resulting unemployment rate.

1976–81

During the recovery and "boom" years of 1976–81, employment grew at an annual average rate of 3.8 percent (see Table 6–6), and the labor

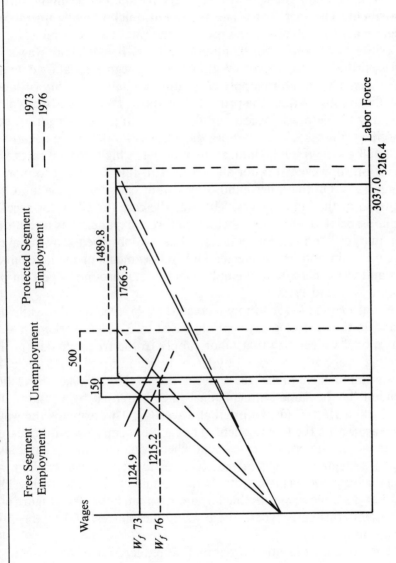

Figure 6–4. Labor Market Adjustment to Changes between 1973 and 1976.

force showed record growth rates of 2.6 percent per year on average. All of this is consistent with a recovery period and declining unemployment. The fact that wages recovered quickly, while unemployment was still well above the past normal rates has been puzzling. A possible explanation will be attempted here. In our view, wages increased due to two forces. Within the free segment, labor demand grew faster than labor supply generating a relative scarcity of labor for those jobs. Within the protected segment, there were two typical scenarios. There was excess supply of certain labor categories, like specific skills associated with all those activities that were negatively affected by the trade liberalization and by the high interest rates. Indexation, however, did not allow wages to fall according to market conditions. On the other hand, other labor categories were in excess demand at the initial wages. This was the case for all sector-specific skills associated with those sectors that were expanding as a result of the market liberalization policies. Thus, we observed growing average wages in both the protected and free segments of the labor market and also a persistent unemployment rate of around 14 percent between 1977 and 1979.

From 1976–81 labor supply increased by 453,000 people, while demand in the protected segment increased by 336,400 workers. Using our model we can say that labor supply to the free segment (at the original wage W_f) increased by 116.6 thousand people ($453 - 336.4$). Since employment in the free segment increased by 228,000, then labor demand in the same segment must have increased by substantially more than 116,600 (at the original wage W_f). This explains the wage increase within the free segment. The fact that employment increased more within the protected segment where wages are higher, and also that free segment wages increased in relative terms, can explain the overall wage recovery in spite of the sustained unemployment. The level of unemployment declined by approximately 100,000. Figure 6–5 represents this case, where the broken lines correspond to the 1981 situation.

The trade liberalization program that reduced tariffs from an average of 94 percent in late 1973 to a 10 percent across-the-board by June of 1979 had its major effect on the allocation of employment and investment throughout this period. The effect of the trade liberalization on the labor market represents a vast and critical area of research. In principle, changes in relative prices of goods would translate in a reallocation of resources, and apart from short-run adjustment lags, we

Figure 6–5. Labor Market Adjustment to Changes between 1976 and 1981.

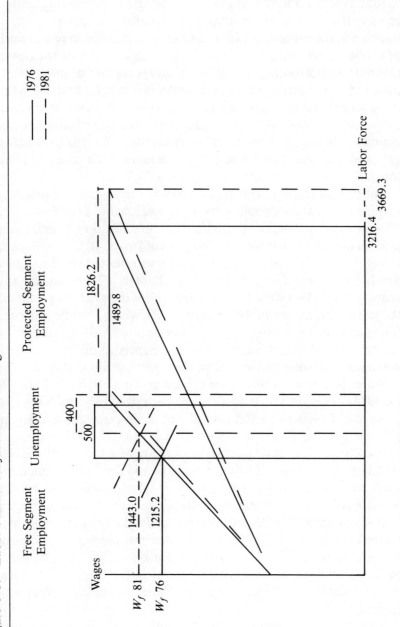

should expect no long-run effect on the rate of unemployment. We can say that the optimum amount of frictional unemployment may increase in the presence of large and sudden changes in relative prices of commodities because individuals have to learn about the new employment opportunities. But if there is wage rigidity of the type introduced by minimum wages, and if capital is immobile in the short run, the liberalization process can result in short-run involuntary unemployment. Along these lines, S. Edwards (1982) reports that the upper bound for the unemployment effect of the trade liberalization between 1975 and 1978 would be 3.5 percent of the labor force (or about 129,000 jobs).

Labor reallocation takes place when workers leave one job to take another, but capital mobility requires investment. Therefore, the reallocation of resources induced by the liberalization policies generated an increase in demand for investment funds. In fact, the scarcity of capital in Chile during this period was reflected by the unprecedently high interest rates analyzed in Chapter 3. The recovery of the economy, and therefore the growth in labor demand, was limited by the degree of capital mobility or in other words, by the amount of funds available for investment. It was only with the opening of the capital account that this process could be speeded up and the level of unemployment due to the reallocation effect could disappear.

Since the liberalization of the capital account started in June 1979, the 1976–79 period can in a way be characterized by immobile capital, while in the 1980–81 period capital was more easily moved. By mid-1979 the construction sector, which until then had still been quite depressed, showed a frantic recovery, and unemployment declined. Nevertheless, at the end of this recovery period (mid-1981), unemployment was still around 11 percent of the labor force. If we take Edwards's estimate of 3.5 percent unemployment associated to the trade liberalization, we are left with an unexplained unemployment rate of around 11 percent (14.5 percent − 3.5 percent) for the 1976–79 period and a slightly higher rate of 11.4 percent on average for the 1980–81 period. Certainly, the level of real wages in the economy was above the level consistent with a historical rate of unemployment of 5 or 6 percent.

These rates of unemployment—two times the historical rates for the Chilean economy—can be explained by the process of wages determination and by a resulting inconsistency between workers' expectations about wages and actual market wages. As is described in Figure

6–5, the recovery of labor demand during this period induced average wage increases, in spite of the unemployment level. Therefore, the actual recovery of employment was relatively moderate.

Moreover, toward the end of this recovery period wages showed a significant real increase. The new labor law and the fixed exchange rate policy favored the growth of real wages in the economy and particularly within the "protected" segment. Real wages increased dramatically in 1980. To give just an indication, the proportion of labor income out of GDP went from 36.1 in 1979 to 38.2 in 1980 to 40.5 in 1981 and 41.2 in 1982.

1981–83

The strong recovery of the preceding period came to an abrupt end by mid-1981. This period has been extensively analyzed in the preceding chapters.

The financial market situation was giving signs of a turning point in 1981 as interest rates climbed. During the second semester of 1981 industrial production started to decline. Nevertheless, nominal wages were officially granted a 14 percent increase in August 1981 – to reestablish the real wage as of October 1980 – and collective bargaining agreements were setting nominal wage readjustments that exceeded the legally required minimum of accumulated past inflation. Firms, especially in the tradables sectors, could afford this wage increase only by borrowing from the financial system. When in 1982 foreign banks decided that Chile was not a good risk any more, bankruptcies mounted. Open unemployment – excluding the emergency program – reached in 1982, 20.4 percent of the labor force.

The labor market adjustment between 1981 and 1983 is represented in Figure 6–6. The 1983 case is represented by the broken lines. In Figure 6–6 we have omitted any change in the protected segment wage. The idea is that between 1981 and 1982 real wages increased above equilibrium and then declined in 1983. But due to the initial downward inflexibility of wages, the reduction in demand that took place was considerable. As an indicator of the disequilibrium that resulted, the unemployment level rose to 700,000 in 1983.

Summarizing, the higher rate of unemployment for the 1974–83 period is explained by the low average rate of growth of the economy for the period coupled with a lack of downward flexibility of wages

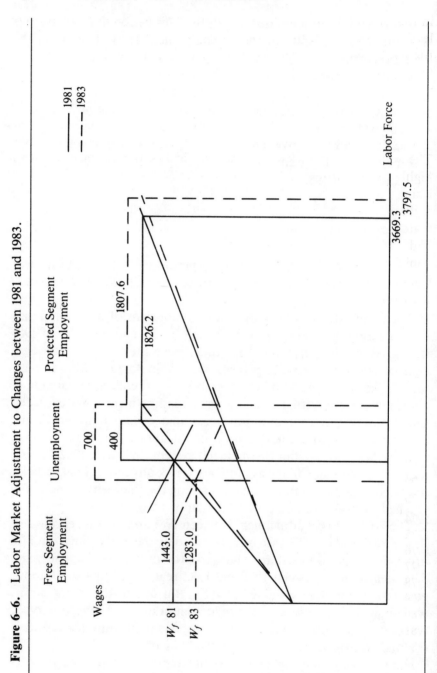

Figure 6-6. Labor Market Adjustment to Changes between 1981 and 1983.

in the "protected" segment of the labor market. The recovery of the
level of economic activity between 1976 and 1981 was not sustained
for a long enough period to succeed in reducing unemployment to
historical levels.

INCOME DISTRIBUTION

The evolution of income distribution during the military rule has been
highly debated by Chilean social scientists and by the popular press.[18]
Using the Gini coefficient as an indicator of the degree of inequality,
and either the individual or the family as the unit of analysis, the estimated degree of inequality increased significantly in 1975 and 1976
and again in 1982–83 (see Table 6–8).[19] The estimated changes in the
Gini coefficient are of course more pronounced if the unit of analysis
is the individual, and in particular, if the entire labor force is included, assuming zero income for the unemployed.[20] There have been

Table 6-8. Gini Coefficient: Income Distribution (Greater
Santiago area).

| Year | Personal Income | | Family Income |
	Working Population	Labor Force	
1958	0.512	0.577	0.466
1964	0.490	0.496	0.462
1970	0.526	0.571	0.501
1974	0.468	0.518	0.450
1975	0.484	0.566	0.471
1976	0.543	0.618	0.438
1977	0.534	0.599	0.526
1978	0.524	0.588	0.520
1979	0.526	0.589	0.518
1980	0.522	0.578	0.526
1981	0.531	0.579	0.521
1982	0.534	0.624	0.539
1983	0.530	0.639	0.542

Source: Heskia (1979) and Riveros (1985).

disagreements on this issue, mainly related to technical aspects and relevance of these summary statistics, but it is clear that the unemployed situation is closely associated to the degree of inequality of the income distribution.[21]

It is well known that the Gini coefficient presents a number of shortcomings as an indicator of income distribution. For this reason the controversy has been lately centered on the effects of social government expenditure on the alleviation of poverty. Two questions have been discussed: the actual level of government expenditure in social areas and the distributional impact of that expenditure.[22]

The primary emphasis of the military government in the area of social expenditures was to increase the cost effectiveness of basic needs' programs — that is, to increase the content value delivered per *peso* spent — and to concentrate resources on those segments of the population in greatest need of these basic goods or services. This increasing emphasis on meeting the needs of the poor was to be financed largely by a reallocation of budgetary resources rather than by significant increases in the level of public sector social expenditure. Nevertheless, some social programs have expanded considerably, mainly as a form to alleviate some of the effects of the unemployment problem. For example, expenditures in social welfare that include, for example, the Minimum Employment Program, were in 1976 three times the 1974 real level and in 1983 ten times the 1974 real level.

As can be seen in column 1 of Table 6-9, social government expenditure in real terms does not show a clear trend but reaches its highest level during the last three years of the period (1981–83). Social fiscal expenditure as a proportion of public sector expenditure shows a growing trend, mainly as a result of a lower aggregate government expenditure. It is interesting to note that the increase in government expenditure as a proportion of GDP in 1982 and 1983 is almost entirely explained by the increase in social government expenditure over GDP.

A study on the distributional impact of social expenditure by Rodriguez (1985) concluded that education and health policies have reduced poverty. But the distributional impact of other programs was not so clear. Government housing programs, for example, had been modified several times in an effort to reach the targeted groups of the population. In the end, they became more efficient, but the final effect was weak. In general, Rodriguez finds a significant bias in favor of the metropolitan region and against the rural areas.

Table 6-9. Social Government Expenditure: 1974-83.

Year	(A) Social Government Expenditure per Capita (1983 U.S. $)	(B) (Social Government Expenditure/ (GDP))	(C) Social Government Expenditure/ Public Sector (Debt Service Excluded)	(D) Public Sector Expenditure (Debt Service Excluded/GDP)
1974	314.8	.181	.500	.362
1975	282.8	.190	.561	.338
1976	254.9	.167	.538	.312
1977	299.6	.183	.590	.310
1978	292.1	.167	.547	.306
1979	304.2	.164	.570	.288
1980	281.8	.165	.574	.288
1981	357.1	.174	.579	.302
1982	375.9	.218	.616	.360
1983	333.8	.199	.586	.339

Source: Cheyre and Symon (1985) and Banco Central de Chile (1984).
Note: Public expenditure refers to all government institutions.

SUMMARY

This chapter analyzed several aspects of employment, wages, unemployment, and income distribution during the period of economic reforms in Chile, 1974-83. The high level of unemployment observed throughout the period responded to a number of interrelated factors. First, the slow average rate of growth of economic activity during the period resulted in a slow rate of employment creation. Second, the labor force grew at rates substantially higher than the historical average. Third, the reduction in the government size generated a major reduction in the number of jobs, contributing to the overall unemployment problem. And fourth, the persistence of unemployment responded to a number of rigidities that precluded a smooth adjustment to various shocks, including the liberalization reforms. In particular, the across-the-board wage indexation mechanism did not allow relative wages to change sufficiently. Our simple model of a segmented labor market highlights the role of these rigidities and is very useful to explain the evolution of employment, unemployment, and wages during the period.

The ten years under study were divided into three subperiods according to the type of reform or external shock affecting the labor market: The years 1973–76 are a period of stabilization effort complicated with a negative external shock; the 1976–81 period experienced the trade liberalization reforms; and finally in 1981–83 another major negative external shock took place.

Unemployment growth in Chile during the period analyzed is associated with two types of episodes: employment reduction within the public sector and negative external shocks. Our explanation is that the replacement of government jobs by new jobs (at the same wage) would take place gradually as the economy builds up the complementary factors to use this labor productively. On the other hand, negative external shocks induce a reduction in aggregate demand for tradables through a reduction in real income. The reduced demand for tradables generates a reduction in labor demand that would generate unemployment unless real wages decline. Therefore, the lack of downward flexibility of real wages is a fundamental explanatory factor behind the unemployment generated in the two types of episodes.

NOTES

1. Analyses of the unemployment problem are provided, for example, in A. Edwards (1985, 1986a, 1986b), Cortes (1983), Riveros (1984, 1985), Meller, Cortazar, and Marshall (1979), Meller (1984), and Arellano (1984).
2. Corbo and Meller (1981) document how the import substitution trade policy resulted in highly capital intensive productive techniques.
3. See Marshall and Romaguera (1981).
4. During the decade of the 1960s, the rate of unemployment was at approximately the average level for Latin America. For example, during the second half of that decade the annual rates of open unemployment (countrywide) were: 1977, 6.8 percent; 1967, 5.5 percent; 1968, 5.0 percent; 1969, 4.1 percent; 1970, 3.5 percent.
5. The existing empirical evidence shows that, although real wages across the economy significantly fluctuated during this period, relative wages between any two sectors for comparable workers (given education and experience) were quite inflexible. This was, to an important degree, a consequence of the indexation mechanism. What the evidence shows is

that there were no significant wage responses to sectoral variations in labor demand throughout the 1974–80 period. (See the econometric cross-sector analysis in A. Edwards (1985). See also Cortazar (1982)). At this point, it is convenient to consider labor as a quasi-fixed factor in the short run (Oi 1962). In response to changes in relative prices of goods or to changes in the employment policy of the public sector, firm- or industry-specific attributes of human capital should experience price changes. Consequently we should observe changes in relative wages across industries or sectors of economic activity. Alternatively, we would observe unemployment in all those labor categories that have experienced demand reductions. It is also reasonable to expect that an economy going through a serious stabilization and liberalization program would present a higher rate of frictional unemployment for a short period of time.

6. The existence of this emergency program introduces some difficulties into the analysis of the employment problem. Since some, but not all, of the participants in the PEM program consider themselves as being employed full time, it is not easy to compute the actual rate of unemployment. On this problem see Meller (1984). On the PEM emergency program see Schmidt-Hebbel (1981).

7. If after sixty days of negotiations there was no new agreement, workers could resume their jobs under the same conditions established by the previous contract, with the exception of nominal wages, which were increased by the rate of inflation incurred since the last contract. According to the law, it was understood that if a worker did not resume his job sixty days after the strike had begun he "would have implicitly resigned" his post.

8. This structure can be altered to consider the presence of a binding minimum wage. In this case in the unprotected segment it is necessary to distinguish between the *covered* sector, which is subject to the legal minimum wage, and the uncovered sector where wage rates are fully set according to market forces. Since workers in the protected or *covered* sectors get rents, labor mobility from these sectors to the free segment is slow, and major shocks to the economy are usually translated into large and persistent unemployment. On segmented labor markets see, for example, Stiglitz (1974), Harberger (1971), Berry and Sabot (1978), and A. Edwards (1984). See also the discussion below.

9. If E is the level of employment and F is the labor force, then $u = 1 - E/F$ is the rate of unemployment. Consequently $du = E/F(dF/F - dE/E)$. Assuming an initial level of unemployment of 6 percent ($E/F = .94$) and the same rate of growth in employment of the 1960s, the higher rate of growth of the labor force in the 1973–83 period explains an annual average increase in the unemployment rate of half of a point, or an

accumulated increase of five points in ten years ($du = .94(.023 - .018) = .0047$). If we assume the same growth in the labor force of the 1960s, the reduction in employment growth explains an annual increase in the unemployment rate of .9 of a point, or an accumulated increase of nine points in ten years ($du = .84(.016 - .007) = 0.085$).

10. Estimates based on World Bank data.

11. The 1979 law established 100 percent backward indexation for workers subject to collective bargaining only, but it added to the overall rigidity of the indexation mechanism in two ways. First, although it legally focused on wages in a particular sector, other wages were also affected via labor mobility and turnover. Second, and more important, by mandating 100 percent wage indexation for unionized workers, the government was in a way forced—to the extent it did not want to be discriminatory—to decree 100 percent indexation for nonunion workers.

12. Recall that in 1979 General Pinochet said that the law "assures workers an increase of remunerations of at least 100 percent of the increase of the cost of life" (Banco Central de Chile, *Boletín Mensual*, (September 1979): 1489). Of course, he was not strictly correct. Whether real wages would decline or increase due to Article 26 depended on whether inflation was increasing or decreasing. How can it be explained that an otherwise sophisticated piece of legislation included an aberration such as the institutionalization of backward indexation? The answer to this probably lies in the realm of politics. The wage floor and indexation clauses were included in the law as a way to show that this piece of legislation was not antilabor as some generals had argued. In fact, it was pointed out that this law was, if anything, prolabor, since it assured that real wages would "never" decline again.

13. Of this 56.9 percent the employer's contribution amounted to 45.4 percent, and the employers contribution was 7.5 percent.

14. An alternative approach to the existence of segmentation is implicit in the "dual" labor market theory (see Doeringer and Piore 1971). According to the "duality" approach, segmentation is a structural failure in the way labor markets function in developing countries, and the evidence of its existence is in the widespread poverty observed in these countries. Empirical analyses of the dual labor market hypothesis have encountered two problems. First, the nonoperational character of the theory that limits the testable hypothesis to the alleged inadequacy of human capital investment in the secondary market. Second, and more important, the theory does not contain a clearly defined criterion to distinguish the two segments.

15. There are a number of reasons why large firms, including *grupo* firms, paid as a matter of policy wages above market levels. For example, firms might be interested in minimizing hiring/training costs. In a context of imperfect information where the firm cannot identify quitters,

a wage above equilibrium will reduce quits. Also, since supervision is costly, wage premiums will induce workers to perform better and to be loyal to the firm. The informational gaps tend to be more important in large firms. Finally, if a firm has market power, it could pay wages above narrowly defined market wages and still survive.

16. Differences in earnings functions across segments persist after controlling for differences in human capital and specific attributes of employment by sectors, like unemployment trends and cyclical variations in labor demand. The persistence of these wages differentials needs an explanation; indexation is a possible one.

17. According to Chilean law throughout period 1973–81, wages of domestic service employees and trainees were not subject to the minimum wage.

18. See, for example, Cortazar (1980, 1982), Heskia (1979), Marshall (1981), Riveros (1985), Rodriguez (1983).

19. The Gini coefficient is a summary statistic calculated from an income distribution representation called Lorenz curve. The closer to 0 (1) is the Gini coefficient, the more (less) even is the distribution of income.

20. Although estimates available indicate that in the period 1974–82, around 20 percent of the unemployed perceived some income. Riveros (1985).

21. See Atkinson (1975).

22. Marshall (1981) and Cheyre and Symon (1985) offer alternative series of government expenditure, different from the official ones. The differences are due both to a more accurate account of what should be included as public sector, central government, or social expenditures and to the choice of the price deflator. The main difference between Marshall and Cheyre-Symon's series is due to the price deflator chosen. Table 6–8 data is based on Cheyre-Symon's estimates because their series covered the entire 1974–83 period.

7 THE SEQUENCING OF THE LIBERALIZATION REFORMS

One lesson that emerges from the Chilean experiment is that a number of issues related to the dynamics of the liberalization of the external sector are not fully understood by the policymakers, economists, and other observers. Some of the most important of these dynamic problems are related to the speed and sequencing of economic liberalization. How fast should an economy be liberalized? In analyzing this aspect of the problem, considerations related to efficiency gains, income distribution, and feasiblity of the attempt should be taken into account. Regarding the sequencing of liberalization, the main question relates to the order in which markets should be liberalized.[1]

The sequencing of liberalization in Chile and the other Southern Cone countries is particularly interesting, since they followed opposite orders — Argentina and Uruguay opened the capital account first, while Chile opened the current account first. An important policy question that has emerged from these experiences has to do with defining liberalization policy packages, including a specific sequencing, that are credible to the public. This issue has recently gained great prominence in specific policy discussions. For example, the recent debate on the liberalization reforms in Korea have focused on the definition of an appropriate sequencing of liberalization for that country. Also, recent policy discussions in Ecuador have evolved around this important issue.[2]

This chapter discusses a particularly important aspect of the sequencing of economic liberalization — the order of liberalizing the current and capital accounts of the balance of payments — within the context of the Chilean experience. The approach followed in this chapter is somewhat different from that of the previous chapters. First, the material presented here is somewhat more analytical. Without resorting to a technical presentation, the discussion rigorously covers different aspects of the sequencing of liberalization. The main conclusion of this chapter is that in a liberalization experience the sequence chosen to reform markets can be crucial. More specifically, the most prudent strategy calls for liberalizing the current account first; only when this phase of the reform has been finalized should the capital account be slowly opened.

THE SEQUENCING OF LIBERALIZATION IN CHILE

As has been discussed in the previous chapters, the liberalization reforms of the more critical markets in Chile were undertaken at different points in time. In this section, and in order to provide some perspective to the analytical discussion that follows, we summarize the order in which the reforms were undertaken.

The domestic goods market was liberalized first. In October 1973 domestic prices of all goods — with the sole exception of fifty-one "necessities" — were freed. This represented a major departure from the Allende regime, where prices of over 3,000 commodities were fixed and closely controlled by the Ministry of Economy and Industry. The freeing of domestic prices was followed by the initial steps toward liberalizing the domestic financial market and international trade in goods. Starting in 1977 with Chile's withdrawal from the Andean Pact, the trade liberalization reform was greatly accelerated. By mid-1979 the trade reform was completed, with tariffs for all but two items reduced to a uniform 10 percent. Significant measures toward lifting controls in international capital movements were enacted for the first time in June 1979. As was explained in detail in Chapter 3, by mid-1981 the liberalization of capital movements had achieved significant proportions. Short-term capital movements, however, were tightly controlled until mid-1982. As pointed out in Chapter 6, although the labor market never attained a very high degree of liberalization, the reforms of 1978, 1979, and 1980 did introduce some changes.

In terms of the external sector, then, Chile liberalized trade in goods first, and only when the desired level of import restrictions was achieved — the uniform 10 percent tariff in June of 1979 — did the process of liberalization of the capital account really start. This sequencing of liberalization of the external sector contrasted with the approach followed by Argentina and Uruguay. Both of these countries opened their economies to capital movements well before their trade accounts were liberalized.[3] The fact that the reforms ultimately failed in the three countries has added considerable interest to the issue of the appropriate sequencing of economic reform.

THE APPROPRIATE SEQUENCING OF LIBERALIZATION OF THE EXTERNAL SECTOR: ANALYTICAL ASPECTS

This section deals with some of the more important analytical issues related to the sequencing of liberalization of the external sector.[4] The discussion draws heavily on the Chilean case. The question that we address is the following: When designing a strategy for the liberalization of the external sector in a particular country, which account — the current account or the capital account — should be opened up first? Of course, from a pure theory perspective the answer to this question is trivial. If there are no rigidities or market failures, all markets should be liberalized simultaneously and instantaneously. In most real world situations, however, there are a number of reasons, both political and economic, why this theoretical first best path is not feasible. The discussion that follows assumes that the initial conditions correspond to those of a country like Chile in the mid-1970s and focuses on three aspects of this problem: (1) the relationship between the sequencing of liberalization, macroeconomic management, and the real exchange rate; (2) welfare aspects of alternative sequencings of liberalization; and (3) the sequencing of liberalization and adjustment costs.

The Sequencing of Liberalization, Macroeconomic Management, and the Real Exchange Rate

The other major liberalization episodes in Chile, Argentina, and Uruguay during the last decade were characterized by a highly unstable macroeconomic environment. There is little doubt that this macroeconomic instability was not completely exogenous but that it was in some sense related to the liberalization strategy followed in these countries. In particular, the effects of the opening of the capital account on the real exchange rate was a major problem that affected the final outcome of these liberalization attempts. (See Chapter 3.)

Under most circumstances the opening of the capital account of the balance of payments will result in the short-run in large destabilizing capital flows — either outflows or inflows. If, for example, the capital account is opened at a stage where the domestic capital market is still repressed, with domestic interest rates fixed at artificially low levels, massive capital outflows will take place. For this reason most if not all authors that have discussed this issue have indicated that the capital account should be opened only after the domestic capital market has been liberalized and domestic interest rates have been raised. This was indeed the case in Chile, where the domestic capital market was reformed well before any important relaxation of exchange controls was taken.

It is also generally accepted that in an inflationary environment the dometic financial market should be liberalized only after the fiscal deficit has been controlled. McKinnon and Mathieson (1981), for example, have pointed out that the existence of a large fiscal deficit, which is financed by an inflation tax, necessitates that banks' reserve requirements are kept high and interest payments on deposits are kept low. In this way it is assured that the base on which the inflation tax is collected — the stock of high-powered money — is not eroded. In fact, as has been suggested by Rodriguez (1983) and Sjaastad (1983) among others, the inability to control the fiscal deficit in Argentina was one of the major causes for the failure of the liberalization with stabilization attempted in that country. Also, as Dornbusch (1983) has recently pointed out, capital flights played a key role toward the latter part of the Argentinian experience of 1978-82.

If, on the other hand, the fiscal deficit has been controlled and the domestic financial market liberalized, the opening of the capital account in a developing country will generally result in large inflows of foreign capital, triggered by portfolio adjustments and the existence of interest rates differentials.[5] These inflows will allow an increase in the level of aggregate expenditure both on tradable and nontradable goods and will generate a real appreciation.

While the opening of the capital account will usually generate a *real appreciation*, a successful liberalization of the trade account will generally require a real *devaluation* of the domestic currency. This real depreciation would help the exportables sector to expand as the new structure of relative prices replaces the old protective structure. In fact, as noted in Chapter 5, the Chilean trade liberalization was indeed accompanied initially by a remarkable real depreciation.[6]

If, however, due to the opening of the capital account this real devaluation is precluded, the transition in the goods sector from a protective to a freer environment will become more difficult. The appreciation generated by the opening of the capital account will tend to squeeze profitability in the tradable goods sector at a moment when this sector (or part of it in the import substitution industries) is going through a costly readjustment. Consequently, it has been suggested by a number of authors that the capital and current accounts should *not* be open simultaneously and that during the transition period after trade has been liberalized capital inflows should be tightly controlled. For example, according to McKinnon (1973: 160),

> unusually large inflows of foreign capital...inhibit the exchange rate to depreciate sufficiently.... [P]reviously protected competing industries, which face a significant adjustment problem, could have their difficulties magnified.... [H]ence the capital inflow could trigger a decline in overall domestic output.

McKinnon then goes on to recommend that an economy that liberalizes its foreign trade should *"deliberately avoid an unusual or extraordinary injection of foreign capital"* (1973: 161, emphasis added). More recently this kind of reasoning has also been made by Dornbusch (1983a), S. Edwards (1984c), and again by McKinnon (1982). As Dornbusch (1983a: 176) has put it: "The worst thing to do is to liberalize the capital account...before the required real depreciation has been achieved."

A critical question regarding this line of argument is to what extent the freeing of the capital account will result in an "extraordinary" injection of foreign capital, in the sense of the McKinnon quote. If the opening of the capital account results in large capital inflows that are sustainable in the long-run, the resulting appreciation should be viewed as a long-run equilibrium phenomenon. Under those circumstances it is not clear that the opening of the capital account should be delayed on the grounds of its effects on the real exchange rate.

It turns out, however, that it is not difficult to build simple models of an economy that restricts capital inflows, where an opening of the capital account will result in short-run overshooting of the level of capital inflows. In order to illustrate this point assume a country with restrictions to capital movements similar to those existing in Chile in the mid- and late 1970s (see Chapter 3). In this case, and assuming that capital has to be imported via domestic banks, capital inflows ΔK can be represented by the following equation:

$$\Delta K = \text{minimum}[\theta(D^* - D_{-1}), \overline{\Delta K}] \qquad (7.1)$$

where D^* is the level of domestic assets that foreign investors want to hold in their portfolios (that is, Chile's sustainable level of foreign debt). D^* will basically depend on the perception that the international financial community has on the longer-run profitability of the domestic economy and on some estimates of political stability. Of course, there is no reason for D^* to be constant through time. In fact in a growing economy D^* will go up as time passes. Also, changes in domestic policies will tend to generate changes in D^*. D_{-1} is the actual stock of debt in the previous period. The term θ is a partial adjustment coefficient that represents the fraction of the disequilibrium between D^* and D_{-1} that can be solved in each period. In the Chilean case it may be useful to think of θ as reflecting the maximum increase of foreign liabilities domestic banks can incur in each period—that is, in the case of Chile, 5 percent of equity or $2 million U.S. per month between June 1979 and April 1980 (see Chapter 3 for further details). $\overline{\Delta K}$ is the maximum (possibly zero) amount of (net) capital inflow allowed by the economic authority in every period.

Clearly, if before the liberalization capital controls are binding, $\overline{\Delta K} < \theta[D^* - D_{-1}]$ an actual capital inflows will be equal to $\overline{\Delta K}$, and in a growing economy as time passes the gap between D^* and D_{-1} will widen. Once the restrictions on capital inflows are lifted, actual inflows will become equal to $\theta[D^* - D_{-1}]$.[7] As a result of this the amount of domestic securities they want to hold (D^*), will increase to a substantially higher level after the liberalization reforms are enacted. Immediately after the opening of the capital account an initial jump in the level of capital inflows as in Figure 7-1 will take place. This indeed was the case in Chile where, as shown in Chapter 3, in 1980–81 foreign capital flows reached unprecedented levels. As capital flows into the country, the gap $(D^* - D_{-1})$ is slowly reduced until it reaches a new equilibrium level.

This sudden increase (that is, overshooting) of capital inflows will initially generate a large current account deficit—as was the case of

Figure 7-1. Real Exchange Behavior following the Liberalization of the Capital Account.

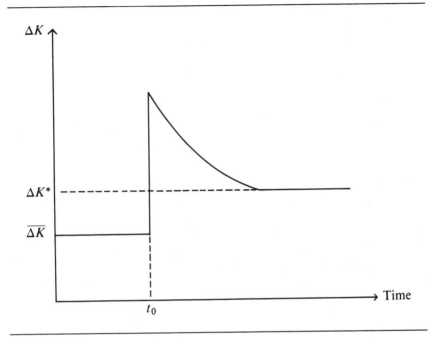

Chile during 1979–81. As was pointed out in Chapter 3, as long as a fraction of these additional foreign funds are spent on nontradable goods, the absorption of these capital inflows will *require* an increase in the relative price of nontradables and real appreciation of the domestic currency. Harberger (1982) has argued that the increase in the level of capital inflows in Chile is capable of explaining a real appreciation of the peso of up to 25 percent between 1979 and 1981.

Once the gap between desired and actual debt begins to close, the relative price of nontradables will decline toward its new long-run equilibrium. This part of the adjustment process, however, can run into some serious problems if the economic structure exhibits some inflexibility. For example, if for some reason the nominal price of nontradables is inflexible downward, the country will run into problems under a fixed exchange rate. A more serious case arises however, if *real* wages are institutionally inflexible downward, as was the case in Chile. In this case, the real depreciation required to attain equilibrium once the level of capital inflows decreases will not take place.

Instead the quantity produced of nontradables will drop, with a resulting important increase in unemployment. In fact, if real wages are rigid, there will be problems with the adjustment process even under a flexible exchange rate (Dornbusch 1984; A. Edwards 1985).[8] As Harberger (1984: 2–3) has pointed out:

> [H]igh rates of capital inflow drive the real exchange rate down (i.e., cause it to be highly appreciated), a situation that then has to be sharply reversed when the rate of capital inflow is curtailed.

The conflicting movements of the real exchange rate as a result of opening the capital and current accounts (that is, real appreciation and depreciation, respectively), captures the fact that these policies will exercise pressures for resources to move in opposite directions. The opening of the capital account will tend to generate, at least in the short-run, an expansion of the nontradable goods sector and a contraction of the importables and exportables sectors. This indeed has been the case in countries that have opened the capital account. As discussed in the preceding chapters, in Chile, after the capital account was opened in 1979, an important fraction of the massive capital inflows was used to finance the expansion of the construction sector. This was also the case of Argentina and Uruguay (see Nogués 1983; Hanson and de Melo 1983). The opening of the current account, on the other hand, will result in an expansion of the exportables sector, a contraction of the production of importables, with the nontradables sector either expanding or contracting (see S. Edwards 1985d). To the extent that there are adjustment costs associated with resource movements between sectors, it is advisable to implement policies that would avoid unnecessary resource switches (that is, resource movements that will be reversed after a short period of time).

Consider, for example, the case where both accounts are opened simultaneously. Since financial markets adjust faster than goods markets, we will observe an immediate inflow of capital (see Figure 7–1). In the goods market sphere, however, nothing or very little in terms of commodity arbitrage will happen in the very short-run. The result, then, will be that at this early stage the capital account effect will dominate, with the real exchange rate appreciating and resources (capital and labor) tending to move into the nontradable goods sector. As time passes, the goods market will begin to adjust and the capital account will enter the phase, after the initial overshooting, where capital inflows will slowly decline toward their new long-run equilibrium (see Figure 7–1). At this point the effect of the tariff reduction will begin to be felt and resource movements will be reversed, with capital and labor now moving out of the nontradables sector. To the extent that there are real economic costs related to those resource movements (that is, adjustment costs), policy measures aimed at reducing these costs should be implemented. In particular, on these macroeconomic grounds, a *synchronization* of the effects of opening the capital and current accounts, in the sense suggested by Frenkel (1982, 1983) will be called for. Frenkel has proposed that given the differential speeds at which the goods and capital markets adjust, this synchronization could be achieved by opening the current account first and only after some time opening the capital account.[9]

As is discussed below in more detail, the real appreciation associated with the opening of the capital account will have two additional disrupting effects. First, it will tend to compromise the credibility of the liberalization episode as a whole. Second, after the initial overshooting of capital inflows, the expected real depreciation will result in higher—and in sometimes exorbitantly high—real interest rates, at a time when the real side is going through the costly adjustment that follows the liberalization of trade restrictions. When deciding on the appropriate sequencing of liberalization, these negative macro effects of opening the capital account before, or simultaneously with, the current account should then be weighted against the positive effects of being able to trade at world intertemporal prices.

The Welfare Effects of Alternative Sequences of Liberalization of the External Sector

In the preceding section we discussed the macroeconomic implications of alternative sequencing of liberalization of the external sector. In the present section we will deal with the welfare effects of alternative sequencings. In fact, welfare considerations are at the center of the analytical discussion on the order of economic liberalization in developing countries. At the level of the simple textbook case of the small economy without rigidities, the answer to the sequencing question is quite trivial: In order to maximize the present value of welfare both accounts should be liberalized simultaneously and instantaneously. In more complicated and realistic cases the answer may be quite different.

We first consider the case where for some reason — political or other — all markets cannot be liberalized simultaneously. Under these circumstances we are in a second-best world, and there may be (negative) welfare implications of reducing or eliminating *one* distortion while other distortions are kept in place. This argument has been made, among others, by McKinnon (1973), Frenkel (1982, 1983), Krueger (1983), S. Edwards (1984a, 1986), and S. Edwards and van Wijnbergen (1986b). These authors have generally concluded that welfare considerations indicate that the current account should be liberalized first, and that after tariffs have been reduced and the adjustment process has been completed, the capital account should be opened. This policy recommendation is based on the belief that the negative indirect welfare effect of opening the capital account in the presence of trade distortions will exceed the negative indirect effects arising from the opposite ordering. McKinnon (1973: 157), for example, has stated that "the liberalization [of] capital inflow[s]. . .increase[s] the basic distortion in the economy. Krueger (1983: 19) has noted that

> Since exchanges of assets are exchanges of capitalized values of income streams, income streams generated by distorted prices are probably the inappropriate ones at which to trade. It would then follow that capital account liberalization should not be undertaken unless both current account and dometic financial transaction are already liberalized.

While according to Frenkel (1983: 167),

> when the trade account is opened first the cost of the remaining distortion (i.e., the closed capital account). . .is likely to be relatively small. On the other hand, when the capital account is opened up first the cost of the remaining distortion (i.e., the close trade account). . .is likely to be very large. Thus a comparison of the costs of distortions. . .supports the proposition that the trade account should be opened first.

This type of reasoning, which focuses on the welfare effects of opening the capital account in the presence of trade distortions, is in some sense related to the argument of immiserizing capital accumulation originally advanced by Harry Johnson (1967). This argument points out that if there are tariffs and the importable good is capital intensive, capital accumulation may be welfare reducing. When capital is accumulated, production of the capital-intensive (that is, the importable) sector will increase (Rybczynski 1955), and the negative welfare effect of the preexisting distortion will be reinforced. This effect can be strong enough, so that the accumulation of capital will result in a reduction of welfare (Johnson 1967). If this is the case, however, why would the recipients of capital flows from abroad use them to accumulate capital? The answer is that the private domestic real return to capital will exceed the world's real interest rate when importables are capital intensive. Therefore, the accumulation of capital will be beneciary from a private perspective but will be less desirable from a social perspective—and could even be immiserizing.[10]

What are the welfare effects of liberalizing trade in the presence of a closed capital account? Are there circumstances under which this particular order of liberalization will result in some indirect negative welfare effects? In principle, it is conceivable that under certain circumstances this result will emerge. Specifically, if the restrictions in the capital account take the form of a tax on foreign borrowing that introduces a wedge between foreign and domestic rates of interest, and the liberalization of the current account results in a reduction (that is, leftward shift) of the demand for foreign borrowing, an indirect negative welfare effects could result.

In practice, however, this case is somewhat inplausible. First, it is unlikely that the reduction of tariffs will generate a reduction of the demand for foreign borrowing. On the contrary, once tariffs are reduced, there will generally be a tendency for the demand for importables to increase, with part of this increase in demand being financed by additional foreign borrowing, as was indeed the case in Chile.[11] Second, in a large number of cases the distortions associated with the capital account take the form of quantitative restrictions, where a given maximum amount of foreign borrowing is allowed. In this case there is no indirect welfare cost (that is, welfare rectangle) in the borrowing market associated with the reduction of trade distortions. These considerations, then, tend to support the presumption that trade liberalization is welfare improving even if distortions in the capital account are maintained.

An important problem related to the welfare effects of economic liberalization in developing countries is whether the external sector should be fully or only partially liberalized. From a theoretical perspective the answer to this question is again clear. Unless the country in question can alter world prices, and in the absence of other distortions, the first best solution is to completely liberalize the economy, eliminating tariffs, quotas, and all restrictions to financial movements. If, on the other hand, the country has a monopoly or monopsony position and can affect world prices, there is a first-best argument for the imposition of some restrictions. This case has been extensively discussed in the trade literature on optimal import tariffs and optimal export taxes (Bhagwati and Srinivasan 1983). From a practical point of view, however, there may be a number of reasons why all restrictions on external transactions should (or could) not be removed. For example, it is possible that, in some instances, there are no superior ways of dealing with other domestic distortions. Even though in these cases trade and capital controls are clearly third-best options, they may be the only alternative available.

While in practice a number of developing countries have a monopoly position in the production of certain commodities, most (if not all) LDCs are small in the world financial market. This, however, does not mean — as the recent experience has forcefully shown — that these countries can borrow infinite amounts at a given interest rate. Quite on the contrary, countries face borrowing limits in the world financial markets, and they are charged a premium that is positively related to the perceived degree of country risk (Eaton and Gersovitz 1980, 1981; Harberger 1983a; Sachs and Cohen 1982). The existence of this country-risk premium implies that even (very) small countries face an upward sloping supply curve for foreign funds, where the interest rate at which they can borrow will increase with a higher level of indebtedness. An empirical study by S. Edwards (1984b) has found a significant and robust positive relation between the spread charged over LIBOR on foreign loans to developing countries and their level of foreign indebtedness. This evidence suggests that there is a negative externality associated with the process of borrowing from abroad in developing countries, stemming from the fact that there is a divergence between the average and marginal cost of foreign borrowing. From a policy perspective the best way of dealing with this problem is by imposing a tax on capital importation.[12] In this case there is a genuine first-best argument for not fully liberalizing the capital account. As Harberger (1982: 13) has put it,

> The corrective for any such externality [the difference between the marginal cost of international credit and its average cost] is something that will lead economic agents to internalize it. In the present case a tax would be the obvious instrument for accomplishing this task.

The Sequencing of Liberalization, Adjustment Costs, and Credibility

The reduction of trade barriers will result in changes in domestic relative prices and in resources' being reallocated across sectors. In general, any process of economic liberalization will require an adjustment period during which firms go through a retooling process and labor acquires new skills. Generally this adjustment process will take time and will be quite costly. Some authors have postulated that in order to increase the probability of success of the trade reform, the adjustment costs (unemployment and others) related to the tariffs reduction should be minimized (see for example, Michaely 1982). The idea of minimizing adjustment costs has been translated into two forms of policy recommendations: (1) Liberalization of trade should be done slowly, and (2) adjustment assistance — usually in the form of foreign funds — should be provided. One possible way of reducing these adjustment costs is through the importation of foreign capital, which would be used to finance a smoother adjustment of the import-competing industries.

According to this view, the capital account should be opened first or simultaneously with the trade account. This would increase the availability of "cheap" funds that could then be used to ease the adjustment process (Little, Scitovsky, and Scott 1970: ch. 10; Michaely 1982: 17). Anne Krueger (1983: 11), for example, while not agreeing with the order "capital account first and trade-account second," has also recognized the possible important role of foreign funds to help achieve a smoother transition. As she puts it,

> [O]ne of the important contributions international lending can make to a country when its leaders are genuinely committed to full liberalization, [is to]...permit higher levels of imports than would otherwise be feasible.... Not only does this reduce the economic and political strains associated with liberalization, it also reduces uncertainty of business as to the likelihood that liberalization will persist.

Paul Clark (1982: 2), on the other hand, argues that the successful liberalization of the Egyptian economy in the 1970s was due, to a large extent, to the adjustment assistance provided by foreign sources: "Egypt's liberalization experience has taken place during a period in which external assistance first rose dramatically."

Arguments for using foreign funds to smooth the adjustment process during a trade liberalization episode are related to arguments in favor of providing adjustment assistance to industries that are negatively affected by (exogenous) changes in the terms of trade.[13] As Bhagwati (1982) has pointed out, the analysis of the adjustment assistance issue requires knowing the path that the economy will take following the change of relative prices (that is, changes in terms of trade and/or tariff reductions). According to the simple textbook case, following a change in relative prices, resources will immediately move out of the sector whose relative price has declined and into the expanding sector. In more complex models, however, there will be adjustment costs, and resource reallocation will take place only slowly and possibly result in short-run losses of output and in unemployment. However, it is important to clearly specify the nature of these adjustment costs before making inferences regarding the desirability of intervening through assistance. If these costs are related to the activity of moving resources between sectors, as in Mussa's (1978) model, and there are no externalities, there is no welfare-related reason to provide adjustment assistance. However, even in the absence of distortions, adjustment assistance might be called for other reasons, like income distribution considerations, as has been argued by Leamer (1980). If, on the other hand, adjustment costs arise from market imperfections—like the existence of minimum wages as in Chile, for example—there is room for intervention. The first-best policy, of course, is to try to eliminate the source of these market imperfections. If, for whatever reason, this first-best policy is not available, second-best solutions should be sought.

McKinnon (1973, 1982) has strongly opposed the idea of using foreign capital flows to assist the trade reform transition period. In fact, in his 1973 book he points out that if capital inflows are allowed the liberalization episodes will generally be aborted. He refers to these cases as "partial liberalization with foreign capital" (1973: 155). This view, of course, is consistent with his position of tightly controlling capital inflows throughout the trade liberalization and is based on the idea that short-term capital movements provide incorrect signals to the private sector. As he has stated (1982: 163):

[T]rade liberalization should proceed *without* relying on unusual short-term inflows of private capital. . . . Such capital inflows are simply not sustainable in the long-run; and during the liberalization process itself they throw out incorrect market signals.

There are two potential problems with this view. First, it is not clear what is meant by "unusual" inflows of capital. Second, there is no theoretical *a priori* reason to believe that these "unusual" capital inflows will provide the wrong signals. In order for this argument to make sense it is necessary to explicitly specify why the private sector will not realize (as the government presumably does in McKinnon's model) that these inflows are temporary and "unusual." If, on the other hand, the private sector does realize the temporary nature of the inflows, they will not throw incorrect signals, and there is no reason, at least on these grounds, to restrict capital movements.

A critical and perhaps even central question regarding this problem is related to the *credibility* of the trade reform. If the public believes that there is some probability that the reform will be reversed in the future, foreign funds, obtained through the opening of the capital account, may be used by the owners of capital in the import substitution industries to maintain their firms functioning at a (temporary?) loss. Alternatively, these funds could be used to finance lobbying activities aimed at convincing government officials of the desirability of reversing the trade reform. This was the case in Argentina where, due to the lack of credibility on the future of the preannounced trade reform, firms used foreign funds in order to survive in the short run. As Carlos Rodriguez (1983: 28) has put it in his evaluation of the Argentina experience of 1978–82,

> As a consequence of the *lack of credibility* on the continuity of the economic program, many firms—which would have disappeared due to the tariff reductions—decided to get into debt in order to remain operating while waiting for a change in the economic strategy [emphasis added].

Also, if agents believe that the trade reform will be reversed, they will tend to borrow heavily today, in order to finance a higher present consumption of imported goods. This, indeed, seems to have been the case in Chile in 1981. This is a perfectly rational strategy if it is expected that importable goods in the future will be more expensive, due to the perceived hike of tariffs. This optimal behavior from a private perspective, however, may result in excessive (that is, nonoptimal) borrowing from the social point of view.

Depending on the degree of credibility a larger availability of foreign funds may either help the adjustment process—by making it politically more pallatable as Krueger suggests—or may frustrate the experience. The degree of credibility, however, should not be viewed as a completely exogenous variable. On the contrary, the strategy followed during the liberalization process will tend to affect this credibility.

A fundamental aspect of establishing credibility is related to the perception that the public has of the internal consistency of the policies being pursued. In that respect, for example, the inconsistency of the Argentinian fiscal policy—which maintained a very large fiscal deficit—and the preannounced exchange rate policy severely undermined the degree of credibility of the reform process. In the case of Chile the markedly overvalued currency in 1981 was seen by large segments of the public as inconsistent with the long-run viability of the liberalized economy. In general, if the real exchange rate experiences an unprecedented real appreciation, the public will think that exports will not be able to develop and that there is a nontrivial probability of the reform's being reversed in the future. Under these circumstances it will be optimal for consumers to get into debt today in order to acquire "cheap" importables.

The present section has focused on some analytical aspects of the sequencing of liberalization of the capital and current accounts of the balance of payments. There are, however, other important issues related to a broadly defined liberalization process that deserve to be briefly mentioned. First, if a liberalization will not completely eliminate all distortions, the question of welfare effects of partial reforms will become critical. Even though theoretically and from a second-best perspective almost anything, in terms of welfare, can happen as a consequence of a partial reform, there are well-founded conjectures that the liberalization of some markets will be welfare improving (see Krueger 1983).

Second, the question of the speed of liberalization is also important. In the simplest textbook case with no market imperfections or externalities, markets should be liberalized very quickly (now). If externalities or market failures are present, however, and the first-best policies to deal with them are not available, a gradual liberalization might be called for (Mussa 1986).

Third, the relationship between liberalization and stabilization is crucial to understand the success or failure of liberalization reforms, since many liberalization attempts have been undertaken in conjunction with major stabilization programs (Krueger 1978; Little 1982).[14] There are some important aspects of the relationship between these two policies that deserve further attention. In particular, in light of the Chilean experience it seems that it may not be desirable to implement an almost complete liberalization at the same time as the economy is going through a major stabilization effect. The reason for this is that, in the public's eyes, it is not clear whether the adjustment costs that have taken place are due to the liberalization or the anti-inflationary programs. Also if the stabilization program relies to any degree on exchange rate management, a real appreciation—which will be detrimental for the liberalization effort—will occur.

THE SEQUENCING OF LIBERALIZATION: LESSONS FROM CHILE

While the analysis presented in this chapter has not yielded a strong *theorem* regarding the appropriate order of liberalizing of the current and capital accounts of the balance of payments, both the historical evidence and the theoretical considerations discussed suggests that a more *prudent* strategy would be based on liberalizing the current account first. Perhaps the strongest case for this ordering is based on the relation between macroeconomic stability, capital flows, the real exchange rate, and credibility. The experience with destabilizing capital flows immediately following a capital account liberalization has generally been negative and has jeopardized other aspects of the reform package. Historical experiences also suggest that the capital account should be opened slowly, so that the possible increase in the stock of foreign debt that will follow the liberalization will be spread through time, reducing the degree of real appreciation and exchange rate deprotection. Also, to the extent that due to the existence of country risk these countries face an upward sloping supply curve of foreign funds, there is an argument for imposing an optimal tax on foreign indebtedness.

The Chilean experiment offers some important lessons for the sequencing debate. First, this episode shows that the destabilizing effects of massive capital movements are much greater than what most observers initially thought. With hindsight we can say that in the Chilean case it would have been advisable to distance even more in time the two reforms. More generally, the experience suggests that in countries whose initial conditions resemble those in Chile in the early 1970s, the capital account should be opened rather slowly and after "sufficient" time has elapsed since the trade reforms have been completed. Of course, it is not possible to state in a precise fashion what "sufficiently after" means. Policymakers, however, should monitor real exchange rate movements and the external sector behavior when deciding how to relax capital movement controls.

Second, the Chilean experiment clearly shows that the destabilizing effects of massive capital movements are greatly magnified in the presence of other distortions like legally imposed wage rigidity.

And third, this experience highlights the crucial role of credibility in the success of an economic reform. Obviously, if the public believes that the reform attempt will be reversed, it will act accordingly and may even be able to frustrate the whole liberalization reform. In the Chilean case the combination of marked exchange rate overvaluation and a passive government macroeconomic policy undermined the public's credibility on the maintenance of both the exchange rate and tariffs policy.[15] It is, we believe, in the credibility sphere where the most important lesson on the sequencing of liberalization lies. In a sense the implementation of a consistent and credible policy package is more important than determining "the correct" order of liberalization.

NOTES

1. A related question — in fact, one that precedes the sequencing of a speedy one — is whether countries should liberalize at all. We believe that as extensive empirical as well as theoretical research has shown, the answer is positive. We discuss the issue in more detail in Chapter 8.
2. See, for example, Park (1985) and World Bank (1986). The issue of the appropriate order of liberalization has also become important in the more analytical literature. See, for example, Rodrick (1985), S. Edwards (1984a, 1986), McKinnon (1982), Frenkel (1983), and Bruno and Sachs (1985).
3. On Argentina see, for example, McKinnon (1982) and Fernandez (1985). On Uruguay see Hanson and de Melo (1985).
4. Parts of this section draw from S. Edwards (1984b).
5. McKinnon (1973) discussed this problem in his classical analysis of economic liberalization policies.
6. From an analytical perspective this is not necessarily the case. Under some circumstances a trade reform may result in a real appreciation. On this issue see the discussion in Chapter 3 of S. Edwards (Forthcoming). However, under the most plausible circumstances in terms of elasticities a trade liberalization will in fact require a real depreciation.

7. An important consequence of a liberalization reform that results in a more extensive use of market mechanisms is that foreign investors will generally perceive an increase in the overall profitability of investing in the domestic country. This point is made, for example, by McKinnon (1986). See also S. Edwards (1985d).

8. The dynamic effect of a capital account liberalization resembles that of the Dutch-Disease. On Dutch-Disease see, for example, the essays collected in Neary and van Wijnbergen (1986). See Chapter 5 of S. Edwards (Forthcoming) for a thorough discussion on the effects of capital movements on the real exchange rate.

9. Deepak Lal (1984) has recently presented an alternative view. According to him, since exchange rate behavior is critical during the transition period from a protected toward a liberalized trade account, it is better *not* to let the government manipulate the nominal exchange rate during this transition. There have been plenty of cases, he argues, where exchange rate management has been inappropriate and has resulted in the trade reform being finally aborted (such as the recent experience of Argentina). For this reason Lal has proposed that a floating exchange rate system with full currency convertibility should be implemented before the trade reform takes place. This, of course, means that the capital account should be liberalized before the trade account. See S. Edwards (1984a) for a discussion of this proposition.

10. The above discussion and the arguments of McKinnon (1973), Frenkel (1982, 1983), and Krueger (1983) focus exclusively on the case where as a consequence of the liberalization of the capital account the additional borrowing is used to increase investment. This, of course, needs not be the case. A fraction (possibly zero) of the new borrowing could be used to increase present consumption. Indeed, that will happen as long as prior to the liberalization the domestic rate of time preferences exceeded the (given) world rate of interest. It is easy to show that under these circumstances and according to the traditional trade model, if all of the (new) foreign borrowing is used for additional present consumption (with the world rate of interest below the domestic rate of the time preferences), welfare will not deteriorate even if there are tariffs.

11. There is an important problem, however, related to the speed of tariff reductions. It is conceivable that if a slow tariff reform is announced today, borrowing will decrease, since the public will postpone consumption to the future, when tariffs will be lower. See S. Edwards and van Wijnbergen (1986a, 1986b).

12. It should be noted that this argument for imposing a first-best optimum tax on capital imports should be qualified in an important way. If borrowers and lenders have the same perception about the probability of default, the country risk premium is not a real part of the cost

of borrowing, and no tax should be imposed on these grounds. If, however, as argued by Harberger (1976, 1980) lenders perceive a larger probability of default than borrowers, there is a first-best reason for imposing such a tax. See also S. Edwards (1986a, 1986b).

13. An important issue, however, is how these additional funds are made available. In one case the capital account is fully opened, and free international borrowing and lending is allowed. Alternatively, the capital account is only partially opened, and some sectors are allowed only to obtain funds from abroad. This latter case is similar to the adjustment assistance literature.

14. There have been, of course, important exceptions to this. For example, the 1983–87 Korean liberalization is being carried out in a framework of great price stability.

15. It is very important to emphasize that from the fact that there are some macroeconomic problems related to the sequencing of reform, it does *not* follow that the capital account should never be opened. Quite on the contrary, there are some obvious benefits from dismantling capital controls — the most important being the possibility of trading intertemporally at world prices. Our discussion points out that in a country like Chile in the early 1970s, there are clear indications that it is more prudent to liberalize the current account first.

8 FROM MIRACLE TO CRISIS
Lessons from the Chilean Experiment

The first decade of the Chilean experiment with free market policies ended in major disappointment. Contrary to what had been expected by the architects of the program and by a number of observers, the economy did not enter a new phase of continuous growth and prosperity. Moreover, the inability to significantly reduce unemployment and the worsening of income distribution represented an important failure of the military social policies. This chapter discusses some of the valuable lessons that have emerged from this experience.

There has been a tendency among some observers, and especially in the popular press, to oversimplify the causes of the collapse of the Chilean economy in 1982. Most of these accounts have tried to single out only one factor as responsible for the failure of the free market attempt.[1] The principal suspects in these searches for "the" failure's cause have usually been the exchange rate policy (that is, the *tablita* and subsequent fixing of the peso) and the marked deterioration of the terms of trade in 1981–82.[2] However, this oversimplified view obscures the important fact that the failure of the Chilean experience was the result of many interwoven factors, which interacted in complex ways to generate yet another disappointment to the Chilean people.

The economy's land-crash of 1982 was the consequence of both domestic policy mistakes and of the greatly deteriorated external environment. Chile, as all the Latin American countries, was hard hit by the 1980–83 world recession, when the value of its exports declined significantly and its debt service ratio increased sharply, in part as a result of the rise in world interest rates. In addition, a number of policy inconsistencies and mistakes — some of which had been mounting since the early years of the experiment — helped magnify the consequences of these foreign disturbances. This chapter analyzes the way in which these domestic and external factors interacted and generated one of the worst recessions the country has ever faced.

EXTERNAL SHOCKS AND THE MAGNITUDE OF THE 1982 CRISIS

In 1981–82 the Chilean economy was hit by three major negative shocks stemming from abroad. First, the terms of trade fell by almost 30 percent between 1980 and 1982. Second, world interest rates skyrocketed. This, plus the lower value of Chilean exports and the rapid accumulation of foreign debt in the preceding years, resulted in an increase in the ratio of debt service to exports from 37 percent in 1980 to almost 60 percent in 1982. And third, the sudden halt in capital inflows from abroad resulted in a large reduction in real expenditure. However, contrary to the rise in world interest rates and the decline in the terms of trade, the drying up of foreign capital inflows was not a completely exogenous factor. It was to a large extent a reaction on behalf of international bankers to the deteriorating domestic conditions and to the policy mistakes.

Although the direct effects of the world recession on the decline of real income in 1982 were not negligible, they were not the dominating force. In Table 8–1 we present data on three alternative indicators on the evolution of economic activity during 1979–83; all of them reflect the seriousness of the 1982 crisis.[3] A comparison of columns A, B, and C in Table 8–1 give a good summary of the extent of the foreign shocks and of the way in which they affected real income in 1982. In that year real gross disposable national income, which is measured in Table 8–1 by real command-basis GNP, declined by 19 percent or 69,076 million of 1977 pesos. It is possible to attribute 8,165 million pesos or 2.2 percentage points of this reduction in real income to the deterioration of the terms of trade in 1982. On the other hand, 6,883

Table 8–1. The Magnitude of the 1982 Crisis.

	(A) Real GDP		(B) Real GNP		(C) Real Command Basis GNP	
	Millions 1977 Pesos	Rate of Change	Millions 1977 Pesos	Rate of Change	Millions 1977 Pesos	Rate of Change
1979	337,207	8.3%	326,386	7.8%	334,026	10.6%
1980	363,446	7.8%	350,456	7.4%	357,818	7.1%
1981	383,551	5.5%	364,181	3.9%	364,240	1.8%
1982	329,523	−14.1%	303,270	−16.7%	295,164	−19.0%
1983	327,180	−0.7%	301,263	−0.7%	297,097	0.7%

Source: Banco Central de Chile (1981, 1983, 1984).

Note: Real GDP measures total production of goods and services, valued at 1977 relative prices. Real GNP adds to real GDP net factor payments from abroad. The real command-basis GNP corrects the real GNP computation by the effects of terms of trade (prices of exports to imports) changes.

million pesos, or 1.9 percent of gross national disposable income, stemmed from the increase in net factor payment to the rest of the world, which was mainly the result of the higher international interest rates.[4] It is interesting to note that in 1982 the adverse external shocks played a significantly less important role than in the 1975 recession. In that year the deterioration of the terms of trade generated a decline in real income of 11 percent — compared to 2.2 percent in 1982 — while the higher net factor payments to the rest of the world reduced real gross national disposable income by 1.7 percent.[5]

Real aggregate expenditure fell even more sharply than real income. The reason for this, of course, was the steep decline in the volume of capital inflows; as the availability of foreign funds was cut, expenditure had to adjust downward. Table 8–2 contains data on the evolution of real expenditure between 1979 and 1983.

The effects of the external shocks on the level of economic activity (that is, output) and employment were greatly compounded by the rigidities introduced into the system by the combination of the fixed exchange rate and the backward indexed wages. Under "normal"

Table 8–2. Real Aggregate Expenditure: 1979–83.

Year	Millions Pesos of 1977	Δ%
1979	354,937	10.5%
1980	387,830	9.3
1981	432,990	11.6
1982	328,832	−24.0
1983	313,669	−4.6

Source: Banco Central de Chile (1981, 1983, 1984).

circumstances a reduction of aggregate domestic demand stemming from negative external factors, such as a decline in the level of capital inflows or deteriorated terms of trade, results in a decline in output and employment in nontradables and in some of the import-competing sectors. As part of the adjustment process the reduction of production in nontradables will be accompanied by a decline in their relative price. However, to the extent that fixed (or increasing) real wages and a fixed nominal exchange rate preclude the relative price of nontradables (which, of course, is the inverse of the real exchange rate) from adjusting, the decline in output and employment will be much higher than under flexible prices. This is indeed what happened in Chile; the reluctance to abandon the inconsistent exchange and wage rate policies in 1981, and the insistence on relying on the automatic adjustment, helped transform what would have been a serious crisis into a catastrophic recession.

Table 8–3 presents data on the behavior of real GDP at the sectoral level between 1980 and 1983. As can be seen, in 1982 two of the main export sectors — mining and fishing — increased production at healthy rates, while production in the agriculture sector declined by only 2.1 percent. On the other hand, production in the manufacturing and services sectors plunged in 1982 and further declined in 1983. Table 8–4 contains data on manufacturing gross domestic product for 1980–83. As can be seen, not all sectors responded in the same way to the 1982 crisis. Production of the most important industrial export sectors — food and paper products — declined by relatively small percentages, while the level of activity in the import-competing sectors were severely affected.

Table 8-3. Rate of Change of Real GDP by Sectors: 1980–83 (percentages).

Sector	1980	1981	1982	1983
Agriculture and forestry	3.6%	2.7%	−2.1%	−3.6%
Fishing	7.5	18.1	9.4	8.8
Mining	5.2	7.7	5.7	−1.9
Manufacturing	6.2	2.6	−21.0	3.1
Electricity, gas, and water	5.0	2.1	0.1	4.3
Construction	23.9	21.1	−23.8	−5.0
Commerce	12.4	4.3	−17.3	−3.5
Transportation and communications	11.1	1.8	−11.8	−1.5
Services	6.7	4.2	−4.8	−9.3
Financial services	22.6	11.9	−5.4	−30.2
Real estate (housing)	1.0	1.5	1.0	0.8
Public administration	−3.2	−1.8	−2.9	2.1
Education	−1.1	−2.3	−0.3	4.3
Health	3.3	3.2	−8.0	0.9
Other services	5.7	3.3	−16.2	−2.6
Minus: Imputed bank service charge	41.0	27.6	−5.4	−57.8
Plus: Import duties	22.4	34.0	−44.2	−17.4
Gross domestic product	7.8	5.5	−14.1	−0.7

Source: Banco Central de Chile (1981, 1983, 1984).

THE CONDUCT OF ECONOMIC POLICY AND THE COLLAPSE OF THE CHILEAN ECONOMY

The foreign shocks conspired with a number of policy inconsistencies and mistakes to generate the great recession of 1982. In fact, in the absence of these policy problems the effects of the external shocks on the Chilean economy would have been significantly less severe and traumatizing. These policy mistakes were related both to the way the economics reforms were implemented and to the way in which macro-economic policy was conducted.

Table 8-4.   Real Manufacturing Gross Domestic Product:
1980-83 (millions of 1977 pesos).

Sector	1980	1981	1982	1983
1. Food, beverages, and tobacco	26.631	27.251	25.564	25.790
2. Textiles, apparel, and leather industries	6.880	6.172	4.165	4.635
3. Wood and wood products, including furniture	4.224	5.061	2.990	3.092
4. Paper and paper products, printing, and publishing	6.877	7.538	6.880	7.191
5. Chemical, petroleum, rubber, and plastic products	11.946	12.655	10.202	10.465
6. Nonmetallic mineral products	2.882	3.003	1.527	2.624
7. Basic metal industries	3.036	2.885	2.484	2.986
8. Metal products, machinery, and equipment	15.001	14.512	8.480	7.419
9. Other manufacturing industries	854	1.259	1.228	1.264
Total	78.331	80.336	63.500	65.466

Source: Banco Central de Chile (1981, 1983, 1984).

A first area of major policy problems relates to the way in which the privatization process and the reform of the financial sector were undertaken — basically with no supervision of the banks' behavior. This allowed the *grupos* to grow at phenomenal rates on the basis of an exceedingly fragile financial structure. This financial fragility affected the economy in several ways. First, as discussed in Chapter 3, it resulted in an almost continuous increase in the *grupos'* demand for credit and in the rolling over of "bad loans" by banks, with the consequent upward pressure on the demand for credit and interest rates. Second, and possibly more important, it greatly increased the vulnerability of the financial and industrial sectors to adverse foreign shocks, such as the reduction in the demand for Chile's exports and the hike in world interest rates. In fact, the financial situation of most of the largest *grupos* was so weak that already in 1980 many of their firms could avoid bankruptcy only because of the continuous injection of debt (ultimately) obtained from abroad. As we have discussed at length in the preceding chapters, the financial condition of firms in the tradables sector was aggravated by the steady real appreciation that took place after mid-1979. The sudden halt of capital inflows from the international financial community in late 1981 merely precipitated the collapse of banks, firms, and *grupos*.

The difficulties faced by the financial sector and some of the major *grupos* had important costs for the economy, which were amplified by the passive views that the authorities had regarding macroeconomic adjustment and by their complacent attitude toward bankruptcy. Moreover, once the financial situation of banks and firms became too serious for the government to ignore, its intervention introduced a series of distortive measures that had important negative effects on the distribution of the adjustment costs across the population. These measures included the imposition of a lower exchange rate for foreign currency debtors after the successive devaluations of 1982 and 1983.

The timing of the opening of the capital account was another mistake. Although contrary to the case of Argentina, care was taken not to lift exchange controls at the same time as import tariffs were lowered, the massive inflow of foreign capital that followed the liberalization of the capital account generated forces that played a major role in the appreciation of the real exchange rate. Of course, the conjunction of relaxed exchange controls with a completely unsupervised domestic banking system—plus *grupos'* competing to grow at the fastest possible pace—set the stage for a situation where substantial "overborrowing" took place. The overborrowing was fueled in part by the public's perceptions about the future. On one hand, during the boom years, the sharp increase in perceived wealth resulted in the use of foreign funds to finance the acquisition of imported goods, mainly durables. Later on, as the combination of high interest rates and sharp overvaluation generated expectations of a reversal of the trade liberalization reform, the acquisition of durables financed by foreign borrowing increased at an even faster pace.[6]

The failure to recognize the dynamics of real exchange rate behavior following the opening of the capital account was another problem. In particular, the authorities did not realize that the large real appreciation that followed the lifting of exchange controls exceeded the new long-run equilibrium real appreciation. When lifting capital controls in a country like Chile in 1979, after an initial "jump" in capital inflows, their level will start to decline toward their new long-run equilibrium, and a real depreciation will have to take place. It was this "required" reversal of the real exchange rate movement that was precluded by the indexation mechanism in late 1981 and 1982. As the real exchange rate could not depreciate to the new level required to maintain macroeconomic equilibrium, there was an adjustment through reduced aggregate supply and employment.

The maintenance, and in some instances even increase, of a number of rigidities in the labor market was another mistake that was translated into a persistent and very high level of unemployment during most of the experiment. The backward wage indexation mechanism was the chief rigidity; it interacted with existing distortions such as labor segmentation and did not allow the labor market to adjust smoothly to the different liberalization reforms and to the exogenous shocks. The basic problem was that imposing an economywide and general wage adjustment mechanism during a period of drastic structural reforms greatly affected the aggregate and sectoral demands for labor, and unnecessarily high adjustment costs were introduced. The combination of these rigidities with the major structural changes introduced an important wage-gap that persisted through the period.[7]

Much of the discussion in this book has revolved around the exchange rate policy followed by the military government. The combination of a fixed exchange rate with the 100 percent indexed wage rate after June 1979 was a serious blunder, which as shown in the simple model of Chapters 2 and 3 was destined to generate a badly overvalued real exchange rate.[8] This policy mishap interacted with problems emanating from other areas to make things worse. For example, the opening of the capital account, started the same month the exchange rate was fixed, generated additional (and fatal) forces that further appreciated the real exchange rate. As the real overvaluation became unsustainable, the expectations of devaluation started to mount and exercise considerable upward pressure on interest rates. These higher real interest rates, in turn, further reduced the level of economic activity.

Much has been speculated on what would have happened if the Chilean authorities had followed different exchange and wage indexation policies. There is little doubt that had the government decided to adopt a floating exchange rate in mid-1979 or early 1980, the real overvaluation would have been somewhat smaller by mid-1981. However, the effect on the real exchange rate of the higher real expenditure made possible by the increase in foreign borrowing would not have disappeared. Under floating or other nonpegged exchange rate policy the magnitude of the capital inflows would have been smaller, but still substantial and still requiring a real appreciation of the peso.[9]

Regarding wages, much of the problem stemmed from having indexed them to past changes of prices, under conditions of rapidly decreasing inflation and changing structural conditions. An alternative would have been to devise a system that would have indexed them to some good proxy of current or, even better, future inflation. The problem with this, of course, is that we don't know the future rate of inflation! An alternative mechanism, fully consistent with the overall spirit of the stabilization policy, would have been to index the wage rate to the *tablita* preannounced rate of devaluation. It is easy to see from the model in Chapter 3 that in this case the inertial component of the rate of overvaluation would tend to disappear.[10]

Although the adoption of a fixed exchange rate in the presence of indexed wages—or was it the maintenance of wage indexation once the exchange rate was fixed?—was a mistake, the passive and even indolent attitude of the government once the macroeconomic disequilibrium became apparent was even more serious. In fact, this area of passive macroeconomic policy is where we believe reside some of the crucial mistakes. By refusing to act on the face of major macroeconomic disequilibria such as the steep climb of interest rates, the increase in bankruptcies, the sustained real overvaluation, and the massive increase in the current account deficit in the first half of 1981, the magnitude of the crisis was unnecessarily deepened. As the crisis unraveled the passive attitude of the government resulted in a loss of credibility on the long-run viability of the experiment and created growing expectations of a major catastrophe and of a reversal of liberalization policies. Even as late as during the first half of 1981 the adoption of a pragmatic and active macro policy, consisting of the abandonment of the fixed rate at the same time as reforming the indexation mechanism and placing a check on the foreign debt, would have helped to reduce the extent of the free-fall. It should be recognized, however, that in many ways it was too late; at that time the economy was already suffering the consequences of the previous policy inconsistencies, and additional supporting active policies at many other levels would have been required. For example, some measures should have been taken to solve the financial crisis faced by most banks, firms, and *grupos*.

LESSONS

Why were these policy mistakes made? Was it, in any way, obvious from the beginning that these were ill decisions, or is it only now that with hindsight we can recognize them? The answer to this is that some of the mistakes were fairly obvious early on — for example, the lack of supervision of the financial sector was manifest in 1976 with the Banco Osorno crisis — and were in fact the subject of some (limited) debate. Others became apparent only slowly through time. However, during the first half of 1981 it became clear that something fundamentally wrong was going on, and it was apparent that the economy had moved to a situation of a major policy-induced macroeconomic disequilibrium. In fact, many of these mistakes were labeled as such by some observers as early as (or as late as) 1980. The political environment had undoubtedly some effect on the type and magnitude of the policy mistakes. The limitations imposed by the military on critical scrutiny by the political opposition allowed the "Chicago boys" to pursue what Carlos Díaz-Alejandro (1983) has called the "practical orthodoxy," including the naive views related to the simplest (that is, textbook) version of the monetary approach to the balance of payments. Moreover, the lack of real political accountability of the economic authorities to a broad spectrum of the population allowed them to stick for a long time to poor policies like the joint wage–exchange rate fixity and the passive macroeconomic automatic adjustment program.[11]

The Chilean experiment has shown that a small liberalized economy is extremely sensitive to policy inconsistencies. In particular, mistakes at the macroeconomic level are paid for dearly. In a liberalized environment policy blunders that would have had very minor effects in highly controlled settings are quickly propagated and affect the functioning of the different markets. Moreover, in a liberalized economy the public quickly becomes quite sophisticated in economic matters and will generally recognize these policy mistakes. In an effort to anticipate their consequences the public may introduce additional destabilizing forces.

A major lesson emanating from this experience is that the transition period from a controlled economy to a liberalized one is much more complex than what economists had thought. The dynamic path of the different variables will depend both on the sequencing of the liberalization reforms and on the accompanying macropolicies. As pointed out in Chapter 7 a lesson of the Chilean case is that the opening of the capital account should be managed with extreme care and should generally follow by a sufficient period of time the removal of restrictions to trade in commodities.[12] An incorrect sequencing of reform can have negative welfare effects and, more seriously, can affect the perceived consistency of the policies and thus the degree of credibility that the public has on the reforms. Once credibility is lost, the public will not undertake the actions sought by the liberalization reforms — that is, resources will not move to the newly liberalized sectors — and the reforms themselves will be in jeopardy.

The Chilean experiment has also shown, once again, that the use of the exchange rate as a stabilization tool entails a number of risks. In the presence of wage rate rigidities a preannounced rate of devaluation at a rate substantially below the ongoing rate of inflation will almost invariably generate a substantial real overvaluation. The Chilean episode was an extreme case where the wage rate rigidities were institutionally imposed in the form of indexation mechanisms.

The key role played by the failure of the financial sector in the unraveling of the Chilean events has brought forward the need to compare the ills of excessive regulation with those of almost complete lack of effective supervision of the financial sector. It turns out that these two concepts are not necessarily antagonistic. In fact, the lesson is that while a serious effort should be made to get rid of the "excessive" regulation (that is, arbitrary allocation of credit and negative real interest rates), there still should be an appropriate degree of bank supervision that would ensure that a fragile financial structure does not emerge, as was the case in Chile. Also, the Chilean experience has made clear that the indiscriminate (implicit) granting of government deposit insurance may lead to serious situations of moral hazard that can have negative effects on the overall stability of the financial system.

Another important lesson is that the liberalization of the financial markets is not necessarily translated in the short- to medium-run into higher savings. The process governing the consumption-savings decisions is a very complex one that depends on a number of variables of which interest rates is only one and maybe not even the most important. More specifically, to the extent that savings respond to wealth in a Metzlerian way, it is likely that, at least initially, as the reforms raise expectations of future income and wealth, domestic savings will fail to increase even in light of higher real interest rates.

The persistence of unemployment was a major shortcoming of the experience and shows that following major structural reforms the adjustment process in the labor market can take a substantial period of time. This suggests that in order to expedite tariff liberalization reforms and reduce their short-run impact on employment, some active government policies, such as retraining programs and moving subsidies, may be desirable.

Although there were serious mistakes, and at the end of the road the economy's performance fell considerably shorter than what had been expected, there were some important achievements during the period 1973–83. Chief among them was the elimination of a great number of atavistic and paralyzing regulations that had penalized the Chilean economy for many decades. The enhanced use of the price system to allocate resources, the tax reform that eliminated numerous distortions and introduced a modern value added tax, the rationalization of the foreign trade regime, and the import tariffs reform that eliminated a number of discriminating laws, were all important accomplishments. In fact, until 1979, in spite of the existence of a number of problem areas such as unemployment, low investment ratios, and increasing unsupervised ownership concentration in the industrial and financial sectors, things had worked quite well on some fronts. The fiscal deficit had been eliminated; while still high, inflation had reached historical levels; exports had been greatly diversified and had grown at a very fast pace; an important modernization of the economic structure — reflected in the very high rates of growth of productivity — was taking place; and output was growing at healthy rates.

The liberalization of international trade and the resulting increase in efficiency, productivity, and export growth until 1980 was possibly the major economic achievement of this period. In fact, there is generalized agreement among economists and experts of different political persuasion that perhaps with some variations, the new liberalized foreign trade regime should be maintained by future democratically elected governments.[13]

In spite of its disappointing final outcome, the Chilean experiment does not constitute a case against the implementation of liberalization reforms aimed at increasing the use of market prices as an incentive system in the developing countries. It shows, however, that implementing a major liberalization is a formidable task that requires careful and, many times, pragmatic policy decisions.[14] More specifically, the Chilean experience constitutes a case for paying particular attention to the evolution and supervision of the financial system after its liberalization.[15] But more important, the Chilean experience presents a very strong case against dogmatic and rigid stances toward macroeconomic policy. In Chile, the application of some simplistic and erroneous macroeconomic ideas with religious zeal created a major disequilibrium that not only resulted in the deceleration of growth and eventual disastrous fall in the level of output but also compromised the continuity of the reforms themselves. The stubborn insistence in maintaining a passive macroeconomic policy during a period of major upheaval in the world economy greatly exacerbated the effects of the adverse foreign shocks. Moreover, the high priests of the "practical orthodoxy" failed to recognize that in an open market-oriented economy, policy inconsistencies are rapidly transmitted to the private sector through the (newly liberalized) price system, generating unsustainable pressures on firms and banks. More than anything, the Chilean reformist experience has shown that it is in fact essential to accompany any liberalization attempt with consistent and credible macroeconomic policies.

Thirteen years after the Pinochet coup, the Chilean economy is once again struggling to get on its feet. To a large extent most of the market oriented reforms are still in place. The backward indexation mechanism and the fixed exchange rate, however, are long gone. Between 1983, the last year covered in this study, and early 1986, inflation has wandered around 25 percent, output has recovered slowly, and unemployment has somewhat declined. Once again, under a high real exchange rate, noncopper exports have grown quite rapidly. The financial system has been reorganized, and some of the collapsed banks have been auctioned to the private sector. This time an effort has been made to avoid the ownership concentration of the 1970s. The medium-run perspectives, however, are not the brightest. The heavy burden associated with the payment of the foreign debt, the low investment ratio of the past decade and a half, and the projections of a depressed price of copper indicate that the growth path of the next years will be moderate at best. There is little doubt that the major problem Chile faces in 1986 is political. The main issue that occupies the minds and efforts of the great majority of the people is the return to democracy. Hopefully, the policymakers of the future democratic governments would have learned that although a coherent program is a requirement for a credible and sustainable policy, dogmatism, religious zeal, and arrogance in policy matters more often than not lead to disaster.

NOTES

1. As noted in Chapter 1, whether the Chilean experience with free market policies was or was not a failure may be a subject of some debate. For example, some authors (Michaely 1982) have defined failure of a liberalization attempt as the reversal of the reform policies. Under that definition the experiment did not fail, since, at least until early 1986, most of the reforms were in place, with only minor amendments. However, if failure is defined as a significant deviation between expected (and publicized) overall results of the policies and actual results, then the Chilean experience was a failure. This, however, does not mean that there were no accomplishments.

2. For a good popular discussion on the collapse of the Chilean economy see "Pinochet Sends the Chicago Boys Back to School" (1985).

3. Since the most traditional measures of economic activity — real gross domestic product (GDP) and real gross national product (GNP) — measure total production of goods and services at given relative prices (those of the base year), it is not possible to learn from them the direct, first-round effect of the decline in terms of trade on the economy. This makes the analysis of the effect of external shocks a somewhat difficult task.

4. These figures give us information on only the direct effect of the exogenous factors on real income, since they ignore the indirect effects related to the exogenously generated reduction of real income on the production of goods and services. The importance of this indirect effect will depend on adjustment costs and on the existence of rigidities.

5. These computations are in agreement with those discussed in Balassa (1985). Díaz-Alejandro (1983) and Sachs (1986) also pointed out that the 1980–83 world recession played a nontrivial role in the dismal performance of the Latin American economies in the first half of the 1980s.

6. We mean *overborrowing* from a social point of view. Using a general equilibrium simulation model Condon, Corbo, and de Melo (1986) have argued that if the capital controls had been relaxed later and more slowly, the extent of the overvaluation would have been reduced and the drop in real output would have been smaller.

7. *Wage-gap* is defined as the difference between actual real wage and the equilibrium value of the marginal productivity of labor compatible with a "normal" rate of unemployment. See Bruno and Sachs (1985).

8. However, as discussed in Chapter 5, during the first years a sustained effort was made to complement the tariff reform with a crawling peg exchange rate system aimed at helping maintain a competitive exchange rate, which helped encourage noncopper exports. Moreover, the adoption of the preannounced rate of devaluation between 1978 and mid-

1979 did not generate the negative effects on the degree of competitiveness suggested by some authors (Corbo 1986a). Obviously, since the real exchange rate is a real variable, its long-run (or steady state) equilibrium value cannot be affected by the nominal exchange rate policy. However, due to the existence of rigidities and adjustment lags the nominal exchange rate policy can have very important effects on the dynamic behavior of the real exchange rate in the short to medium run.

9. Recall the discussion in Chapter 3. See Morandé (1986) empirical analysis.

10. McKinnon (1986) has proposed this mechanism of "forward looking indexation." A question that emerges at this point is, Why index at all? Obviously, under conditions of rapid inflation, even in the absence of government intervention, periodic wage adjustments of magnitudes related in some way to inflation will take place via private agreements. A government-regulated indexation mechanism, if flexible enough, would be helpful and would reduce transaction and negotiations costs. A more difficult question, however, has to do with the frequency and magnitude of the wage adjustment.

11. It is indeed ironic that these free market policies were pushed by an authoritarian dictatorship that had openly manifested disdain for the political principles of free democratic systems (see "Declaracion de Principios de la Junta de Gobierno," in Mendez (1979)). However, it is important to note that as Díaz-Alejandro (1983) forcefully argued, historically there has been no clear correlation between liberalization attempts and repressive political regimes. Moreover, the probability of a free market attempt to survive in the longer run is higher under (more stable) democratic regimes.

12. A possible way to deal with the effects of the opening of the capital account on the real exchange rate is by imposing a dual exchange rate. Interestingly enough, this system was proposed in 1955 by the Klein-Saks Mission. For a comparison of the monetarist experience in the 1950s and in the 1970s see S. Edwards (1985d).

13. Senior economic experts from the opposition have in fact argued for basically maintaining a liberalized low tariffs and export-oriented external sector. For example, in a volume suggestively titled *Economic Reconstruction for Democracy,* Ffrench-Davis (1983) has pointed out that in the future policymakers should make sure that commercial policies are export oriented and that import tariffs should have an average between 20 and 30 percent, with a range between 10 and 50 percent. Tironi (1985), on the other hand, has argued that an adequate tariff system should have an average of approximately 25 percent with a range of 10 to 35 percent. Both authors have also suggested the implementation of surcharges for "luxury" imports in the form of consumption

taxes and of a system that would reduce the price volatility of agricultural products. Although these propositions diverge from the uniform 10 percent import tariff implemented by the military, they are clearly on the "liberalized" side and represent a major improvement over the abominable levels of protection of the 1960s and of the early 1970s.

14. An important issue has to do with the degree of reform. Most other liberalization attempts that have been scrutinized in the literature have been relatively timid (see Krueger 1978). The Chilean case, on the other hand, was a major attempt that "went all the way."

15. The practical aspects related to privatization have become a subject of debate in a number of countries. See, for example, Kay and Thompson (1986) and Brittan (1986).

BIBLIOGRAPHY

Aedo, C., and F. Lagos. 1984. "Protección Efectiva en el Sector Manufacturero" ["Effective Protection in the Manufacturing Sector"]. Working Paper. Santiago: Universidad Católica de Chile.

Ahumada, J. 1958. *En Vez de la Miseria* [*An Alternative to Misery*]. Santiago: Editorial del Pacifico.

Alaluf, D., ed. 1972. *La Economía Chilean en 1972* [*The Chilean Economy in 1982*]. Santiago: Instituto de Economía Universidad de Chile.

Allende, S., et al. 1971. *El Pensamiento Económico del Gobierno de Allende* [*The Economic Program of the Allende Government*]. Santiago: Editorial Universitaria.

Aranda, S., and A. Martínez. 1970. "Estructura Económica: Algunas Características Fundamentales" ["Economic Structure: Some Basic Characteristics"]. In *Chile Hoy*, edited by A. Pinto, pp. 55–172. Santiago, Chile: Editorial Universitaria.

Arellano, J., ed. 1982. *Modelo Económico Chileno: Trayectoria de una Crítica. [Chilean Economic Model: The Critics]*. Santiago: Editorial Aconcagua.

———. 1984. "Una Nota sobre las Causas del Desempleo en Chile" ["A Note on the Causes of Unemployment in Chile"]. *Colección Estudios Cieplán* 14 (September): 99–104.

————. 1985. "De la Liberalización a la Intervención: El Mercado de Capitales en Chile, 1974–83" ["From Liberation to Intervention: The Capital Market in Chile"]. *El Trimestre Económico* 48: 721–72.

Arellano, J., and J. Ramos. 1986. "Capital Flight in Chile." Paper presented at the Institute for International Economics Conference on "Capital Flight and Third World Debt." Washington, D.C.

Arriagada P. 1986. "Adjustment by Agricultural Exporters in Chile During 1974–82." In *Scrambling for Survival,* edited by Vittorio Corbo and Jaime de Melo, pp. 119–54. Working Paper 764. Washington, D.C.: The World Bank.

Atkinson, A. 1975. *The Economics of Inequality.* Oxford: Oxford University Press.

Balassa, B. 1971. *The Structure of Protection in Developing Countries.* Baltimore: Johns Hopkins University Press.

————. 1982. *Development Strategies in Semi-Industrial Economies.* Oxford: Oxford University Press.

————. 1985. "Policy Experiments in Chile, 1973–1983." In *The National Economic Policies of Chile,* edited by G.M. Walton, pp. 203–38. Greenwich, Conn.: JAI Press.

Ballesteros, M., and T. Davis. 1963. "The Growth of Output and Employment in Basic Sectors of the Chilean Economy, 1908–1957." *Economic Development and Cultural Change* 12 (March): 152–76.

Banco Central de Chile. 1981. *Indicadores Económicos, 1960–1980.* [*Economic Indicators*]. Santiago.

————. 1983. *Indicadores Económicos y Sociales 1960–1982* [*Social and Economic Indicators*]. Santiago.

————. 1984. *Cuentas Nacionales de Chile, 1960–1983* [*National Accounts*]. Santiago.

————. *Boletín Mensual* [Monthly Bulletin]. Various issues.

Barandiarán, E. 1977. "Una Nota sobre Política Cambiaria" ["A Note on Exchange Policy"]. Documento no. 50. Departamento Estudios B.H.C. Santiago.

————. 1983. "La Crisis Financiera Chilena" ["The Chilean Financial Crisis"]. Documento de Trabajo no. 6. Centro de Estudios Publicos. Santiago.

Barandiarán, E.; F. Montt; and M. Pollack. 1982. *Noveno Informe de Coyuntura* [*9th Economic Report*]. Departamento Estudios B.H.C. Santiago.

Bardón, A., and F. Bacigalupo. 1980. "Algunos Puntos Referentes al Manejo Monetario en Chile" ["Some Aspects of Monetary Management in Chile."] *Boletín Banco Central* 53 (July): 1947–54.

Bardón, A.; C. Carrasco; and A. Vial. 1985. *Una Década de Cambios Económicos: La Experiencia Chilena 1973–1983* [*A Decade of Economic Changes*]. Santiago: Ed. Andres Bello.

Barletta, A.; M. Blejer; and L. Landau, eds. 1984. *Economic Liberalization in Argentina, Chile and Uruguay: The Monetary Approach to the Balance of Payments.* Washington, D.C.: World Bank.

Behrman, J. 1976. *Foreign Trade Regimes and Economic Development.* Cambridge, Mass.: Ballinger Publishing Co.

———. 1977. *Macroeconomic Policy in a Developing Country: The Chilean Experience.* New York: North-Holland.

Berry, A., and R. Sabot. 1978. "Labor Market Performance in Developing Countries: A Survey." *World Development* 6 (December): 1199–2421.

Bhagwati, J. 1978. *Anatomy and Consequences of Exchange Control Regimes.* Cambridge, Mass.: Ballinger.

———. 1982. "Directly Unproductive Profit-Seeking Activities." *Journal of Political Economy* 90 (October): 934–48.

Bhagwati, J., and T.N. Srinivasan. 1979. "Trade Policy and Development." In *International Economic Policy: Theory and Evidence,* edited by R. Dornbush and J.A. Frenkel, pp. 1–34. Johns Hopkins University Press.

———. 1980. "Revenue Seeking: A Generalization of the Theory of Tariffs." *Journal of Political Economy* 88 (December): 1069–87.

———. 1983. *Lectures in International Trade.* Cambridge, Mass.: MIT Press.

Bolsa de Comercio Santiago, Chile. "Estadísticas" ["Statistics"]. Various issues.

Brock, P.L. "Financial Controls and Economic Liberalization in Latin America." *Journal of Interamerican Studies and World Affairs* 27, no. 4 (Winter): 125–40.

Brittan, S. 1986. "Privatisation: A Comment on Kay and Thompson." *The Economic Journal* 96 no. 381 (March): 33–38.

Bruno, M. 1985. "The Reforms and Macroeconomic Adjustment. Introduction." *World Development* 13 no. 8. (August): 867–70.

Bruno, M., and J. Sachs. 1985. *Economics of Worldwide Stagflation.* Oxford: Basil Blackwell.

Calvo, G.A. 1986a. "Fractured Liberalism: Argentina under Martinez de Hoz." *Economic Development and Cultural Change* (April): 511–34.

———. 1986b. "Welfare, Banks, and Capital Mobility: The Case of Predetermined Exchange Rates." In *Economic Adjustment and Exchange Rates in Developing Countries,* edited by S. Edwards and L. Ahamed. Chicago: University of Chicago Press.

Castaneda, T. 1983. "Evolución del Empleo y Desempleo y el Impacto de Cambios Demográficos sobre la Tasa de Desempleo en Chile: 1960–1983" ["Employment and Unemployment and the Effect of Demographic Changes of the Unemployment Rate in Chile"]. Documento Serie Investigación no. 64. Departamento de Economía, Universidad de Chile. Santiago.

Cauas, J., and V. Corbo. 1972. "La Economía Chilena en 1971 y Perspectivas para 1972" ["The Chilean Economy in 1971 and Projections for 1972"]. Serie Informes de Coyuntura no. 1. Departamento de Economía. Universidad Católica. Santiago.

Chenery, H. 1960. "Patterns of Industrial Growth." *American Economic Review* 51 (March): 18–51.

——. 1975. "The Structuralist Approach to Development Policy." *Papers and Proceedings of the American Economic Association* 65 (May): 310–16.

Cheyre H., and E. Symon. 1985. "Evolución del Gasto Público en la Década 1974–1983" ["The Evolution of Public Expenditure during 1974–1983"]. *Revista de Economia* 33 (April): 20–28.

Clark, P. 1982. "Step by Step Liberalization of a Controlled Economy: Experiences in Egypt." Unpublished paper. Washington, D.C.

Cline, W., and S. Weintraub, eds. 1981. *Economic Stabilization in Developing Countries.* Washington, D.C.: Brookings Institution.

Coeymans, J.E. 1978. "Liberalización del Comercio Exterior y sus Efectos sobre la Asignación de Recursos y Empleo" ["Trade Liberalization and Its Effects on the Allocation of Resources and Employment"]. *Cuadernos de Economía* 15: 183–246.

Condon, T.; V. Corbo; and J. de Melo. 1983. *A Simulation Analysis of the Macroeconomic Effects of Capital Inflows and Wage Indexation in Chile, 1977–81.* DRD Working Paper no. 108. Washington, D.C.: World Bank.

——. 1986. "Capital Inflows, the Current Account, and the Real Exchange Rate: Tradeoffs for Chile." Washington, D.C.: World Bank.

Connolly, M., and C. Gonzales. 1986. *Economic Resources and Stabilization in Latin America.* New York: Praeger.

Corbo, V. 1974. *Inflation in Developing Countries.* New York: North-Holland.

——. 1982. "Inflación en una Economía Abierta: El Caso de Chile" ["Inflation in an Open Economy: The Chilean Case"]. *Cuadernos de Economía* no. 56 (April): 5–16.

——. 1985a. "Reforms and Macroeconomic Adjustment in Chile during 1974–1983." *World Development* 13, no. 8 (August): 893–916.

——. 1985b. "Chilean Economic Policy and International Economic Relations since 1970." In *The National Economic Policies of Chile,* edited by G.M. Walton, pp. 107–44. Greenwich, Conn.: JAI Press.

——. 1986a. "The Use of the Exchange Rate for Stabilization Purposes: The Case of Chile." Discussion paper no. DRD132. Washington, D.C.: The World Bank.

——. 1986b. "The Role of the Real Exchange Rate in Macroeconomic Adjustment: The Case of Chile, 1973–82." Discussion Paper no. DRD145. Washington, D.C.: The World Bank.

————. 1986c. "International Prices, Wages and Inflation in an Open Economy: A Chilean Model." *The Review of Economic and Statistics* 67 (November): 564–73.

Corbo, V.; J. de Melo; and J. Tybout. 1986. "What Went Wrong with the Recent Reforms in the Southern Cone?" *Economic Development and Cultural Change* 34, no. 3 (April): 607–40.

Corbo, V., and P. Meller. 1979. "Trade and Employment: Chile in the 60s." *American Economic Review* (February): 112–16.

————. 1981. "Alternative Trade Strategies and Employment Implications: Chile." In *Trade and Employment in Developing Countries,* vol. 1, edited by A.O. Krueger, H.B. Lary, T. Monson, and N. Akrasanee, pp. 83–134. Chicago, Illinois: University of Chicago Press.

Corbo, V., and J.M. Sánchez. 1985. "How Firms Adjusted to the Reforms in Chile." Working paper. Washington, D.C.: World Bank.

Cortázar, R. 1980. "Distribución del Ingreso, Empleo y Remuneraciones Reales en Chile, 1970–1978" ["Income Distribution, Employment, and Real Wages"]. *Coleccion Estudios Cieplan* 3 (June): 5–24.

————. 1982. "Chile: Distributive Results." Working paper. Cieplan.

Cortázar, R., and J. Marshall. 1980. "Indice de Precios al Consumidor en Chile, 1970–1978" ["Consumers' Price Index in Chile, 1970–1978"]. *Colección Estudios Cieplán* no. 4 (November): 159–201.

Cortés, H. 1983. "Stabilization Policies in Chile: Inflation, Unemployment and Depression 1975–1982." Documento de Trabajo no. 85. Santiago: Instituto de Economía, Universidad Catolica.

Cortés, H.; A. Butelmann; and P. Videla. 1981. "Proteccionismo en Chile: Una Visión Retrospectiva" ["Protectionism in Chile: A Retrospective View"]. In "La Economía Política de la Reforma Comercial en Chile", edited by L. Sjaastad and H. Cortes-Douglas. *Cuadernos de Economía* nos. 54–55 (August/December): 141–94.

CORFO. *Cuentas Nacionales* [*National Accounts*]. Various issues.

Cumby, R., and S. van Wijnbergen. 1983. "Fiscal Policy and the Collapse of Preannounced Rate of Devaluation: Argentina." Working paper. Washington, D.C.: World Bank.

Dahse, F. 1979. *Mapa de la Extrema Riqueza* [*Identifying High Income Groups*]. Santiago: Editorial Aconcagua.

Davis, T. "Eight Decades of Inflation in Chile, 1879–1959: A Political Interpretation." *Journal of Political Economy* 71 (August): 389–97.

de Castro, S. 1981. *Exposición de la Hacienda Publica* [*Minister of Finance Yearly Economic Report*]. Santiago: Ministerio de Hacienda.

de Gregorio, J. 1984. "Comportamiento de las Exportaciones e Importaciones en Chile: Un Estudio Econométrico" ["Exports and Imports in Chile: An Econometric Study"]. *Colección Estudios Cieplán* 13 (June): 53–86.

de la Cuadra, S. 1969. "La Protección Efectiva en Chile" ["Effective Protection in Chile"]. Working paper. Santiago: Universidad Católica de Chile.

―――. 1980. "Inflación y Tipo de Cambio: Experiencia Reciente" ["Inflation and the Exchange Rate: The Recent Experience"]. *Boletín Mensual Banco Central* 53 (October): 1955–64.

―――. 1981. "Política Cambiaria y Deuda Externa" ["Exchange Rate Policy and Foreign Debt"]. *Boletín Mensual Banco Central* 53 (May): 1021–26.

de la Cuadra, S., and D. Hachette. 1986. "The Timing and Sequencing of a Trade Liberalization Policy: The Case of Chile." Santiago: Universidad Católica.

de Melo J., and S. Urata. 1984. "Market Structure and Performance: The Role of International Factors in a Trade Liberalization." World Bank DRD Discussion Paper no. 71. Washington, D.C.: World Bank.

Díaz-Alejandro, C. 1970. *Essays on the Economics of the Argentine Republic.* New Haven: Yale University Press.

―――. 1982. "Latin America in Depression, 1929–39." In *The Theory and Experience of Economic Development,* Essays in Honor of Sir W. Arthur Arthur Lewis, edited by M. Gersovitz, C. Díaz-Alejandro, G. Ranis, and M.R. Rosenzweig, pp. 334–55. London: George Allen & Unwin.

―――. 1983. "¿Economía Abierta y Política Cerrada?" ["Liberalized Economy and Repressed Politics?"]. *El Trimestre Económico* 50, no. 197 (January/March): 207–44.

Doeringer, P.B., and M.J. Piore. 1971. *Internal Labor Markets and Manpower Analysis.* Lexington, Mass.: Heath.

Dornbusch, R. 1983a. "Real Interest Rates, Home Goods and Optimal External Borrowing." *Journal of Political Economy* 91 (February): 141–53.

―――. 1983b. "Remarks on the Southern Cone." *IMF* Staff Papers no. 30 (March): 173–76.

―――. 1984. "External Debt, Budget Deficits, and Disequilibrium Exchange Rates." *NBER Working Paper* no. 1336. Cambridge, Mass.

―――. 1985. "External Debt, Budget Deficits and Disequilibrium Exchange Rates." In *International Debt and the Developing Countries,* edited by G. Smith and J. Cuddington, pp. 213–35. Washington, D.C.: World Bank.

Dornbusch, R., and S. Fischer. 1986. "Stopping Hyperinflations: Past and Future." NBER Working Paper no. 1810. Cambridge, Mass.

Eaton, J., and M. Gersovitz. 1980. "LDC Participation in International Financial Markets: Debt and Reserves." *Journal of Development Economics* 7 (March): 3–21.

―――. 1981. "Debt with Potential Repudiation: Theoretical and Empirical Analysis." *Review of Economics and Statistics* 48 (April): 289–310.

Edwards, A. Cox. 1984. "Three Essays on Labor Markets in Developing Countries." Ph.D. dissertation, University of Chicago.

———. 1985. "Wage Indexation and Real Wages: Chile 1974–1980." Unpublished paper. Washington, D.C.: World Bank.

———. 1986a. "The Chilean Labor Market 1970–1983: An Overview." Discussion Paper no. DRD152. Washington, D.C.: World Bank.

———. 1986b. "Economic Reform, External Shocks and the Labor Market: Chile 1973–1983." Paper presented at World Bank Conference on Labor Markets in Developing Countries, Washington, D.C., June 27–28.

Edwards, S. 1980a. "El Problema del Empleo en Chile: Un Análisis Preliminar" ["The Employment Problem in Chile: A Preliminary Analysis"]. Documento de Trabajo no. 146. Santiago: Departamento Estudios B.H.C.

———. 1980b. "Condicionantes del Desempleo en Chile" ["The Determinants of Unemployment in Chile"]. Documento de Trabajo no. 145. Santiago: Departamento Estudios B.H.C.

———. 1981. "El Mercado Accionario en Chile: Análisis Empírico del Periodo 1977–1981" ["The Stock Market in Chile: An Empirical Analysis of the 1977–1981 Period"]. Documento no. 197. Santiago: Departamento de Estudios B.H.C.

———. 1982. "Trade Liberalization, Minimum Wages and Employment in the Short Run: Some Reflections Based on the Chilean Experience." Working paper. Los Angeles: UCLA.

———. 1984a. "The Role of International Reserves and Foreign Debt in the External Adjustment Process." In *Adjustment Conditionality and International Financing,* edited by J. Muns, pp. 143–73. Washington, D.C.: International Monetary Fund.

———. 1984b. "LDC Foreign Borrowing and Default Risk: An Empirical Investigation 1976–1980." *American Economic Review* 74 (September): 726–34.

———. 1984c. *The Order of Liberalization of the External Sector in Developing Countries.* Princeton, N.J.: Princeton Essays in International Finance.

———. 1985a. "Stabilization with Liberalization: An Evaluation of Ten Years of Chile's Experiment with Free Market Oriented Policies." *Economic Development and Cultural Change* 33 (January): 223–54.

———. 1985b. "Economic Policy and the Record of Economic Growth in Chile, 1973–1982." In *The National Economic Policies of Chile,* edited by G.M. Walton, pp. 11–46. Greenwich, Conn.: JAI Press.

———. 1985c. "Review of Foxley's." *Journal of Development Economics* 17 (September): 321–25.

———. 1985d. "Money, Devaluation and Interest Rates in a Semiopen Economy: Colombia 1968–1972." *Journal of Money, Credit and Banking* 17 (February): 59–68.

———. 1986. "Monetarism in Chile, 1973–1983: Some Economic Puzzles." *Economic Development and Cultural Change* 34, no. 3 (April): 535–60.

————. Forthcoming. *Exchange Rates in Developing Countries.* Cambridge, Mass.: MIT Press.

Edwards, S., and M. Khan. 1985. "Interest Rate Determination in Developing Countries." *IMF Staff Papers* 32 (September): 377–403.

Edwards, S., and F. Ng. 1985. "Trends in Real Exchange Rate Behavior in Selected Developing Countries." CPD Discussion Paper no. 1985-16. Washington, D.C.: World Bank.

Edwards, S., and van Wijnbergen. 1986a. "The Welfare Effects of Trade and Capital Account Liberalization." *International Economic Review* 27 (February): 141–48.

————. 1986b. "On the Appropriate Speed and Timing of Economic Liberalization." In *Economic Reform in Latin America,* edited by M. Conolly and C. Gonzales. New York: Praeger.

Elías, V. 1978. "The Sources of Growth in Latin America." *Review of Economics and Statistics* 60 (August): 362–70.

Felix, D. 1960. "Structural Imbalances, Social Conflict and Inflation: An Appraisal of Chile's Recent Anti-Inflationary Effort." *Economic Development and Cultural Change* 8 (January): 113–47.

Fetter, F.W. 1932. *La Inflación Monetaria en Chile* [*Monetary Inflation in Chile*]. Santiago: Dirección General de Prisiones.

Fernandez, R. 1985. "The Expectations Management Approach to Stabilization in Argentina during 1976–82." *World Development* 13 (August): 781–92.

Ffrench-Davis, R. 1973. *Políticas Económicas en Chile 1952-1970* [*Economic Policies in Chile 1952-1970*]. Santiago: Editorial Nueva Universidad.

————. 1981. "Liberalización de Importaciones" ["Imports Liberalization"]. *Estudios Cieplán* no. 4 (November): 39–78.

————. 1983. "Una Estratergia de Apertura Externa Selectiva" ["A Strategy for a Selective Opening of the External Sector"]. In A. Foxley, *Reconstrucción Económica para la Democracia,* pp. 237–98. Santiago: Editorial Aconcagua.

Fontaine, J.A. 1983. "El Rol Macroeconómico del Estado" ["Macroeconomic Rol of the State"]. *Estudios Públicos* 9 (Summer): 19–42.

Foxley, A. 1981. "Stabilization Policies and Their Effects on Employment and Income Distribution: A Latin American Perspective." In *Economic Stabilization in Developing Countries,* edited by W. Cline and S. Weintraub, pp. 191–225. Washington, D.C.: Brookings Institution.

————. 1982. "Towards a Free Market Economy: Chile, 1974–1975." *Journal of Development Economics* (February): 3–29.

————. 1983. *Latin American Experiments in Neo-conservative Economics.* Berkeley: University of California Press.

Frankel, J., K. Froot, and A. Mizala-Salces. 1986. "Credibility, the Optimal Speed of Trade Liberalization, Real Interest Rates, and the Latin American Debt." Berkeley: University of California.

Frenkel, J. 1982. "The Order of Economic Liberalization: Discussion." In *Economic Policy in a World of Change*, edited by K. Brunner and A.H. Meltzer, pp. 199–202. Amsterdam: North-Holland.

———. 1983. "Remarks on the Southern Cone." *IMF Staff Papers* 30 (March): 164–73.

Frenkel, J., and H. Johnson. 1976. *The Monetary Approach to the Balance of Payments*. Toronto: University of Toronto Press.

Furtado, C. 1970. *La Economía Latinoamericana* [*The Latin American Economy*]. Santiago: Editorial Universitaria.

Galvez, J., and J. Tyebout. 1985. "Microeconomic Adjustments in Chile during 1977–81: The importance of being a *Grupo*." *World Development* 13 no. 8 (August): 969–94.

Guardia, A. 1979. "Structural Transformations in Chile's Economy and Its System of External Economic Relations." In *Chile 1970–1973*, edited by S. Sideri, pp. 45–102. The Hague: Martinus Nijhoff.

Guardia, A.; A. Martinez; and J. Ramos. 1979. "General Considerations on the Chilean Economic Structure." In *Chile 1970–1973*, edited by S. Sideri, pp. 11–43. The Hague: Martinus Nijhoff.

Guzmán, J.F. ed. 1975. *La Reforma Tributaria: Sus Efectos Económicos* [*The Tax Reform: Its Economic Effects*]. Santiago: Universidad de Chile, Departamento de Economia.

Hachette, D. 1978. "Aspectos Macroeconómicos de la Economía Chilena 1973–1976" ["Macroeconomic Aspects of the Chilean Economy"]. Documento de Trabajo no. 55. Santiago: Instituto de Economía, Universidad Católica.

Hanson, J. 1985. "What Went Wrong in Chile?" Paper presented at the World Bank Conference on Economic Liberalization: Adjustments during the Transition. Washington, D.C., October 1983.

Hanson, J., and J. de Melo. 1983. "The Uruguayan Experience with Stabilization and Liberalization: 1974–81." *Journal of Interamerican Studies and World Affairs* 25, no. 4 (November): 563–81.

———. 1985. "External Shocks, Financial Reforms, and Stabilization Attempts in Uruguay during 1974–1983." *World Development* 13, no. 8 (August): 917–40.

Harberger, A.C. 1959. "Using the Resources at Hand More Efficiently." *American Economic Review* 49 (May): 134–46.

———. 1963. "The Dynamics of Inflation in Chile." In *Measurement in Economics: Studies in Mathematical Economics and Econometrics*, edited by C. Christ, p. 248. California: Stanford University Press.

———. 1971. "On Measuring the Social Opportunity Cost of Labor." *International Labor Review* no. 103 (June): 559–79.

———. 1976. "On Country Risk and the Social Cost of Foreign Borrowing by Developing Countries." Unpublished manuscript. Chicago: University of Chicago.

———. 1980. "Vignettes on the World Capital Market." *American Economic Review Papers and Proceedings* 70 (May): 331–37.

———. 1981a. "Comment on Foxley." In *Economic Stabilization in Developing Countries,* edited by W. Cline and S. Weintraub, pp. 226–28. Brookings Institution.

———. 1981b. "The Real Exchange Rate in Chile." Unpublished manuscript. University of Chicago.

———. 1982. "The Chilean Economy in the 1970's: Crisis, Stabilization, Liberalization, Reform." In *Economic Policy in a World of Change,* edited by K. Brunner and A. Meltzer, pp. 115–52. Carnegie-Rochester Conference Series on Public Policy, vol. 17. New York: North-Holland.

———. 1983a. "A Primer on the Chilean Economy 1973–1983." Unpublished paper. University of Chicago.

———. 1983b. "Welfare Consequences of Capital Inflows." Paper presented at World Bank Conference. Washington, D.C., October 1983.

———. 1984. "Lessons for Debtor Country Managers and Policy Workers." Paper presented at World Bank Conference.

———. 1985. "Observations on the Chilean Economy, 1973–1983." *Economic Development and Cultural Change* 33 (April): 451–62.

Harberger, A.C., and M. Selowsky. 1966. "Las Fuentes del Crecimiento en Chile: 1940–62" ["Sources of Growth in Chile"]. *Cuadernos de Economía* 3 (December): 1–16.

Harris, J., and M. Todaro. 1970. "Migration, Unemployment and Development: A Two Sectors Analysis." *American Economic Review* 60 (March): 126–43.

Heskia I., 1979. "Distribución del Ingreso en el Gran Santiago 1957–1978" ["Income distribution in the Greater Santiago Area"]. Documento de Investigacin no. 41. Santiago: Departamento de Economía, Universidad de Chile.

Hirschman, A.O. 1961. *Journeys towards Progress: Studies of Economic Policy Making in Latin America.* New York: Twentieth Century Fund.

Hoy. 1981. May and June. Santiago, Chile.

IMF. *International Financial Statistics.* Washington, D.C.: IMF, various issues.

Instituto de Economía y Planificación, Universidad de Chile, 1973. *La Economía Chilena en 1972* [*The Chilean Economy in 1972*]. Santiago: Universidad de Chile.

Johnson, H. 1965. "Optimal Trade Intervention in the Presence of Domestic Distortions." In *Trade Growth and Balance of Payments,* edited by R. Caves, pp. 3–34. Chicago: Rand-McNally.

———. 1967. "The Possibility of Income Losses from Increase Efficiency or Factor Accumulation in the Presence of Tariffs." *Economic Journal* 77 (March): 151–54.

Kay, J.A., and D.T. Thompson. 1986. "Privatisation: A Policy in Search of a Rationale." *The Economic Journal* 96, no. 381 (March): 18–32.

Khan, M. 1974. "Import and Export Demand in Developing Countries." *IMF Staff Papers* 21 (July): 389–413.

Kindleberger, 1978. *Manias, Panics, and Crashes: A History of Financial Crisis.* New York: Basic Books.

Klein–Sacks Mission. *El Programa de estabilización de la Economía Chilena y el trabajo de la Misión Klein–Sachs* [*The Chilean Stabilization Program and The Work of the Klein and Sacks Economic and Financial Mission to Chile*]. Santiago: Editorial Universitaria.

Kouri, P., and M. Porter. 1974. "International Capital Flows and Portfolio Equilibrium." *Journal of Political Economy* 82 (May): 312–25.

Krueger, A. 1978. *Foreign Trade Regimes and Economic Development: Liberalization Attempts and Consequences.* Cambridge, Mass.: Ballinger.

———. 1983. "The Problems of Liberalization." Unpublished paper. Washington, D.C.: World Bank.

Lagos, R. 1961. *La Concentración del Poder Económico* [*The Concentration of Economic Power*]. Santiago: Editorial del Pacífico.

Lal, D. 1984. "The Real Aspects of Stabilization and Structural Adjustment Policies: An Extension of the Australian Adjustment Model." Staff Working Paper no. 636. Washington, D.C.: World Bank.

Leamer, E. 1980. "Welfare Computations and the Optimal Staging of Tariff Reductions in Models with Adjustment Costs." *Journal of International Economics* 10 (February): 21–36.

Leff, N. 1978. "Industrial Organization and Entrepreneurship in the Developing Countries: The Economic Groups." *Economic Development and Cultural Change* 26, no. 4 (July): 661–75.

———. 1979. "Monopoly Capitalism and Public Policy in Developing Countries." *Kiklos* 32, no. 4 (December): 718–38.

Le Fort, 1985. "The Real Exchange Rate and Capital Flows: The Case of the Southern Cone Countries." Ph.D. dissertation. University of California, Los Angeles.

Little, I. 1982. *Economic Development.* New York: Basic Books.

Little, I.; T. Scitovsky; and M. Scott. 1970. *Industry and Trade in Some Developing Countries.* Oxford: Oxford University Press.

Luders, R. 1968. "Monetary History of Chile: 1925–1958." Unpublished Ph.D. dissertation. University of Chicago. Department of Economics.

Luders, R., and B. Arbildua. 1969. "Una Evaluación Comparada de tres programas antinflacionarios en Chile" ["A Comparative Analysis of Three Stabilization Programs in Chile"]. *Cuadernos de Economía* 14 (April): 25–105.

Mamalakis, M. 1978. *Historical Statistics of Chile.* Westport, Conn.: Greenwood Press.

Mamalakis, M.; O. Munoz; and J.A. Fontaine. 1984. "Los Ultimos Diez Años de Historia Económica" ["The Last Ten Years of Economic History"]. *Estudios Públicos* 15 (Winter): 191–206.

Mamalakis, M., and C.W. Reynolds. 1965. *Essays on the Chilean Economy.* Homewood, Illinois: Richard Irwin.

Mardones, J.L.; I. Marshall; and E. Silva. 1984. "Chile y el CIPEC en el Mercado del Cobre" ["Chile and the Group of Copper Exporters in the World Copper Market"]. *Estudios Públicos* no. 15 (Winter): 5–38.

Marshall, J. 1981. "El Gasto Público en Chile, 1969–1979" ["Public Expenditure in Chile, 1969–1979"]. *Colección Estudios Cieplán* 5 (July): 53–84.

Marshall, J., and P. Romaguera. 1981. "La Evolución del Empleo Público en Chile, 1970–78" ["The Evolution of Public Employment in Chile"]. *Notas Tecnicas* no. 26. Santiago: Cieplán.

Martinez, V. 1979. "Las Variables Motivacionales que Influyen en el Comportamiento del Empresario" ["Motivation and Entrepreneurs' Behavior"]. Unpublished dissertation, Facultad de Ciencias Economicas y Administrativas. Universidad de Chile.

Martner, ed. 1971. *El Pensamiento Económico del Gobierno de Allende* [*The Economic Thought of the Allende Government*]. Chile: Editorial Universitaria.

McKinnon, R. 1973. *Money and Capital in Economic Development.* Washington, D.C.: Brookings Institution.

———. 1982. "The Order of Economic Liberalization: Lessons from Chile and Argentina." In *Economic Policy in a World of Change,* edited by K. Brunner and A.H. Meltzer, pp. 159–86. Amsterdam: North-Holland.

———. 1986. "Comment on Corbo." Paper presented at Conference on Southern Cone Experiences with Liberalization. Quito, Ecuador, January 28–30.

McKinnon, R., and D.J. Mathieson. 1981. *How to Manage a Repressed Economy.* Essays in International Finance no. 145. Princeton, N.J.: Princeton University.

Meller, P. 1984. "Análisis del Problema de la Elevada Tasa de Desocupación Chilena" ["Analysis of the Unemployment Problem in Chile"]. *Colección de Estudios Cieplán* no. 14 (September): 9–42.

Meller, P.; R. Cortázar; and J. Marshall. 1979. "Estancamiento del Empleo, 1974–1978" ["Employment Stagnation"]. *Colección de Estudios Cieplan* no. 2 (December): 141–58.

Meller, P.; E. Livacich; and P. Arrau. 1984. "Una Revisión del Milagro Económico Chileno (1976–1981)" ["A Revision of the Chilean Economic Miracle"]. *Colección Estudios de Cieplán* no. 15 (December): 5–109.

Mendez, J.C., ed. 1979. *Chilean Economic Policy.* Chile: Calderón.

Michaelly, M. 1982. "The Sequencing of a Liberalization Policy: A Preliminary Statement of Issues." Unpublished Paper. Washington, D.C.

Milgrom P., and J. Roberts. 1982. "Limiting Pricing and Entry under Incomplete Information: An Equilibrium Analysis." *Econometrica* 50, no. 2 (March): 443–60.

Morandé, F. 1986. "Domestic Currency Appreciation and Foreign Capital Inflows: What Comes First (Chile, 1977–1982)." Paper presented at VI Latin American Meetings of the Econometric Society. Córdoba, Argentina, July 22–26, 1986.

Muñoz, O. 1966. *Crecimiento Industrial de Chile 1914–1965* [*Industrial Growth in Chile*]. Santiago: Universidad de Chile.

Mussa, M. 1978. "Dynamic Adjustment in the Hecksher-Ohlin-Samuelson Model." *Journal of Political Economy* 86 (November): 775–92.

———. 1986. "On the Optimal Speed of Liberalization." In *Economic Liberalization in Developing Countries,* edited by A. Choksi and D. Papageorgiou. Oxford: Basil Blackwell.

Neary, P., and van Wijnbergen. 1986, eds. *Natural Resources and the Macroeconomy.* Oxford: Basil Blackwell.

Nogués, J. 1983. "Política Comercial y Cambiaria: Una Interpretación de la Experiencia Argentina 1976–1981" ["Commercial and Exchange Policies: An Interpretation of the Argentinian Experience"]. Unpublished paper. Buenos Aires, Banco Central de Argentina.

Obstfeld, M. 1986. "The Capital Inflows Problem Revisited: A Stylized Model of Southern Cone Disinflation." *Review of Economic Studies* 52 (December).

Oi, W. 1962. "Labor as a Quasi-Fixed Factor." *Journal of Political Economy* 70 (December): 538–55.

ODEPLAN. 1972. *Cuentas Nacionales de Chile 1960–1971* [*National Accounts, Chile 1960–1971*]. Santiago, Chile: Oficina de Planificacion Nacional.

Park, Y.C. 1985. "Financial Repression, Liberalization, and Development in Developing Countries." Unpublished paper. Seoul: Korea University.

Parkin, V. 1983. "Economic Liberalization in Chile 1973–82: A Model of Growth and Development or a Recipe for Stagnation and Impoverishment?" *Cambridge Journal of Economics* 7 (June): 101–24.

"Pinochet Sends the Chicago Boys Back to School." 1985. *The Economist* 296 (August 16): 60–62.

Pinto, A. 1964. *Chile: Una Economía Difícil* [*Chile: A Difficult Economy*]. Mexico City: Fondo de Cultura Económica.

———. 1959. *Chile: Un Caso de Desarrollo Frustrado* [*Chile: A Case of Frustrated Development*]. Santiago: Editorial Universitaria.

Pollack, M. 1980. "El Sector Industrial en el Periodo 1960–1979" ["The Industrial Sector in the 1960–1979 Period"]. Documento no. 144. Santiago: Departamento Estudios B.H.C.

Qué Pasa. 1977. April. Santiago, Chile.

Ramos, J. 1984. *Estabilización Económica en el Cono Sur* [*Stabilization and Liberalization in the Southern Cone*]. Estudios e Informes de la Cepal no. 38. Santiago: Naciones Unidas.

Riveros, L. 1984. "Un Análisis sobre el Problema del Empleo en Chile en la decada del 70" ["Analysis of the Employment Problem in Chile during the 70s"]. *Estudios de Economía* no. 23 (October) 3–27.

―――. 1985. "Desempleo, Distribución del Ingreso y Política Social" ["Unemployment, Income Distribution, and Social Policy"]. *Estudios Públicos* no. 20 (Spring): 315–47.

Robischeck, W. 1981. "Some Reflections About External Public Debt Management." In *Estudios Monetarios VII. Alternativas de Políticas Financieras en Economías Pequeñas y Abiertas al Exterior* [Financial Policies in Small Open Economies], edited by Banco Central de Chile, pp. 169–84. Santiago: Alfabeta.

Rodrick, D. 1985. "Trade and Capital-Account Liberalization in a Keynesian Economy." Discussion Paper Series no. 136D. Cambridge, Mass.: Kennedy School, Harvard University.

Rodriguez, C.A. 1983. "Políticas de Estabilización en la Economía Argentina 1978–1982" ["Stabilization Policies in the Argentinian Economy"]. *Cuadernos de Economía* 20 (April): 21–42.

Rodriguez, J. 1985. "El Papel Redistributivo del Gasto Social: Chile 1983" ["Redistributive Role of Social Expenditure in Chile"]. *Estudios Públicos* no. 19 (Winter): 37–70.

Rybczynski, T.M. 1955. "Factor Endowments and Relative Commodity Prices." *Economica* 22 (November): 336–54.

Sachs, J. 1985. "External Debt and Macroeconomic Performance in Latin America and Asia." *Brookings Papers on Economic Activity.* 2. 1985: 523–73.

Sachs, J., and D. Cohen. 1982. "LDC Borrowing with Default Risk." Working Paper no. 925. Cambridge, Mass.: NBER.

Sargent, T.J. 1983. "The Ends of Four Big Inflations." In *Rational Expectations and Inflation,* edited by T.J. Sargent, pp. 40–109. New York: Harper & Row.

Schmidt-Hebbel, K. 1981. "El Programa del Empleo Mínimo en Chile" ["The Minimum Employment Program in Chile"]. Documento no. 199. Santiago: Departamento de Estudios B.H.C.

Sideri, S., ed. 1979. *Chile 1970–1973: Economic Development and its International Setting—Self-Criticism of the Unidad Popular Government's Policies.* The Hague: Martinus Nijhoff.

Sierra, E. 1970. *Tres Ensayos de Estabilización en Chile* [*Three Stabilization Efforts in Chile, The Policies Applied between 1956 and 1966*]. Santiago: Editorial Universitaria.

Singleton, K.J. 1986. "Speculation and the Volatility of Foreign Currency Exchange Rates." Paper presented at Carnegie-Rochester Conference on Public Policy, Rochester, N.Y., April 11.

Sjaastad, L. 1983. "Failure of Economic Liberalism in the Cone of Latin America." *World Economy* 6 (March): 5-27.

Sjaastad, L., and Cortes, H. 1981. "Protección y Empleo" ["Employment and Protection"]. *Cuadernos de Economía* no. 54-55 (August/December): 318-36.

Sjaastad, L., and H. Cortes-Douglas, eds. 1981. "La Economía Política de la Reforma Comercial en Chile" ["The Political Economy of the Commercial Reform in Chile"]. *Cuadernos de Economía* nos. 54-55 (August/December).

Stiglitz, J. 1974. "Wage Determination and Unemployment in LDCs." *Quarterly Journal of Economics* 88 (May) 194-227.

Subercaceaux, G. 1922. *Monetary and Banking Policy of Chile.* Oxford: Clarendon Press.

Sunkel, O. 1958. "Inflación: Un Enfoque Hetereodoxo" ["An Heterodox Approach to Inflation"]. *El Trimestre Económico* 25 (October): 612-37.

Superintendencia de Bancos. "Información Estadística" ["Statistical Information"]. Various issues.

Tironi, E. 1985. "¿Por Qué Chile Necesita Aranceles Diferenciados?" ["Why Does Chile Need Tariffs at Different Rates?"]. *Estudios Públicos* 19 (Winter): 21-36.

Tockman, V. 1984. "Reactivación con Transformación: El Efecto Empleo" ["Recovery with Reforms: The Employment Effect"]. *Colección Estudios Cieplán* no. 14 (September): 105-28.

Tybout, J. 1985. "Microeconomic Adjustments during the Reforms: Introduction." *World Development* 13, no. 8 (August): 941-48.

Unidad Popular. 1970. *Prorama Básico de la Unidad Popular.* Santiago de Chile: Impresora Horizonte.

Varas, J.I. 1975. "El Impacto de una Liberalización del Comercio en el Sector Agrícola Chileno" ["A Trade Liberalizacion and the Agricultural Sector in Chile"]. *Cuadernos de Economía* 12 (August): 121-34.

Vergara, P. 1981. "Las Transformaciones de las Funciones Económicas del Estado en Chile bajo el Régimen Militar" ["Changes in the Role of the State in Chile under the Military Regime"]. *Colección Estudios Cieplán* 5 (July): 117-54.

Vuskovic, P. 1970. "Distribución del Ingreso y Opciones de Desarrollo" ["Income Distribution and Development Options"]. *Cuadernos de la Realidad Nacional* no. 5 (September): 41-60.

———. 1975. "Dos Años de Política Económica del Gobierno Popular" ["Two Years of Economic Policy of the Socialist Government"]. In *El Golpe de Estado en Chile,* Edited by Centro de Estudios Latinoamericanos, Universidad Nacional Autónoma de Mexico. Mexico City: Fondo de Cultura Economica.

Walton, G., ed. 1985. *The National Economic Policies of Chile.* Greenwich, Conn.: JAI Press.

"Will General Pinochet Sink the Copper Market?" 1984. *The Economist* 295 (December 22): 71–72.

Wisecarver, D. 1985. "Economic Regulation and Deregulation in Chile, 1973–1983." In *National Economic Policies of Chile,* edited by G.A. Walton, pp. 145–202. Greenwich, Conn.: JAI Press.

World Bank. 1980. *Chile: An Economy in Transition.* Washington, D.C.: World Bank.

――――. 1986. "Korea: Managing the Industrial Transition." Washington, D.C.: World Bank.

Yañez, J. 1978. "Una Corrección del Indice de Precios al Consumidor durante el Periodo 1971–1973" ["A Correction of the Consumers' Price Index for the 1971–1973 Period"]. In *Comentarios sobre la Situación Económica,* edited by F. Contreras, pp. 205–57. Santiago: Universidad de Chile.

Zahler, R. 1980. "The Monetary and Real Effects of the Financial Opening Up of National Economies to the Exterior." *Cepal Review* 10 (April): 127–54.

――――. 1985. "Las Tasas de Interés en Chile: 1975–1982" ["Interest Rates in Chile: 1975–1982"]. Unpublished manuscript. CEPAL: Santiago de Chile.

Zorrilla, A. 1971. "Exposición de la Hacienda Pública, 27 de Noviembre de 1970" ["Minister of Finance Yearly Economic Report, 1979"]. In *El Pensamiento Económico del Gobierno de Allende,* edited by G. Martner, pp. 11–36. Santiago: Editorial Universitaria.

INDEX

ABOUT THE AUTHORS

Sebastian Edwards is an associate professor of economics at the University of California, Los Angeles, and a faculty research fellow at the National Bureau of Economic Research. He received his Ph.D. from the University of Chicago. He is the editor of *Economic Adjustment and Exchange Rates in Developing Countries,* a conference volume published by the National Bureau of Economic Research, and the coeditor of *Growth, Trade and Adjustment: Latin America in the 1970s and 1980s.* His numerous articles on international economics, economic development, and the economics of Latin America have been published in leading national and international journals. He has been a consultant to the World Bank and the International Monetary Fund.

Alejandra Cox Edwards is an assistant professor at California State University, Long Beach. She has a Ph.D. in economics from the University of Chicago. Her work focuses on labor markets issues with special relation to developing countries. She has been a consultant to the World Bank. She has also held teaching positions at the University of California, Los Angeles, and at the University of California, Irvine.